ACCA
PRACTICE & REVISION KIT

Professional Paper 11

Tax planning
(Finance Act 1999)

BPP Publishing
January 2000

First edition 1994
Eighth edition January 2000

ISBN 0 7517 0855 0 (Previous edition 0 7517 0885 2)

British Library Cataloguing-in-Publication Data
A catalogue record for this book
is available from the British Library

Published by

BPP Publishing Limited
Aldine House, Aldine Place
London W12 8AW

www.bpp.com

Printed in Great Britain by
WM Print Ltd
Frederick Street
Walsall
West Midlands WS2 9NE

All our rights reserved. No part of this publication may be reproduced, stored in a retrieval system or transmitted, in any form or by any means, electronic, mechanical, photocopying, recording or otherwise, without the prior written permission of BPP Publishing Limited.

We are grateful to the Association of Chartered Certified Accountants for permission to reproduce in this Kit the syllabus and the pilot paper questions of which the Association holds the copyright.

We are also grateful to the Association of Chartered Certified Accountants, the Chartered Institute of Management Accountants and the Institute of Chartered Accountants in England and Wales for permission to reproduce past examination questions. The answers to the past examination questions have been prepared by BPP Publishing Limited.

©
BPP Publishing Limited
2000

Contents

CONTENTS	Page number
Question and Answer Checklist/Index	(iv)
The BPP Effective Study Package	(vi)
The 2000 exams	(vii)
Revision	
How to revise	(ix)
What to revise for the 2000 exams	(x)
Practice	
Exam technique	(xi)
Practising tutorial questions	(xii)
Practising exam standard questions	(xiii)
Doing the Mock Exam	(xiii)
Analysis of past papers 1997-1999	(xiv)
The Official 2000 Syllabus	(xvii)
Rates and allowances	(xxiii)
Question Bank	3
Answer Bank	83
Mock Exam: questions	213
Mock Exam: answers	223
Review Form & Free Prize Draw	
Order Form	

Question and answer checklist/index

The headings indicate the main topics of questions, but questions often cover several different topics.

Tutorial questions, listed in italics, are followed by guidance notes. These notes show you how to approach the question, and thus ease the transition from study to examination practice.

A date alone (12/98, say) or 'pilot paper' after the question title refers to a current syllabus paper.

Questions preceded by * are **key questions** which we think you must attempt in order to pass the exam. Tick them off on this list as you complete them.

		Marks	Time allocation (mins)	Page number Question	Answer

PART A: PERSONAL TAXATION

Personal computations, employment and investment income

		Marks	Time (mins)	Question	Answer
1	*Tutorial question: Car and travel*	–	–	5	83
* 2	Techno plc (6/96)	25	45	5	83
3	Clifford Jones (12/94)	25	45	6	86
* 4	Charles Choice (6/97)	25	45	8	90
5	William Wiles (6/97)	25	45	9	93
* 6	Duncan McByte (12/98)	25	45	10	96

Capital gains tax and inheritance tax

		Marks	Time (mins)	Question	Answer
7	*Tutorial question: A chattel, land and shares*	–	–	15	99
8	Ken Sing (12/94)	25	45	15	101
9	Desmond and Myrtle Cook (6/94)	25	45	17	103
* 10	Bluetone Ltd (6/98)	25	45	18	107
11	Monty Noble (12/97)	25	45	19	111
* 12	Ming Wong (12/98)	25	45	20	114
* 13	Dorothy Lake (6/97)	25	45	21	117
* 14	Michael Earl (12/95)	25	45	22	121
* 15	Maud Smith (6/95)	25	45	24	124

Investments and finance

		Marks	Time (mins)	Question	Answer
* 16	Ming Lee (6/94)	25	45	29	127
17	Muriel Grand (6/96)	25	45	30	129
* 18	Mary Mole (6/98)	25	45	30	132

Trusts

		Marks	Time (mins)	Question	Answer
19	Mr Rowe	25	45	31	135

PART B: BUSINESS TAXATION

Self assessment and payment of tax, Schedule D cases 1 and 11

		Marks	Time (mins)	Question	Answer
20	Tony Tort (12/98)	25	45	35	138
21	*Tutorial question: Change of Accounting date*	–	–	36	140
22	Cecile Grand (12/97)	25	45	36	141
23	Clark Kent (6/94)	25	45	37	143
* 24	Basil Nadir (12/95)	25	45	39	145
25	Garden Ltd (6/95)	25	45	40	147
* 26	Alex Zong (12/97)	25	45	41	149
27	Chow Tong (12/97)	25	45	42	151

Question and answer checklist/index

			Marks	Time allocation (mins)	Page number Question	Answer
Partnerships. National insurance						
*	28	Ming Khan and Nina Lee (6/97)	25	45	44	154
*	29	Smart and Sharp (6/96)	25	45	45	157
*	30	Sally and Trevor Acre (12/98)	25	45	46	160
Capital gains tax and businesses						
	31	Tutorial question: Choosing assets to sell	–	–	51	163
	32	Velo Ltd (6/98)	25	45	51	165
	33	Sally Jones	25	45	53	168
Value added tax						
	34	Tutorial question: Registration and accounting	–	–	53	170
*	35	Schooner Ltd (12/98)	25	45	54	172

PART C: CORPORATE TAXATION

			Marks	Time allocation (mins)	Question	Answer
Computations of profits and tax						
	36	Highrise Ltd (12/95)	25	45	59	174
Close companies						
	37	Bargains Ltd	25	45	60	177
Groups						
*	38	Target Ltd (6/97)	25	45	60	178
*	39	Hydra Ltd (6/96)	25	45	61	181
*	40	Ongoing Ltd (12/96)	25	45	62	183
*	41	Ocean plc (6/95)	25	45	63	185
*	42	Star Ltd (12/98)	25	45	64	187

PART D: OVERSEAS ASPECTS AND TAX PLANNING

			Marks	Time allocation (mins)	Question	Answer
Overseas aspects						
	43	Tutorial question: Double taxation relief for individuals	–	–	69	189
	44	Tutorial question: Double taxation relief for companies	–	–	69	190
*	45	Barney Hall (6/98)	25	45	70	191
*	46	Eyetaki Inc (6/97)	25	45	71	194
	47	Magee plc (pilot paper)	25	45	72	197
*	48	Paddington Ltd (12/97)	25	45	73	199
Tax planning						
	49	Lucy Lee (12/96)	25	45	74	200
	50	Li and Ken Wong	25	45	75	203
	51	White Stallion Ltd (6/94)	25	45	76	205
*	52	Fred Barley (12/95)	25	45	78	208

The BPP effective study package

Recommended period of use	Elements of the BPP Effective Study Package
3-12 months before exam	**Study Text** Acquisition of knowledge, understanding, skills and applied techniques.
1-6 months before exam	**Practice & Revision Kit** Tutorial questions and helpful checklists of the key points lead you into each area. There are then numerous Examination questions to try, graded by topic area, along with realistic suggested solutions prepared by BPP's own authors in the light of the Examiner's Reports. June 2000 examinees will find the 2000 edition of the Kit essential for bringing them up-to-date for the Finance Act 1999.
last minute - 3 months before exam	**Passcards** Short, memorable notes focused on what is most likely to come up in the exam you will be sitting.
1-6 months before exam	**Success Tapes** Audio cassettes covering the vital elements of your syllabus in less than 90 minutes per subject. Each tape also contains exam hints to help you fine tune your strategy.
3-12 months before exam	**Breakthrough Videos** These supplement your Study Text, by giving you clear tuition on key exam subjects. They allow you the luxury of being able to pause or repeat sections until you have fully grasped the topic.

THE 2000 EXAMS

Format of the June and December 2000 exams

	Marks
4 (out of 6) optional 25 mark questions	100

Time allowed: 3 hours

Pass rates

The pass rate for Paper 11 in recent sittings has been in the region of 40%-45%.

The examiner

The examiner for Paper 11 is David Harrowven. He has been setting the exams for many years. The exams can be time pressured and you must learn to be organised and disciplined in your approach to your work.

Mr Harrowven has a preference for examining topics in respect of which there has been a recent change and/or on which he has written a recent article in the *Students' Newsletter*.

Core syllabus areas

The following are core syllabus areas:

- Overseas taxation, both corporate and personal including double taxation relief;
- Taxation of groups of companies including group relief and transfer of assets;
- Inheritance tax, including valuation of an estate, business property relief.

Other important areas of the Paper 11 syllabus are:

- Personal finance, including pension planning, individual savings accounts, the enterprise investment scheme and venture capital trusts;
- Schedule DI/II (including opening and closing year rules, change of accounting date and partnerships);
- Self assessment;
- Capital gains tax, particularly in business situations
- VAT is of increasing importance and you can now expect the VAT part of a question to be worth up to 15 marks.

Hot topics for 2000 exams

Given the examiner's track record and in the light of the 1999 exams, we believe there is a strong likelihood that the following 'hot topics' will come up in either or both of the 2000 exams:

Inheritance tax	Partnerships
Overseas aspects	Groups
CGT reliefs (including taper relief)	Self assessment and payments on account for companies
Personal finance	VAT
Benefits in kind (including cars)	National insurance contributions
Incorporation	

The 2000 exams

If you wish to concentrate on particular areas of the syllabus whilst maximising your chances of passing, you could start with the topics above. Questions on these are highlighted as 'key questions' in the Question and Answer Checklist on page (iv) ; we look at them in more detail on page (x).

Disclaimer of liability

Please note that we have based our predictions of the content of the 2000 exams on our long experience of the ACCA exams. We do not claim to have any endorsement of the predictions from either the examiner or the ACCA and we do not guarantee that either the specific questions, or the general areas, that are forecast will necessarily be included in the exams, in part or in whole.

We do not accept any liability or responsibility to any person who takes, or does not take, any action based (either in whole or in part and either directly or indirectly) upon any statement or omission made in this book. We encourage students to study all topics in the ACCA syllabus and the mock exam in this book is intended as an aid to revision only.

Examinable material

The Finance Act 1999 is examinable in both June 2000 and December 2000. This Kit fully reflects the provisions of this Act.

The following syllabus exclusions now apply.

- Farmer's averaging relief where the lower profits are between 70% and 75% of the higher profits.

    Averaging where the lower profits are 70% or less of the higher profits remains examinable. However, students would be pointed in the right direction if this relief was included in a question.

- The 5% rollover rules for small part disposals.

    The rules for the small part disposals of land will be added to the list of excluded topics.

- The 5% rollover rules for the sale of rights nil paid and for takeovers remain examinable.

- Capital sums received in respect of damage to non-wasting assets/capital sums received in respect of the loss or destruction of non-wasting assets.

- Migration of companies resident the UK under the central management and control test.

Students' Newsletter

Students are advised to read the 'Exam Notes' published in the Students' Newsletter as these contain details of examinable legislation, changes in the syllabuses and other useful information. In particular, the notes state the Finance Act applicable to each examination session.

REVISION

How to revise

This is a very important time as you approach the exam. You must remember three things.

> **Use time sensibly**
> **Set realistic goals**
> **Believe in yourself**

Use time sensibly

1. **How much study time do you have?** Remember that you must EAT, SLEEP, and of course, RELAX.

2. **How will you split that available time between each subject?** What are your weaker subjects? They need more time.

3. **What is your learning style?** AM/PM? Little and often/long sessions? Evenings/weekends?

4. **Are you taking regular breaks?** Most people absorb more if they do not attempt to study for long uninterrupted periods of time. A five minute break every hour (to make coffee, watch the news headlines) can make all the difference.

5. **Do you have quality study time?** Unplug the phone. Let everybody know that you're studying and shouldn't be disturbed.

Set realistic goals

1. Have you set a **clearly defined objective** for each study period?
2. Is the objective **achievable**?
3. Will you **stick to your plan**? Will you make up for any **lost time**?
4. Are you **rewarding yourself** for your hard work?
5. Are you leading a **healthy lifestyle**?

Believe in yourself

Are you cultivating the right attitude of mind? There is absolutely no reason why you should not pass this exam if you adopt the correct approach

- **Be confident** - you've passed exams before, you can pass them again
- **Be calm** - plenty of adrenaline but no panicking
- **Be focused** - commit yourself to passing the exam

Revision

What to revise for the 2000 exams

Ideally you should revise all areas of the syllabus thoroughly, using your BPP Study Text (and any notes you've made from it), this kit and, if you wish, the BPP Passcards. If your time is limited, however, you could concentrate on revising the areas covered by our hot topics highlighted on page (vii).

Topic	1999 Study Text Chapter/2000 Passcard Chapter	Key questions in this Kit	Key articles in Students' Newsletter
Inheritance tax	9, 10, 11	8, 10, 12, 13, 14, 15, 45, 52	March 1999
Overseas aspects	28, 29	4, 8, 12, 44, 45, 46, 48	December 1998 and January 1999
CGT reliefs including taper relief	4, 7, 19	8, 10, 13, 14, 15, 26, 30, 52	
Personal finance	3, 12	4, 15, 16, 18, 48	
Benefits-in-kind (including cars)	2	2, 4, 6	
Incorporation	19, 30	16, 26, 29,	
Partnerships	18	28, 29, 30	
Groups	27, 20	38, 39, 40, 41, 42	February 1999
Self assessment and payments on account for companies	24	40	
VAT	20, 21	24, 26, 28, 35, 39, 41, 42, 46	February 1999 April 1999
National Insurance contributions	2, 18	4, 6, 24, 29	

Note that although the above articles are very useful, they are not all up to date for the Finance Act 1999. The examiner wrote an article covering Finance Act 1999 in the September 1999 edition of the Students' Newsletter

PRACTICE

Exam technique

Passing professional examinations is half about having the knowledge, and half about doing yourself full justice in the examination. You must have the right technique.

> **The day of the exam**

1. Set at least one **alarm** (or get an alarm call) for a morning exam

2. Have **something to eat** but beware of eating too much; you may feel sleepy if your system is digesting a large meal

3. Allow plenty of **time to get to the exam hall**; have your route worked out in advance and listen to news bulletins to check for potential travel problems

4. **Don't forget** pens, pencils, rulers, erasers

5. Put **new batteries** into your calculator and take a spare set (or a spare calculator)

6. **Avoid discussion** about the exam with other candidates outside the exam hall

> **Technique in the exam hall**

1. *Read the instructions (the 'rubric') on the front of the exam paper carefully*

   Check that the exam format hasn't changed. It is surprising how often examiners' reports remark on the number of students who attempt too few - or too many - questions, or who attempt the wrong number of questions from different parts of the paper. Make sure that you are planning to answer the **right number of questions**.

2. *Select questions carefully*

   Read through the paper once, then quickly jot down key points against each question in a second read through. Select those questions where you could latch on to 'what the question is about' - but remember to check carefully that you have got the right end of the stick before putting pen to paper.

3. *Plan your attack carefully*

   Consider the **order** in which you are going to tackle questions. It is a good idea to start with your best question to boost your morale and get some easy marks 'in the bag'.

4. *Check the time allocation for each question*

   Each mark carries with it a **time allocation** of 1.8 minutes (including time for selecting and reading questions). A 25 mark question should be completed in 45 minutes. When time is up, you *must* go on to the next question or part. Going even one minute over the time allowed brings you a lot closer to failure.

5. *Read the question carefully and plan your answer*

   Read through the question again very carefully when you come to answer it. Plan your answer to ensure that you **keep to the point**. Two minutes of planning plus eight minutes of writing is virtually certain to earn you more marks than ten minutes of writing.

6. *Produce relevant answers*

   Particularly with written answers, make sure you **answer the question set**, and not the question you would have preferred to have been set.

Practice

7   *Gain the easy marks*

   Include the obvious if it answers the question and don't try to produce the perfect answer.

   Don't get bogged down in small parts of questions. If you find a part of a question difficult, get on with the rest of the question. If you are having problems with something, the chances are that everyone else is too.

8   *Produce an answer in the correct format*

   The examiner will **state in the requirements** the format in which the question should be answered, for example in a report or memorandum.

9   *Follow the examiner's instructions*

   You will annoy the examiner if you ignore him or her. The **examiner will state** whether he or she wishes you to 'discuss', 'comment', 'evaluate' or 'recommend'.

10 *Lay out your numerical computations and use workings correctly*

   Make sure the layout fits the **type of question** and is in a style the examiner likes.

   Show all your **workings** clearly and explain what they mean. Cross reference them to your solution. This will help the examiner to follow your method (this is of particular importance where there may be several possible answers).

11 *Present a tidy paper*

   You are a professional, and it should show in the **presentation of your work**. Students are penalised for poor presentation and so you should make sure that you write legibly, label diagrams clearly and lay out your work neatly. Markers of scripts each have hundreds of papers to mark; a badly written scrawl is unlikely to receive the same attention as a neat and well laid out paper.

12 *Stay until the end of the exam*

   Use any spare time **checking and rechecking** your script.

13 *Don't worry if you feel you have performed badly in the exam*

   It is more than likely that the other candidates will have found the exam difficult too. Don't forget that there is a competitive element in these exams. As soon as you get up to leave the exam hall, *forget* **that exam** and think about the next - or, if it is the last one, celebrate!

14 *Don't discuss an exam with other candidates*

   This is particularly the case if you **still have other exams to sit**. Even if you have finished, you should put it out of your mind until the day of the results. Forget about exams and relax!

Practising tutorial questions

A total of 7 tutorial questions are included in the Question Bank. If you read through the revision topics and feel confident that you know what they are about, try to produce at least a plan for the tutorial questions, using the guidance notes to ensure your answer is structured so as to gain a good pass mark.

Practising exam standard questions

Once you are confident with the revision topics and the tutorial questions, you should try as many as possible of the exam standard questions; at the very least, you should attempt the 'hot topic' questions identified in the Question and Answer Checklist. Try to produce full answers under timed conditions; you are practising exam technique an much as knowledge recall here.

Doing the Mock Exam

The Mock Exam includes the style and content of the questions we think are most likely to be set in the June 2000 exam. You should attempt the paper under exam conditions, so that you gain experience of selecting and sequencing your questions, and managing your time, as well as of writing answers. Applying our marking scheme will help you get an idea of how you will fare in your exam.

ANALYSIS OF PAST PAPERS 1997-1999

The analysis below shows the topics which have been examined in the six most recent sittings of the syllabus.

December 1999

1. Income tax: overseas aspects
2. IHT on death
3. Schedule D Case I assessments. VAT. Tax planning for married couples
4. Employment v self employment. Schedule E. Distributions to close company participators
5. CGT retirement relief. Income tax losses. Tax avoidance/evasion
6. Corporation tax: groups

> **Examiner's comments** were not available at the time of going to print.

June 1999

1. Overseas matters. Controlled foreign companies. Quarterly payments of corporation tax.
2. Sale of business to company
3. CGT and IHT implications of various gifts. IHT on discretionary trusts
4. Calculation of income tax liability including DTR. Investment in ISA
5. VAT: Computation; Annual/cash accounting scheme. Provision of company car
6. Badges of trade. Corporation tax computation

> **Examiner's comments**
>
> The performance at this diet was very encouraging, with many candidates achieving pass marks in the seventies and eighties. The overall performance is reflected in the high pass percentage, and it was apparent that may candidates had benefited by studying my series of articles in the *Students' Newsletter*. Those candidates that did not achieve a pass mark generally indicated a lack of knowledge and poor examination technique.

Analysis of past papers 1997 - 1999

December 1998

		Question reference in this Kit
1	IHT and income tax for a non-domiciled individual.	12
2	Income tax self-assessment. Personal pension scheme.	20
3	Corporation tax: groups and capital gains. VAT group registration.	42
4	CGT: retirement relief. Partnership. Income tax losses	30
5	VAT. Raising finance. Schedule D profits.	35
6	Schedule E and Schedule A for individuals.	6

Examiner's comments

It was disappointing that the performance at this diet was not up to the standard of recent sittings. this was largely due to the number of candidates who did not appear to have prepared themselves sufficiently to answer four questions at a pass standard. Typically marginal fail candidates answered two or three questions at the required standard but were then unable to obtain a pass mark because of a poor attempt at the final question.

June 1998

1	Capital allowance and CGT aspects of the relocation of the business, sale and purchase of assets	32
2	Income Tax and CGT aspects of working overseas plus proposed sales and gifts of assets	45
3	Corporation tax group of companies with loss relief	Mock exam
4	Sole trader commencing in business; income tax and VAT consequences. Employed versus self employed discussion. Annual accounting scheme and consequences of late VAT returns	Mock exam
5	Investments; tax consequences of various investments plus discussion of tied adviser and independent adviser and ACCA Statement of Principle on standards expected of an authorised person	18
6	IHT and CGT on lifetime gifts and death estate. Purchase of own shares	10

Examiner's comments

Considering that this paper included relatively straightforward questions on overseas personal tax, group taxation and personal finance, all of which are regularly examined, those candidates who failed to achieve a pass mark can only blame a lack of adequate preparation.

Question 1 dealt with a number of recent changes covered in a Students' Newsletter article. It was therefore disappointing that answers to this question were considerably below the standard of the other five.

Questions 2, 3 and 6 were popular with reasonably good answers. Question 5 was also fairly popular but the answers were not as good as expected for what is an important topic that is regularly examined.

Question 4 was not a popular question but when attempted it was reasonably well answered.

Analysis of past papers 1997 - 1999

December 1997

		Question reference in this Kit
1	Income tax self assessment and change of accounting date	22
2	IHT including the sale of land after death and the variation of a will. Accumulation and Maintenance trusts	11
3	Incorporation of a business. VAT: bad debts, errors, discounts	26
4	Corporation tax: groups and controlled foreign companies	48
5	Trading v not trading. Enterprise investment scheme and reinvestment relief	27
6	Benefits in kind including the provision of a car, credit cards and redundancy payments. Pensions	Mock Exam

> **Examiner's comments**
>
> Many candidates continue to sit this paper without adequate preparation.
>
> Virtually every aspect of question 1 was covered in a recent students' newsletter article. There was therefore little excuse for not being able to make a reasonable attempt at it.
>
> Questions 2 and 6 were popular but the majority of candidates answered them badly. Questions 3 and 4 were also popular and were well answered.
>
> Question 5 was not popular and part (b) was badly answered. Part (a) was, in general, well answered.

June 1997

1	Schedule E; company car versus cash alternative. Profit related pay. Pensions	4
2	Schedule A. Tax reliefs and allowances	5
3	Corporation Tax: Acquisition of new subsidiary	38
4	IHT and CGT on gift of an asset/death. IHT instalment option	13
5	Partnerships. Income tax losses. VAT	28
6	Corporation tax and VAT for overseas company. Industrial buildings allowances. Income tax for director of overseas company working in the UK	46

> **Examiner's comments**
>
> It was difficult to pass this paper without having adequately covered most of the syllabus and it was apparent that many candidates had not spent much time studying Schedule A, consortium relief, partnership losses and the tax treatment of non-UK resident companies and individuals.
>
> Question 1 was not answered as well as would be expected given that all the topics covered are examinable at Paper 7.
>
> Question 2 was not popular although candidates who attempted it often scored high marks. Question 3 was also not popular and resulted in some varied answers, whilst question 6 was the least popular question on the paper and was generally answered badly.
>
> Questions 4 and 5 were generally well answered, although poor presentation resulted in a loss of marks in some cases.

THE OFFICIAL 2000 SYLLABUS

Aim of Paper 11

To equip students with the ability to solve unstructured problems which draw on the interaction of taxes between income, profits and capital.

On completion of this paper students should be able to:

- display an awareness of the impact of all major taxes on the transactions of individuals, partnerships and companies
- apply that knowledge to practical situations involving computation, explanation, discussion and advice
- appreciate the importance of taxation in personal and corporate financial planning and decision making
- demonstrate an understanding of the regulations associated with the provision of suitable investment advice to individuals
- identify opportunities to minimise potential tax liabilities by making full use of available options, reliefs and exemptions
- demonstrate the skills expected at the Professional Stage

Syllabus

Below is reproduced the detailed syllabus as published by the ACCA.

1 Overview of personal business taxation

(a) Interactions between different taxes in a range of situations or transactions

(b) Tax planning; the application of tax planning measures appropriate to the particular situation

2 Capital gains tax

Application of capital gains tax to individuals and corporate taxpayers, with emphasis on business situations.

3 Inheritance tax

(a) Principles and scope.

(b) Rules, basis and application.

(c) Calculating the tax due by clients.

(d) Minimising/deferring tax liabilities by identifying/applying relevant exemptions, reliefs and allowances.

4 Trusts

Application to trusts of income tax, capital gains tax and inheritance tax.

5 Value Added Tax

The application of Value Added Tax to transactions and other activities of corporate taxpayers.

6 Corporate taxation

(a) Groups and consortia.

(b) The provisions covering liquidations and areas such as disincorporations, purchases of own shares, sales and acquisitions of subsidiaries and share for share amalgamations.

(c) Implications of a company being classed as an investment or close company.

7 Overseas activities giving rise to taxation liabilities

(a) Definition of residence, ordinary residence and domicile.

(b) The taxation of UK income and gains of non-domiciled individuals.

(c) Overseas income and gains: the UK tax treatment of overseas income and gains of UK resident individuals and companies, including relief for double taxation.

(d) Overseas persons, the UK tax treatment of income and gains arising within the UK to non resident individuals and companies.

(e) The inheritance tax position regarding overseas assets of UK individuals and UK assets of non resident individuals.

(f) Business structures, including a UK branch/subsidiary of a foreign company/group and a foreign branch/subsidiary of a UK company/group.

(g) Anti-avoidance legislation relating to overseas activities, income or persons.

8 General

(a) Inter-relationship of taxes: the effect of any of the taxes in a given situation or on a particular transaction.

(b) Anti-avoidance: appreciation of the main areas of anti-avoidance legislation and of the enquiry and investigation procedures of the Inland Revenue and Customs and Excise.

9 Personal finance

(a) Assisting clients in the determination of personal financial objectives, taking into account such factors as individual circumstances, expectations and the economic environment.

(b) Determining financial needs of clients (how much, when, for how long, and for what purpose?).

(c) Regulations affecting investment advisers, and ethical considerations, including the definition of investment business.

(d) Advising on sources and costs of different forms of finance and their applicability to different circumstances including:

    (i) bank borrowing;
    (ii) finance houses;
    (iii) mortgages;
    (iv) money and capital markets.

The official 2000 syllabus

(e) Advising on investment of clients' personal funds.

    (i) Insurance policies
    (ii) Pension funds
    (iii) Unit and investment trusts
    (iv) TESSAs
    (v) PEPs
    (vi) Equity shares
    (vii) Gilt edged securities and other bonds
    (viii) Real property
    (ix) Banks and building societies
    (x) National savings

Standard of the paper

The standard of the paper is comparable to that required in the examinations for the second year of a three year UK honours degree course.

Prerequisite knowledge

A thorough understanding of Paper 7 *Tax Framework* is essential for the study of Paper 11.

Paper 11 builds on topics introduced in Paper 7 by:

- applying the knowledge of income tax to tax planning problems for personal and business situations
- interacting knowledge of National Insurance with other taxes
- extending the coverage of corporation tax to include groups and consortia, liquidations and investment and close companies
- applying capital gains tax to individuals and corporate taxpayers, with emphasis on business situations
- applying VAT to transactions and other activities of corporate taxpayers

The teaching guide for Paper 11 assigns the revision of basic areas covered in Paper 7 (income tax, capital gains tax, corporation tax and VAT) to self study to allow sufficient contact time to be allocated to the more advanced subject matter.

In addition, Paper 11 introduces some new areas - overseas considerations, inheritance tax, trusts and personal finance.

List of excluded topics

National Insurance

- The calculation of directors' NIC on a month by month basis
- For the purposes of Class 4 NIC: the offset of trading losses against non-trading income
- Social security: the areas of benefit

Income tax

- Profit related pay schemes
- Pre 5 April 1988 maintenance payments and deeds of covenant
- Relief for interest on home improvement loans

The official 2000 syllabus

- Detailed computations in respect of share options, share incentives, profit sharing and profit related pay. An employee share ownership plan (ESOP) will not be examined in its own right
- A detailed knowledge of the conditions which must be met to obtain Inland Revenue approval for an occupational pension scheme
- Commercial woodlands
- Computations in respect of a non-qualifying life assurance policy or a qualifying policy which is surrendered within ten years
- The PYB rules for Schedule D
- The transitional rules applicable to Schedule D
- Retirement annuities
- A question would not be set involving the cessation of an old business (pre 6.4.94) during 1996/97, 1997/98 or 1998/99.

Capital gains tax

- The rules applicable to assets held on 6 April 1965
- The grant of a lease or sub-lease out of either a freehold, long lease or short lease
- A detailed knowledge of the statements of practice on partnership capital gains
- A question would not be set in respect of a principal private residence where the taxpayer was not in occupation on 31 March 1982
- A detailed question will not be set on the pooling provisions for shares (post 6/4/98 acquisitions)
- Reinvestment relief
- A detailed question will not be set on the relief available where gains are re-invested in enterprise investment scheme shares or in venture capital trusts.

Inheritance tax

- A detailed knowledge of gifts with reservation
- Double grossing up on death
- Valuation of an interest in possession trust where there is an annuity and requiring the use of higher and lower income yields
- Double tax relief calculation involving $\frac{A}{A+B} \times C$ formula
- An accumulation and maintenance trust ceasing to qualify
- Conditional exemption for heritage property
- Woodlands relief
- A question will not be set involving the computation of a principal or an exit charge for a discretionary trust (note that a written question could be set on the principles involved)
- The relief on BPR/APR given to exempt legacies

Trusts

- Tax liabilities arising during a period of administration
- The 'tax pool' where insufficient 34% income tax has been paid by a discretionary trust
- The IHT implications of adding property to discretionary trust
- Retirement relief
- The residence of trusts
- The overseas aspects of trusts

Value Added Tax

- The special VAT schemes for retailers
- The capital goods scheme
- In respect of property and land: leases, do-it-yourself builders and demolition
- A detailed knowledge of penalties (apart from the default surcharge, serious misdeclarations and default interest)

Corporation tax

- Advance corporation tax (ACT)
- The carryback of a loss arising in an accounting period commencing prior to 2 July 1997
- S 242 ICTA 1988 loss relief
- A question will not be set on the interaction of consortium relief and group relief, although this does not preclude the situation where a (loss making) company has both a (profit making) 75% subsidiary and is also a consortium member (re a profit making consortium company)
- The definition of a close company (although the consequences of being a close company are examinable)
- Demergers and reconstructions (other than share for share amalgamations). On disincorporations, a question is unlikely to be set on the sale of a trade or business in return for shares. A question involving a double charge to CGT would not be set
- On liquidations, a question would not be set on the more complex areas such as the different types of liquidation, the preference of debts, or income and expenses arising during the liquidation. A question involving a double charge to CGT would not be set
- A computational question involving the carry back of a loss arising from a loan relationship for non trading purposes

Overseas activities

- A detailed knowledge of double tax agreements
- The 100% relief for 365 day qualifying periods
- Foreign income dividends and international headquarters companies

The official 2000 syllabus

General

- The names of cases or a detailed knowledge of the judgements, although a knowledge of the principles derived from the leading cases is required
- A question will not be set requiring a knowledge of anti-avoidance legislation (eg artificial transactions in land). However, a question might be set requiring comment as to the Inland Revenue's possible attitude towards a particular transaction/situation taking into account the principles from decided cases

RATES AND ALLOWANCES

A INCOME TAX

1 Rates

	1998/99 £	%	1999/00 £	%
Lower rate	1 - 4,300	20	1 - 1,500	10
Basic rate	4,301 - 27,100	23	1,501 - 28,000	23
Higher rate	27,101 and above	40	28,001 and above	40

In 1999/00 savings (excl. Dividend) income is taxed at 20% if it falls within the lower and basic rate bands. Dividend income within these bands is taxed at 10%. Dividend income within the higher rate band is taxed at 32.5%.

2 Allowances and tax reducers

	1998/99 £	1999/00 £
Personal allowance	4,195	4,335
Personal allowance (65 - 74)	5,410	5,720
Personal allowance (75 and over)	5,600	5,980
Married couple's allowance	1,900	1,970
Married couple's allowance (65 - 74)	3,305	5,125
Married couple's allowance (75 and over)	3,345	5,195
Income limit for age-related allowances	16,200	16,800
Additional personal allowance	1,900	1,970
Widow's bereavement allowance	1,900	1,970
Blind person's allowance	1,330	1,380

3 Car fuel scale charges

	1999/00 Petrol £	1999/00 Diesel £
Cars having a cylinder capacity		
1,400 cc or less	1,210	1,540
1,401 cc to 2,000 cc	1,540	1,540
More than 2,000 cc	2,270	2,270
Cars not having a cylinder capacity	2,270	2,270

4 Fixed profit car scheme - 1999/00 rates

	On first 4,000 miles	On each mile over 4,000
Size of car engine		
Up to 1,000 cc	28p	17p
1,000 cc - 1,500 cc	35p	20p
1,501 cc - 2,000 cc	45p	25p
Over 2,000 cc	63p	36p

Rates and allowances

5 *Personal pension contribution limits*

Age	Maximum percentage %
Up to 35	17.5
36 – 45	20.0
46 – 50	25.0
51 – 55	30.0
56 – 60	35.0
61 or more	40.0

Subject to earnings cap of £87,600 for 1998/99 and £90,600 for 1999/00

6 *Capital allowances*

	%
Plant and machinery	
Writing down allowance*	25
First year allowance (acquisitions 2.7.97 - 1.7.98)**	50
First year allowance (acquisitions 2.7.98 - 1.7.00)	40
Industrial buildings allowance	
Writing down allowance: post 5.11.62	4
pre 6.11.62	2
Agricultural buildings allowance	
Writing down allowance	4

* 6% reducing balance for certain long life assets.
** 12% for certain long life assets.

B CORPORATION TAX

1 *Rates*

Financial year	Full rate %	Small companies rate %	Marginal relief fraction	Upper limit £	Lower Limit £
1992	33	25	1/50	1,250,000	250,000
1993	33	25	1/50	1,250,000	250,000
1994	33	25	1/50	1,500,000	300,000
1995	33	25	1/50	1,500,000	300,000
1996	33	24	9/400	1,500,000	300,000
1997	31	21	1/40	1,500,000	300,000
1998	31	21	1/40	1,500,000	300,000
1999	30	20	1/40	1,500,000	300,000

2 *Marginal relief*

$(M - P) \times I/P \times$ Marginal relief fraction

Rates and allowances

C VALUE ADDED TAX

1 *Registration and deregistration limits*

	To 31.3.99	From 1.4.99
Registration limit	£50,000	£51,000
Deregistration limit	£48,000	£49,000

2 *Scale charges for private motoring*

1999/2000 and 1998/99 (VAT inclusive)

	12 months Petrol	Diesel
Up to 1400 cc	850	785
1401 to 2000 cc	1,075	785
Over 2000	1,585	995

D INHERITANCE TAX

6.4.96 - 5.4.97	6.4.97 - 5.4.98	6.4.98 - 5.4.99	6.4.99 onwards	Rate
£1 - £200,000	£1 - £215,000	£1 - £223,000	£1 - £231,000	Nil
Excess	Excess	Excess	Excess	40%

E RATES OF INTEREST

Official rate of interest: 10% (assumed)

Rate of interest on unpaid/overpaid tax: 10% (assumed)

F CAPITAL GAINS TAX

1 *Lease percentage table*

Years	Percentage	Years	Percentage	Years	Percentage
50 or more	100.000	33	90.280	16	64.116
49	99.657	32	89.354	15	61.617
48	99.289	31	88.371	14	58.971
47	98.902	30	87.330	13	56.167
46	98.490	29	86.226	12	53.191
45	98.059	28	85.053	11	50.038
44	97.595	27	83.816	10	46.695
43	97.107	26	82.496	9	43.154
42	96.593	25	81.100	8	39.399
41	96.041	24	79.622	7	35.414
40	95.457	23	78.055	6	31.195
39	94.842	22	76.399	5	26.722
38	94.189	21	74.635	4	21.983
37	93.497	20	72.770	3	16.959
36	92.761	19	70.791	2	11.629
35	91.981	18	68.697	1	5.983
34	91.156	17	66.470	0	0.000

Rates and allowances

2 *Retail prices index (January 1987 = 100.0)*

	1982	1983	1984	1985	1986	1987	1988	1989
Jan		82.6	86.8	91.2	96.2	100.0	103.3	111.0
Feb		83.0	87.2	91.9	96.6	100.4	103.7	111.8
Mar	79.4	83.1	87.5	92.8	96.7	100.6	104.1	112.3
Apr	81.0	84.3	88.6	94.8	97.7	101.8	105.8	114.3
May	81.6	84.6	89.0	95.2	97.8	101.9	106.2	115.0
Jun	81.9	84.8	89.2	95.4	97.8	101.9	106.6	115.4
Jul	81.9	85.3	89.1	95.2	97.5	101.8	106.7	115.5
Aug	81.9	85.7	89.9	95.5	97.8	102.1	107.9	115.8
Sept	81.9	86.1	90.1	95.4	98.3	102.4	108.4	116.6
Oct	82.3	86.4	90.7	95.6	98.5	102.9	109.5	117.5
Nov	82.7	86.7	91.0	95.9	99.3	103.4	110.0	118.5
Dec	82.5	86.9	90.9	96.0	99.6	103.3	110.3	118.8

	1990	1991	1992	1993	1994	1995	1996	1997	1998	1999*
Jan	119.5	130.2	135.6	137.9	141.3	146.0	150.2	154.4	159.5	164.5
Feb	120.2	130.9	136.3	138.8	142.1	146.9	150.9	155.0	160.3	165.0
Mar	121.4	131.4	136.7	139.3	142.5	147.5	151.5	154.4	160.8	165.5
Apr	125.1	133.1	138.8	140.6	144.2	149.0	152.6	156.3	162.6	166.0
May	126.2	133.5	139.3	141.1	144.7	149.6	152.9	156.9	163.5	166.5
Jun	126.7	134.1	139.3	141.0	144.7	149.8	153.0	157.5	163.4	167.0
Jul	126.8	133.8	138.8	140.7	144.0	149.1	152.4	157.5	163.0	167.5
Aug	128.1	134.1	138.9	141.3	144.7	149.9	153.1	158.5	163.7	168.0
Sept	129.3	134.6	139.4	141.9	145.0	150.6	153.8	159.3	164.4	168.5
Oct	130.3	135.1	139.9	141.8	145.2	149.8	153.8	159.6	164.5	169.0
Nov	130.0	135.6	139.7	141.6	145.3	149.8	153.9	159.6	164.4	169.5
Dec	129.9	135.7	139.2	141.9	146.0	150.7	154.4	160.0	164.4	170.0

* Estimated figures.

3 *Annual exemption (individuals)*

	£
1993/94	5,800
1994/95	5,800
1995/96	6,000
1996/97	6,300
1997/98	6,500
1998/99	6,800
1999/00	7,100

4 Taper relief

Number of complete years after 5.4.98 for which asset held	Business assets % of gain chargeable	Non business assets % of gain chargeable
0	100	100
1	92.5	100
2	85	100
3	77.5	95
4	70	90
5	62.5	85
6	55	80
7	47.5	75
8	40	70
9	32.5	65
10 or more	25	60

G NATIONAL INSURANCE (NOT CONTRACTED OUT RATES) 1999/00

Class 1 contributions

	£
Lower earning limit (LEL)	3,432 (£66 pw)
Upper earnings limit (UEL)	26,000 (£500 pw)
Employee contributions	10% on earnings between LEL and UEL (8.4% if contracted out)
Employer contributions	Not contracted out 12.2% on earnings in excess of earnings threshold of £4,335 pa (£83 pw)

Class 1A and Class 1B contributions

Rate 12.2%

Class 2 contributions

Rate	£6.55 pw
Small earnings exception	£3,770 pa

Class 4 contributions

Rate	6%
Lower earnings limit	£7,530
Upper earnings limit	£26,000

Question bank

DO YOU KNOW - PERSONAL COMPUTATIONS, EMPLOYMENT AND INVESTMENT INCOME

- Check that you can fill in the blanks in the statements below before you attempt any questions. If in doubt, you should go back to your BPP Study Text and revise first.

- In a personal computation, we must add up the individual's income from all sources and deduct charges to arrive at ...Statutory Total Income..., and then deduct the personal allowance to arrive at ...TAXABLE INCOME...

- Income from employment is taxed under Schedule E, on a ...receipts... basis.

- Expenses are generally deductible only if they are incurred ...wholly..., ...exclusively... and ...necessary... in the performance of the duties of the employment.

- The general measure of a benefit for an employee earning £8,500 or more per annum or a director is the ...cost to the employer of providing it...

- For employees earning £8,500 or more per annum and directors:
  - The taxable benefit for cars is cost × a % ((35%, 25% or 15%) which depends on the number of ...business... miles travelled × a factor (1 or 3/4) which depends on the ...age... of the car. A partial contribution by the employee ...reduces... the benefit.
  - There is a set scale benefit for fuel for private motoring. A partial contribution by the employee ...not allowable... the benefit.
  - Loans may give rise to taxable benefits based on the official rate of interest, but there is an exemption for loans under ...5000...
  - The taxable value of assets made available for use is the higher of
    (i) ...20...% of the asset's ...Market Value..., and
    (ii) any ...rent... paid by the employer
  - The first ...500... of any benefit arising in respect of the private use of computer equipment is exempt.
  - If ownership of an asset is subsequently transferred, the benefit is based on the higher of ...cost less amount already taxed + M.V. at the date..., and ...of transfer...

- Accommodation can give rise to a taxable benefit for ...all... employees
  - The basic benefit is the ...Annual Value... of the property.
  - There is an additional benefit where the accommodation cost over ...75,000... There is an exemption for ...Job related... accommodation.

- There is a ...30,000... exemption for termination payments.

- Employees pay ...Class 1... NICs. Employers pay ...Secondary Class 1... NICs, and also ...Class 1A... NICs on car and fuel benefits and Class 1B NICs.

- Most interest income is received net of ...20...% tax and is taxed in the year of ...receipt... Basic rate taxpayers have ...no... further liability.

- Dividends are received net of a ...10%... tax credit. The tax credit can be offset against a taxpayer's tax liability but it cannot be repaid to a non taxpayer.

- Income from renting out land and buildings is taxed under Schedule A, on an ...accruals... basis as if the owner were running a business.

TRY QUESTIONS 1 TO 6

DID YOU KNOW - PERSONAL COMPUTATIONS, EMPLOYMENT AND INVESTMENT INCOME

- *Could you fill in the blanks? The answers are in bold. Use this page for revision purposes as you approach the exam.*

- In a personal computation, we must add up the individual's income from all sources and deduct charges to arrive at **statutory total income**, and then deduct the personal allowance to arrive at **taxable income**.

- Income from employment is taxed under Schedule E, on a **receipts** basis.

- Expenses are generally deductible only if they are incurred **wholly**, **exclusively** and **necessarily** in the performance of the duties of the employment.

- The general measure of a benefit for an employee earning £8,500 or more per annum or a director is the **cost to the employer of providing it**.

- For employees earning £8,500 or more per annum and directors:

    o The taxable benefit for cars is cost × a % (35%, 25% or 15%) which depends on the number of **business** miles travelled × a factor (1 or $^3/_4$) which depends on the **age** of the car. A partial contribution by the employee **reduces** the benefit.

    o There is a set scale benefit for fuel for private motoring. A partial contribution by the employee **does not reduce** the benefit.

    o Loans may give rise to taxable benefits based on the official rate of interest, but there is an exemption for loans under **£5,000**.

    o The taxable value of assets made available for use is the higher of

        (i) **20%** of the asset's **market value,** and

        (ii) any **rent** paid by the employer

    o The first **£500** of any benefit arising in respect of the private use of computer equipment is exempt.

    o If ownership of an asset is subsequently transferred, the benefit is based on the higher of **the original cost of the asset less amounts already taxed**, and **the market value at the date of transfer.**

- Accommodation can give rise to a taxable benefit for **all** employees

    o The basic benefit is the **annual value** of the property.

    o There is an additional benefit where the accommodation cost over **£75,000**. There is an exemption for **job related** accommodation.

- There is a **£30,000** exemption for termination payments.

- Employees pay **primary Class 1** NICs. Employers pay **secondary Class 1** NICs, and also **Class 1A** NICs on car and fuel benefits and Class 1B NICs.

- Most interest income is received net of **20%** tax and is taxed in the year of **receipt**. Basic rate taxpayers have **no** further liability.

- Dividends are received net of a **10%** tax credit. The tax credit can be offset against a taxpayer's tax liability but it cannot be repaid to a non taxpayer.

- Income from renting out land and buildings is taxed under Schedule A, on an **accruals** basis as if the owner were running a business.

TRY QUESTIONS 1 TO 6

1 TUTORIAL QUESTION: CAR AND TRAVEL

R Robb was appointed Sales Director of Wirral Widget plc, a UK company, on 1 April 1999, at a salary of £20,000 a year. The company also provided him with the following.

(a) A new petrol engined company car, a 2,500 cc model, costing £17,000. Mr Robb's annual mileage is 25,000 miles, of which 20% is non-business. Total annual expenditure on the car, paid by the company, is £2,800 including all fuel.

(b) Company-owned computer equipment for both business and private use. The equipment cost the company £3,300 on 6.4.99.

He contributes 4% of his salary (excluding benefits in kind) to an approved superannuation scheme.

In the three months to 30 June 1999 Mr Robb was primarily working from the company's offices in Aberdeen. However, he was, from time to time, required to work at a client's premises in Inverness. The company reimbursed Mr Robbs travel expenses of £800 which was the full cost he incurred in travelling directly from his home to the client's premises. The cost of travelling from the company's offices in Aberdeen to Inverness would have been £600.

On 1 July 1999 he flew from London to Egypt on the first stage of a sales visit from which he returned to London on 12 September 1999. For the month of August 1999 he was joined by his wife Sally and their young son. The company reimbursed him £1,600 for their fares and £1,000 for their accommodation.

On 1 November 1999, the company made him a loan of £25,000 at 4% a year, with interest payable monthly in arrears, to assist his purchase of a new home. He has no other mortgage. Assume an official rate of interest of 10%.

He has a pension of £750 a year from a German company for whom he worked in Africa for ten years.

Required

Compute R Robb's taxable income for 1999/00. Do not calculate tax payable.

Guidance notes

1. When a taxpayer receives several benefits, you can take them one by one. Your first step should be to jot down the benefits (car, computer equipment, etc) and then search the question for relevant information on each one. You should also note separately other information, such as pension contributions.

2. You can then work out the value of each item of income separately. Do not try to do two things at once. Get each item right and then move on to the next one.

3. You can then combine all the components of income to arrive at statutory total income and then at taxable income.

2 TECHNO PLC (6/96)   *45 mins*

Techno plc is a rapidly expanding quoted company involved in management consultancy. The company is looking at ways of both motivating and retaining its 10 directors and 70 key personnel, of which several have recently been lost to competitors. The company has 400 other full-time employees, of whom 120 have joined the company during the past two years. One of the directors, Martin Thatch, owns 35% of the ordinary share capital of Techno plc. The other nine directors are 2% shareholders. None of the directors are connected to each other. The average remuneration of the directors and the key personnel is £100,000 pa and £40,000 pa respectively.

The proposals under consideration are as follows.

(a) In January of each year paying an annual bonus based on the increase in profit made by Techno plc compared to the previous year. It is likely that payments of up to £15,000 pa would be payable to each employee.

(b) Setting up a profit sharing scheme whereby directors and key personnel would receive fully paid up ordinary shares in Techno plc free of charge each year. Techno plc would set up a trust to run the scheme, with the trust purchasing the shares required through the Stock Exchange, using funds provided by Techno plc.

(c) Providing each of the directors and key personnel with a new 2400cc petrol powered company motor car. The list price of each motor car is £27,500. In addition, each motor car will be fitted with a mobile telephone costing £500, and other optional accessories costing £2,000. Techno plc will also pay for private petrol, private telephone calls, and will provide free car parking spaces near its offices. The car parking spaces will be rented by Techno plc at a cost of £350 pa each. The motor cars will be driven between 5,000 and 10,000 miles on business each year.

(d) Providing each of the directors and key personnel with an interest free loan of £25,000. This loan will be written off in two years time, provided that the director or the key person is still employed by Techno plc at that date. The loan will be immediately repayable should a director or key person resign from Techno plc's employment.

(e) Setting up a share option scheme whereby directors and key personnel would receive options to purchase fully paid up ordinary shares in Techno plc at their present value. The options would be provided free, and would be exercisable in five years time.

Techno plc's ordinary shares are presently fully paid and quoted at £1.00 each, and are likely to be worth £4.00 each in five years time. Techno plc is a close company.

Required

(a) Explain the income tax, CGT and NIC implications for the directors and key personnel in respect of each of the five proposals. You should ignore the implications of VAT, and should assume that Inland Revenue approval, where applicable, *is not obtained* in respect of any of the proposals. (13 marks)

(b) (i) Briefly state the conditions that must be met in order for the profit sharing scheme (proposal (b)) and the share option scheme (proposal (e)) to obtain Inland Revenue approval. Your answer should indicate whether or not the proposed schemes will qualify for approval.

You are not expected to discuss employee share ownership plans (ESOPs).

(7 marks)

(ii) Advise the directors and key personnel of the potential tax saving if Inland Revenue approval is obtained for the profit sharing scheme and the share option scheme. (5 marks)

(25 marks)

CLIFFORD JONES (12/94) *45 mins*

Clifford Jones and Dinah Smith, both of whom are divorced, are to marry on 30 April 1999. You should assume that today's date is 15 April 1999. Clifford is aged 43, whilst Dinah is aged 42. They have asked for your advice, and the following information is available:

(a) Clifford and Dinah are both self-employed practitioners in alternative medicine. Clifford's practice is in London, and he makes tax adjusted profits of £55,000 pa. Dinah's practice is in Glasgow, and she makes tax adjusted profits of £15,000 pa. Clifford's business is valued at £125,000, whilst Dinah's is valued at £40,000. They will continue to run both practices once they are married although they are unsure as to whether or not it would be beneficial to do so in partnership with each other.

Each year, Clifford and Dinah both contribute the maximum possible amounts qualifying for tax relief into personal pension schemes.

(b) Clifford has a son, aged 22, from his previous marriage, who is presently studying full-time at university but lives with Clifford during the university holidays. Dinah has two daughters, aged 10 and 13, from her previous marriage, who both live with her.

(c) Clifford has a house in London worth £220,000 with an outstanding endowment mortgage of £90,000, which was bought in 1993. Dinah has a house in Glasgow worth £85,000 with an outstanding endowment mortgage of £35,000, which was bought in 1995. Clifford and Dinah are paying gross mortgage interest under MIRAS of £7,200 pa and £3,500 pa respectively. Although they will continue to live in their separate houses after marrying, they will spend weekends and holidays together.

(d) Clifford and Dinah jointly own a holiday cottage in Scotland worth £40,000, which produces taxable income of £5,000 pa. The cottage is 75% owned by Clifford and 25% by Dinah.

(e) Dinah plans to sell a number of assets during March 2000, and this will result in chargeable gains before taper relief of £6,500, £4,200 and £9,000, and an allowable loss of £2,400. The gains of £6,500 and £4,200 will arise on non-business assets whilst the gain of £9,000 and the loss will arise on the disposal of business assets. All of the assets were acquired before 17 March 1998. Neither Clifford nor Dinah will dispose of any other chargeable assets during 1999/00.

(f) Clifford has £50,000 in a building society deposit account, which will produce interest of £1,920 (net) during 1999/00.

(g) Clifford and Dinah have other assets worth £95,000 and £10,000 respectively.

(h) Clifford and Dinah will both draw up new wills when they get married. Clifford is to leave one half of his London house to his son, with all of his remaining assets passing to Dinah, or his son if Dinah predeceases him. Dinah is to leave all of her assets to her daughters.

Clifford and Dinah do not feel that they are wealthy enough for either of them to make any substantial lifetime gifts of assets to their children. They are both concerned that their own children should ultimately inherit the majority of their respective assets.

Required

(a) Advise Clifford and Dinah of the income tax implications arising from their forthcoming marriage on 30 April 1999. (5 marks)

(b) Advise Clifford and Dinah of tax planning measures that they could take following their marriage on 30 April 1999. Your answer should be confined to the implications of income tax, capital gains tax and NIC and should include a calculation of their tax liabilities for 1999/00 prior to your advice. You are not expected to advise on tax-free investments such as ISAs. (8 marks)

(c) Briefly discuss the inheritance tax implications arising from Clifford and Dinah's proposed new wills. Your answer should outline tax planning measures that they could take in order to reduce their potential IHT liability. (5 marks)

(d) Clifford is concerned that should Dinah outlive him, his son should inherit upon her death any assets that Clifford has bequeathed to Dinah under the terms of his will. Explain how this could be achieved by the use of an interest in possession trust. Your answer should include a brief description of how such a trust would be subject to income tax, capital gains tax and IHT up to, and including, the time that its assets are distributed to Clifford's son. (7 marks)

(25 marks)

4 CHARLES CHOICE (6/97) *45 mins*

Charles Choice, aged 47, is an assistant manager with the Northwest Bank plc on a gross annual salary of £23,500.

You should assume that today's date is 2 April 2000, and that the tax rates and allowances for 1999/00 apply throughout. You are *not* expected to take the time value of money into account in any of your answers.

(a) As from 6 April 2000, Charles will be required to drive 8,000 miles each year for business purposes. The Northwest Bank plc have offered him a choice of either a company car or a cash alternative, as follows.

  (i) A new 1298cc diesel powered motor car with a list price of £14,400. All running costs, including private fuel, will be paid for by the Northwest Bank plc. Charles will be required to contribute £50 per month towards the private use of the motor car, of which £15 will be partial reimbursement of private fuel. Under this alternative, Charles would not run a private motor car.

  (ii) Additional salary of £2,800 pa. Charles would then use his private motor car for business mileage. The private motor car is leased at a cost of £285 per month, and has a list price of £11,500. The annual running costs including fuel, are £1,650. He will drive a total of 12,000 miles per year. The Northwest Bank plc pays a business mileage allowance of 23 pence per mile for the type of car run by Charles. The relevant rates allowed under the fixed profit car scheme are 35 pence per mile for the first 4,000 miles, and 20 pence per mile thereafter.

Required

Advise Charles as to which of the two alternatives will be the most beneficial from his point of view. Your answer should include:

  (i) calculations of the additional tax liabilities that will arise under each alternative, and

  (ii) a comparison of a claim for business expenditure and a claim based on the fixed profit car scheme. (13 marks)

(b) Charles joined the Northwest Bank plc four years ago, but has not joined the company's Inland Revenue approved occupational pension scheme. He has been offered the chance to join on 6 April 2000.

Before joining the Northwest Bank plc, Charles regularly changed employers. He has therefore saved for a pension by contributing into a personal pension plan. For 1999/00 he made the maximum amount of tax deductible contributions based on his salary of £23,500.

Under the Northwest Bank plc's occupational pension scheme, Charles would contribute 6% of his salary (you should assume that this is £23,500), and the company would contribute a further 6%. The benefits payable on retirement will be based on final salary.

Required

(i) Advise Charles of the factors that he will have to take into account when deciding whether or not to join the Northwest Bank plc's occupational pension scheme. (5 marks)

(ii) Charles is concerned that if he joins the Northwest Bank plc's occupational pension scheme, his tax deductible contributions will be less than under a personal pension scheme.

Advise Charles of how he could make additional voluntary contributions in order to increase his entitlement to a pension. (2 marks)

(c) David Spence is resident, ordinary resident and domiciled in the UK. On 1 June 1999 he left the UK and went to work in Australia. David expects to return to the UK in March 2004.

David is considering selling a French holiday cottage whilst he is absent from the UK. This sale would result in a gain for capital gains tax purposes of £100,000.

Required

Advise David on whether the gain arising on the sale of the holiday cottage will be subject to UK CGT if he sells the cottage in (i) March 2000 or (ii) September 2000.

(5 marks)

(25 marks)

5 **WILLIAM WILES (6/97)** *45 mins*

(a) William Wiles acquired three houses on 6 April 1999. Houses 1 and 2 were acquired freehold, and are let as furnished holiday accommodation. House 3 was acquired on a 25 year lease, and is let furnished. During 1999/00 the houses were let as follows.

House 1 was available for letting for 42 weeks during 1999/00, and was actually let for 14 weeks at £375 per week. During the 10 weeks that the house was not available for letting, it was occupied rent free by William's sister. Running costs for 1999/00 consisted of business rates £730, insurance £310, and advertising £545.

House 2 was available for letting for 32 weeks during 1999/00, and was actually let for eight weeks at £340 per week. The house was not available for letting for 20 weeks due to a serious flood. As a result of the flood, £6,250 was spent on repairs. The damage was not covered by insurance. The other running costs for 1999/00 consisted of business rates £590, insurance £330, and advertising £225.

House 3 was unoccupied from 6 April 1999 until 31 December 1999. On 1 January 2000 the house was sub-let on a four year lease for a premium of £8,000, and a rent of £8,600 pa payable annually in advance. William had paid a premium of £85,000 for the 25 year lease. During 1999/00 he paid the rent of £6,200 due annually in advance on 6 April 1999, and spent £710 on redecorating the property during June 1999.

Immediately after their purchase, William furnished the three houses at a cost of £6,500 per house. With the exception of the 10 week rent-free letting of house 1, all the lettings are at a full rent.

During 1999/00 William also rented out one furnished room of his main residence. he received rent of £4,600, and incurred allowable expenditure of £825.

Required

(i) Briefly explain why both house 1 and house 2 qualify to be treated as a trade under the furnished holiday letting rules. State the tax advantages of the houses being so treated. (5 marks)

(ii) Calculate William's allowable Schedule A loss for 1999/00, and advise him as to the possible ways of relieving the loss. (14 marks)

(b) On 30 June 1999 William permanently separated from his wife. William and his wife are both aged 39, and they have a son, aged 15, who is in full-time education. The son spends an average of two days each week living with William. Since 1 July 1999 William had been paying his wife maintenance of £475 per month. He has also been paying his son's school fees of £1,800 per term, and the mortgage interest of £550 (gross) per month on a mortgage of £80,000 that was used to purchase a new property for his wife. Until 31 December 1999, these payments were made voluntarily, but on 1 January 2000 they were confirmed by a written agreement as part of the divorce settlement. Under the agreement, William made a lump sum payment of £25,000 to his wife, and will continue the regular payments until the son completes his full-time education in three year's time.

Required

(i) Explain the tax implications arising in 1999/00 from the payments made by William to support his wife and son

(1) voluntarily between 1 July 1999 and 31 December 1999, and
(2) under the divorce settlement from 1 January 2000 onwards. (4 marks)

(ii) State what personal allowances William will be entitled to for 1999/00.

(2 marks)

(25 marks)

6 DUNCAN MCBYTE (12/98) *45 mins*

Duncan McByte is a computer programmer currently living in Scotland. As a result of the 'millennium problem' Duncan's services are in great demand, and he has recently accepted the offer of a contract of employment with Mainframe plc for a period of three years commencing on 1 July 1999 and ceasing on 30 June 2002. Duncan will be based in London during the period of the contract. The remuneration package comprises:

(1) A salary of £65,000 pa together with a termination bonus of £40,000 upon satisfactory completion of the three year contract.

(2) Mainframe plc is providing accommodation for Duncan in London. This is an apartment that was purchased in 1988 for £94,000, and was improved at a cost of £35,000 during 1996. The apartment has a rateable value of £6,700 and is currently valued at £170,000. The furniture in the apartment cost £21,000 and Mainframe plc is paying for the annual running costs of £6,200.

(3) Duncan using his private motor car for business mileage. The motor car is leased at a cost of £380 per month, and the annual running costs, including fuel, are £1,800. He drives a total of 1,200 miles per month, of which 1,000 miles are for business purposes. Mainframe plc pays a mileage allowance of 40 pence per mile for business mileage. The relevant rates allowed under the Fixed Profit Car Scheme are 63 pence per mile for the first 4,000 miles, and 36 pence per mile thereafter.

(4) On 1 July 1999 Mainframe plc provided Duncan with a loan of £60,000 that he has used to purchase a holiday cottage in France. The loan has an interest rate of 4% pa. and will be repaid by six half-yearly instalments of £10,000 commencing on 31 December 1999.

(5) Mainframe plc will pay for Duncan's annual subscription of £125 to the Institute of Chartered Computer Consultants, a sports club membership of £800 pa, an annual premium of £650 for liability insurance, and £1,200 pa. for computer training courses that will keep him up to date with the latest software developments. These amounts will all be paid during January of each year.

(6) On 1 July 1999 Duncan was granted options to purchase 15,000 £1 ordinary shares in Mainframe plc at their value on that date. The options were provided free, and will be exercised by Duncan upon the termination of his contract on 30 June 2002. Mainframe plc's shares were valued at £1.75 on 1 July 1999, and are forecast to be worth £5.00 by 30 June 2002.

Duncan's options have been granted under the Inland Revenue approved company share option scheme that is operated by Mainframe plc.

From 1 July 1999, Duncan has rented out his main residence in Scotland as furnished holiday accommodation. The forecast rental income for 1999/2000, based on 32 weeks letting is £21,000, of which 22.5% will be paid to a letting agency. Running costs will amount to £900. The house was furnished at a cost of £24,000 during June 1999. Duncan has a mortgage of £60,000 on which interest of £5,400 (gross) will be paid during 1999/2000. The mortgage is under MIRAS.

Required

(a) Explain the income tax and NIC implications arising from the remuneration package that Mainframe plc has given to Duncan.

Your answer should include calculations of the amounts assessable under Schedule E for 1999/2000. Assume the official rate of interest is 10%. (17 marks)

(b) Explain why it was beneficial for Duncan's share options (see note (6)) to be granted under an Inland Revenue approved company share option scheme. (3 marks)

(c) Advise Duncan of the Schedule A profit that he will be assessed on for 1999/2000.

(5 marks)

(25 marks)

DO YOU KNOW? - CAPITAL GAINS TAX AND INHERITANCE TAX

- *Check that you can fill in the blanks in the statements below before you attempt any questions. If in doubt, you should go back to your BPP Study Text and revise first*

- The basic CGT computation is: proceeds – cost – indexation allowance = gain.

- The indexation allowance cannot create or increase a .... For individuals the indexation allowance is not available after 6 April 1998, instead a .... relief is available.

- Losses brought forward are deducted before taper relief. However, brought forward losses should only be deducted to the extent that the .... is not wasted.

- Special rules apply to assets acquired before 31 March 1982.

  o Two computations are done, one deducting cost and the other deducting the 31 March 1982 value.

  o The indexation allowance is based on the .... of cost and March 1982 value

  o The final result is the .... gain, the .... loss or (if there is one gain and one loss) ....

  o A global election to use only .... values may be made.

- For companies, shares acquired before .... are included in the 1982 pool. Shares acquired from this date are put in the .... pool.

- Enhancement expenditure is deductible if it is reflected in the .... at the time of disposal.

- On a reorganisation, the original cost of shares is apportioned to new types of capital using the .... of the new capital on the first day of quotation after reorganisation

- Wasting chattels are .... (unless capital allowances were available on them). For other chattels, both gains and losses may be restricted. The key figure is ....

- On a part disposal cost/March 82 value must be apportioned using the formula ....

- A non-domiciled individual is only taxable on foreign gains to the extent that they are .... to the UK.

TRY QUESTION 7

- Inheritance tax (IHT) is charged on the amount which an individual or a trust loses through giving property away, or selling it for less than its value. This is known as the .... principle. Transfers are cumulated for .... years.

- The charge on an individual is basically on all his property at death. IHT is also charged on amounts given away in the .... years before death. Tapering relief reduces the tax charged on gifts made more than .... years before death.

- Practically all gifts during lifetime which are not exempt for other reasons (as, for example, gifts to charities are), and are not to discretionary trusts, are potentially exempt transfers. If the donor survives for seven years after a PET, it is ....; otherwise it is ....

- An annual exemption of .... is available each year. Unused annual exemption may be carried forward .... year. The current year annual exemption is used .... the annual exemption brought forward.

- Business property relief (BPR) is available on businesses, partnership shares and shareholdings. The rate of relief is ....% or ....%. Agricultural property relief (APR) applies to the .... value of farmland. It is at ....%.

TRY QUESTIONS 8 TO 15

DID YOU KNOW? - CAPITAL GAINS TAX AND INHERITANCE TAX

- *Could you fill in the blanks? The answers are in bold. Use this page for revision purposes as you approach the exam.*

- The basic CGT computation is: proceeds – cost – indexation allowance = gain.

- The indexation allowance cannot create or increase a **loss**. For individuals the indexation allowance is not available after 6 April 1998, instead a **taper** relief is available.

- Losses brought forward are deducted before taper relief. However, brought forward losses should only be deducted to the extent that the **annual exemption** is not wasted.

- Special rules apply to assets acquired before 31 March 1982.

  o Two computations are done, one deducting cost and the other deducting the 31 March 1982 value.

  o The indexation allowance is based on the **higher** of cost and March 1982 value

  o The final result is the **lower** gain, the **lower** loss or (if there is one gain and one loss) **no gain/no loss.**

  o A global election to use only **31 March 1982** values may be made.

- For companies, shares acquired before **1 April 1982** are included in the 1982 pool. Shares acquired from this date are put in the **FA 1985** pool.

- Enhancement expenditure is deductible if it is reflected in the **state and nature of the asset** at the time of disposal.

- On a reorganisation, the original cost of shares is apportioned to new types of capital using the **market values** of the new capital on the first day of quotation after reorganisation

- Wasting chattels are **exempt** (unless capital allowances were available on them). For other chattels, both gains and losses may be restricted. The key figure is **£6,000**.

- On a part disposal cost/March 82 value must be apportioned using the formula $\frac{A}{A+B}$.

- A non-domiciled individual is only taxable on foreign gains to the extent that they are **remitted** to the UK.

TRY QUESTION 7

- Inheritance tax (IHT) is charged on the amount which an individual or a trust loses through giving property away, or selling it for less than its value. This is known as the **diminution in value** principle. Transfers are cumulated for **seven** years.

- The charge on an individual is basically on all his property at death. IHT is also charged on amounts given away in the **seven** years before death. Tapering relief reduces the tax charged on gifts made more than **three** years before death.

- Practically all gifts during lifetime which are not exempt for other reasons (as, for example, gifts to charities are), and are not to discretionary trusts, are potentially exempt transfers. If the donor survives for seven years after a PET, it is **exempt**; otherwise it is **chargeable**.

- An annual exemption of **£3,000** is available each year. Unused annual exemption may be carried forward **one** year. The current year annual exemption is used **before** the annual exemption brought forward.

- Business property relief (BPR) is available on businesses, partnership shares and shareholdings. The rate of relief is **100%** or **50%**. Agricultural property relief (APR) applies to the **agricultural** value of farmland. It is at **100%**.

TRY QUESTIONS 8 TO 15

7 TUTORIAL QUESTION: A CHATTEL, LAND AND SHARES

Price supplied the following information in order that his accountant could compute his capital gains tax position for 1999/00.

(i) He sold a vase on 1 August 1999 for £10,900 which he had purchased for £8,400 on 31 March 1982.

(ii) He sold a piece of land on 5 July 1999 for £54,000. He had purchased the land as an investment on 6 December 1974 for £2,000, and had improved it on 1 June 1984 for £3,000. Incidental costs of sale were £985. The market value on 31 March 1982 was £15,000.

(iii) He sold 12,000 shares in Index plc (a quoted company) on 1 July 1999 for £42,000. He had acquired and sold shares in the company on the following dates.

Purchases	Number of shares	Cost £
1 May 1981	10,000	9,000
1 March 1982	2,000	2,000
1 May 1998	2,000	5,314

The market value of Index plc shares at 31 March 1982 was £1.40 per share.

(iv) On 10 September 1999 he sold a property for £60,000, which he had purchased for £25,000 on 1 February 1984. The property had always been used in Price's business.

Price is a single man aged 40, and his income for 1999/00 comprises salary of £6,000 and dividends of £16,875 net.

Required

(a) Compute his income tax and capital gains tax position for 1999/00.
(b) State the due date for payment of capital gains tax for 1999/00.

Guidance notes

1. This question involves a number of separate disposals. They should be dealt with one at a time, and any gains and losses only combined at the end.

2. Indexation is only given to individuals to April 1998.

3. The vase is a chattel (tangible movable property). Special rules apply to non-wasting chattels, based on their value. What are the value-based rules, and how (if at all) do they affect this case?

4. The land was acquired before 31 March 1982 so two calculations are needed.

5. Shares acquired after 6.4.98 are not pooled. After this date each acquisition is dealt with separately.

6. The amount of taper relief available on the disposal of the business asset depends on the number of years of ownership of the asset.

8 KEN SING (12/94) *45 mins*

Ken Sing, aged 59, has been living in the UK since July 1993, working for the London branch of the Pajan National Bank. Ken was born in the country of Pajan, where he is domiciled, and he plans to return there when he retires in June 2000. You should assume that today's date is 5 April 2000.

Ken is paid a salary of £75,000 pa by the Pajan National Bank, and is provided with an 1,800cc motor car which cost £38,000 in 1997. During 1999/00 Ken drove 15,000 miles of which 20% were for business purposes. All running costs, including petrol, are paid for by the bank. The Pajan National Bank also pays for Ken's private medical insurance premiums of £1,200 pa, and for his £1,500 pa membership of a golf club which is used to meet clients of the bank. Ken has an interest free loan of £90,000 from the bank, which was used to purchase his private residence in London. This cost £115,000 in July 1993, and is currently worth £175,000. PAYE of £33,500 was deducted from Ken's salary during 1999/00.

Ken also owned the following assets as at 5 April 2000.

(a) A house situated in Pajan worth £120,000, which is rented out for £10,000 pa. Pajanese tax at the rate of 30% is payable on the rental income. Ken remits £3,500 of the income to the UK each year, and invests the remainder in Pajan. In December 1999 Ken sold a plot of land attached to the house for £40,000. All of the proceeds from the disposal were remitted to the UK. The house and land were purchased in March 1985 for £50,000. The house has never been Ken's principal private residence.

(b) 100,000 £1 ordinary shares in High-Growth plc, an investment trust quoted on the UK Stock Exchange at 102 - 110. High-Growth plc has an issued share capital of 10,000,000 shares, and paid a dividend of nine pence per share during 1999/00. Ken inherited the shares as a specific gift on the death of an uncle in September 1996 when they were worth £45,000. The uncle was domiciled in the UK and paid IHT of £80,000 on an estate valued at £350,000.

(c) 20,000 £1 ordinary shares in Small-Time Ltd, an unquoted UK resident trading company with an issued share capital of 250,000 shares. Ken has sat on the board of the company as a non-executive director since June 1995. This post is unpaid, and Small-Time has not paid a dividend in recent years. Ken's shareholding is worth £65,000, and was subscribed for at par in December 1993. Small-Time Ltd has assets worth £1,050,000, of which £50,000 are investments in quoted shares.

(d) Bank deposits of £80,000 with the Pajan National Bank, of which £60,000 is held at the London branch and £20,000 at the main branch in Pajan. Interest has been credited to these accounts in 1999/00 as follows: London branch £2,240; Pajan branch £850.

Interest is stated net of tax, which in the case of the Pajanese branch is at the rate of 15%. All of the interest arising in respect of the Pajanese branch has been remitted to the UK.

In December 1999 Ken sold a set of paintings situated in his Pajan residence for £8,000. The paintings were purchased in March 1985 for £2,800. Ken deposited the proceeds from the disposal in his bank account in Pajan.

Under the Pajanese tax system, capital gains are not subject to taxation. There is no double taxation treaty between the United Kingdom and Pajan.

Ken has been a widower for a number of years, and has left all of his assets to his children under the terms of his will.

Assume that the official rate of interest is 10%.

Required

(a) Calculate Ken's income tax and CGT payable for 1999/00. (9 marks)

(b) Advise Ken of his liability to IHT were he to die before returning to Pajan in June 2000. You answer should include an explanation of why Ken's assets are or are not subject to IHT, and should assume that he has no outstanding tax liabilities. (9 marks)

(c) When he return to Pajan, Ken plans to dispose of all of his assets situated in the UK. Advise him of his liability to CGT if he were to dispose of these assets (i) before returning to Pajan, and (ii) after returning to Pajan. You should assume that all disposals are made in June 2000, and that Ken will be liable to CGT at the rate of 40% during 2000/01. (7 marks)

You should use the tax rates and allowances for 1999/00 throughout, and should assume that the value of Ken's assets will not materially alter in the foreseeable future.

(25 marks)

9 DESMOND AND MYRTLE COOK (6/94) *45 mins*

Desmond and Myrtle Cook, aged 62 and 67 respectively, are a wealthy couple who are each planning to make a gift to their only child, Judy aged 33. The gifts are to be made on 31 March 2000 (you should assume that today's date is 10 March 2000), and are as follows.

Desmond is to give his furnished holiday cottage worth £115,000. During 1999/00 rental income of £14,200 accrued in respect of the cottage, whilst the running costs amounted to £1,340. In addition, the roof of the cottage had to be replaced during May 1999 at a cost of £1,600 due to storm damage. The cottage was bought on 1 October 1984 for £23,000, and from that date until 31 March 1997 it was rented out as unfurnished accommodation. On 1 April 1997 the cottage was furnished at a cost of £10,098, and from that date onwards has been rented out as furnished holiday accommodation, meeting the conditions for treatment as a 'trade' throughout the whole of this period.

Myrtle is to give 8,000 of her 20,000 £1 ordinary shares in Artic Ltd, an unquoted investment company. Her 20,000 shares represent a shareholding of exactly 8%. The remainder of the company's share capital is held by unconnected persons. Artic Ltd's shares are worth £15.00 each for a holding of less than 5%, and £16.50 each for a holding of between 5% and 10%. Myrtle inherited the shares on 30 March 1994 when they were valued at £78,000. Myrtle has never worked for Arctic Ltd.

Both Desmond and Myrtle have made previous lifetime transfers of assets. Desmond made a gift of £98,000 in May 1993 to his brother. Myrtle made a gift of £114,000 in July 1993 to a discretionary trust for the benefit of her nephews, the trustees paying any IHT. The couple's other assets consist of their jointly owned main residence which is worth £270,000, and interest-bearing investments held by Myrtle worth £125,000. These investments produce taxable income of £10,000 pa (gross). Apart from Desmond's pension of £6,000 pa and Myrtle's salary of £40,000 pa, the couple have no other income or outgoings. Under the terms of their wills, both Desmond and Myrtle have left all of their assets to Judy.

Required

(a) Assuming that Desmond and Myrtle make their gifts to Judy on 31 March 2000:

    (i) calculate their taxable income and taxable gains for 1999/00; (11 marks)

    (ii) calculate the inheritance tax liabilities that would arise if they were both to die during June 2001. You should assume that the holiday cottage and the 8,000 shares in Artic Ltd are still owned by Judy at that date. (7 marks)

(b) Outline tax planning measures that Desmond and Myrtle could take in order to reduce their overall liability to income tax, capital gains tax, and potential liability to inheritance tax. The couple *do not* wish to change their overall portfolio of investments. (7 marks)

You should assume that the tax rates and allowances for 1999/00 apply throughout.

(25 marks)

10 BLUETONE LTD (6/98) *45 mins*

Bluetone Ltd is an unquoted trading company that manufactures compact discs. The company has four full-time working directors, each of whom owns 25% of its share capital of 200,000 £1 ordinary shares. These are currently valued as follows:

Shareholding	Value per share £
15%	9.00
25%	11.00
35%	12.50
50%	15.00

Melody Brown

Melody has recently been appointed a director after inheriting her father's 50,000 shares in Bluetone Ltd. Melody's father purchased the shareholding on 12 November 1999, but died on 15 February 2000. At the date of his death he also owned the following assets:

(a) 42,000 50p ordinary shares in Expanse plc quoted at 312 - 320, with bargains of 282, 288, 306 and 324.

(b) 26,000 units in World-Growth, a unit trust. The bid price was 80 and the offer price was 84.

(c) Building society deposits of £32,000 of which £3,000 was in an ISA.

(d) His main residence valued at £125,000 with an outstanding repayment mortgage of £42,000.

(e) A life assurance policy on his own life with an open market value of £53,000. Proceeds of £61,000 were received on 4 March 2000.

On 15 February 2000, Melody's father had an income tax liability of £6,600 and gambling debts of £1,200. Funeral expenses came to £3,460. Under the terms of his will, Melody was left the shares in Bluetone Ltd. The shares are to bear their own IHT. Melody wants to retain the full 25% holding so she is to personally account for the IHT liability. The residue of the estate was left to Melody's brother. Melody's father made the following lifetime gifts:

(a) On 10 February 1996 he made a wedding gift of £30,000 to Melody.
(b) On 4 June 1996 he made a gift of £161,000 into a discretionary trust.

Liam and Opal White

Liam and Opal, a married couple aged 37 and 32 respectively, have been directors and shareholders of Bluetone Ltd since its incorporation on 1 October 1990 when they acquired their shares at par. On 20 March 2000 Liam is to sell 30,000 of his shares in Bluetone Ltd to their son for £75,000. Liam is a 40% taxpayer, and has not previously made any lifetime gifts of assets.

Noel Green

Noel is aged 52 and has been a director and shareholder of Bluetone Ltd since its incorporation on 1 October 1990. For the past two years he has disagreed with the other directors of Bluetone Ltd over the company's business policies. He is therefore to resign as a director on 31 March 2000, and it has been agreed that Bluetone Ltd will purchase his shareholding for £550,000. The Inland Revenue has given advance clearance that the purchase qualifies for the special treatment applying to a company's purchase of its own shares, and can therefore be treated as a capital gain.

Noel acquired the shares at par, and is a 40% taxpayer.

For the year ended 31 March 2000 Bluetone Ltd is forecast to have profits chargeable to corporation tax of £1,100,000. The company has no chargeable non-business assets.

Required

(a) Calculate Melody's IHT liability and state when this will be due. (10 marks)

(b) Advise Liam of the CGT and IHT implications of selling the 30,000 shares in Bluetone Ltd to his son. You should assume that reliefs are claimed in the most favourable manner on the basis that Liam wishes to defer gains where possible.

(9 marks)

(c) Advise both Bluetone Ltd and Noel of whether it will be beneficial to have the purchase of Noel's 25% shareholding treated as a capital gain under the special treatment, rather than as a distribution by Bluetone Ltd. (6 marks)

The rates and allowances for 1999/00 should be used throughout.

(25 marks)

11 MONTY NOBLE (12/97) *45 mins*

Monty Noble, aged 72, died on 15 July 1999. You should assume that today's date is 31 October 1999. At the date of his death Monty owned the following assets.

(a) His main residence valued at £255,000.

(b) Three holiday cottages valued at £55,000 each.

(c) Building society deposits of £285,000

(d) 20,000 50p ordinary shares in Congo Ltd, an unquoted trading company. The shares were acquired by Monty on 1 May 1999 and on 15 July 1999 were valued at £3.50. Congo Ltd has 20% of the value of its total assets invested in property which is let out.

(e) Agricultural land and buildings valued at £225,000, but with an agricultural value of £180,000. Monty purchased the land on 1 January 1991, and it has always been let out to tenant farmers. The most recent tenancy commenced on 1 January 1999.

Monty was survived by his wife, Olive, and their two children Peter and Penny. Penny has three children aged 6, 15 and 17. Under the terms of his will, Monty left all of his estate to Olive. She is aged 70 and does not own any assets. Olive is not in good health, and does not expect to live past 31 December 2002. Under the terms of her will, Olive has left all of her estate to Peter and Penny. The Noble family appreciate that Monty's estate has not been distributed in a tax efficient manner, and had therefore agreed the following plan.

(a) The three holiday cottages are to be sold on 10 December 1999. The expected selling prices are £47,500, £58,100 and £54,400. Professional fees of £500 will be incurred in respect of each sale.

(b) A field adjoining the existing farmland and buildings is to be purchased for £27,000 on 18 December 1999. Professional fees of £600 are included in the purchase price.

(c) The terms of Monty's will are to be varied so that Olive is left the main residence and £270,000 in cash. The agricultural land and buildings, together with the field purchased on 18 December 1999, will be put into a trust for the benefit of Penny's children. Under the terms of the trust, the income will be used to pay the children's school fees, with the balance being accumulated until the youngest child reaches the age of 18. The assets of the trust will then be distributed as the trustees so decide at that date. The remaining assets will be left to Peter and Penny.

(d) On 25 December 1999, Olive will make a gift of the main residence to Peter. She will continue to live in two rooms of the house, but will pay Peter a commercial rent.

With the exception of the holiday cottages, the only asset which is likely to change in value before 31 December 2002 is the main residence which will then be worth £330,000. Neither Monty nor Olive have made any lifetime transfers of value prior to 15 July 1999.

Required

(a) Advise the Noble family of the inheritance tax implications of the proposed plan. Your answer should consist of:

(i) a calculation of the inheritance tax that will be saved as a result of implementing the plan. (16 marks)

(ii) An explanation of the conditions that must be met for the plan to be valid for inheritance tax purposes. (2 marks)

(iii) Advice as to any improvements that could be made to the plan. (3 marks)

You should assume that Olive dies on 31 December 2002, and that the tax rates and allowances for 1999/00 apply throughout. You should ignore the instalment option.

(b) Explain whether or not the proposed trust for the benefit of Penny's children will qualify to be treated as an accumulation and maintenance trust. Briefly state the tax advantages of the trust being treated as an accumulation and maintenance trust rather than a discretionary trust. (4 marks)

(25 marks)

12 MING WONG (12/98) *45 mins*

Ming Wong aged 63, was born in the country of Yanga, but has lived in the UK since 6 April 1985. Ming is a resident and ordinarily resident in the UK, but is not domiciled in the UK. Following her marriage to a UK citizen Ming is planning to become UK domiciled.

Ming is employed by the Yangan National Bank in London and was paid a salary of £29,000 during 1999/2000. At 5 April 2000 Ming owned the following assets.

(1) A main residence valued at £245,000. This is situated in the UK, and has an outstanding endowment mortgage of £80,000.

(2) A house in Yanga worth £60,000, from which rental income of £7,500 (gross) was received during 1999/2000. Yangan tax at the rate of 35% was paid on the rental income.

(3) 40,000 shares in Ganyan Inc., a company quoted on the Yangan Stock Exchange at 308-316. Dividends of £5,950 (net) were received during 1999/2000, after the deduction of Yangan tax at the rate of 15%.

(4) Antiques worth £35,000. These were bought in Yanga, but are now situated in Ming's UK residence.

(5) Bank deposits of £50,000 with the Yangan National Bank of which £30,000 is held at the London branch and £20,000 at the main branch in Yanga. During 1999/2000 interest of £1,680 (net) was credited to the account in London, and £1,530 (net of Yangan tax at the rate of 15%) was credited to the account in Yanga.

(6) An interest-free loan of £15,000 to Ming's brother who is resident in Yanga. The loan was used to purchase property situated in the UK.

(7) Ming has recently become the beneficiary of a trust set up by her father. Under the terms of the trust, she is entitled to receive all of the trust income, although no income was actually received during 1999/2000. The trust owns UK government stocks with a nominal value of 20,000, quoted at 92-94. Ming's father was domiciled in Yanga at the time of setting up the trust.

None of the income arising in Yanga has been remitted to the UK.

Under the terms of her will, Ming has left all of her assets to her three children. If she were to die, Yangan death duty of £48,000 would be payable in respect of the house situated in Yanga and the 40,000 shares in Ganyan Inc., irrespective of her domicile.

There is no double taxation agreement between the UK and Yanga. All of the above figures are in Pounds sterling.

Ming has not made any previous chargeable transfers.

Required:

(a) Advise Ming of

    (i) when she will be treated as domiciled in the UK for the purpose of IHT, and

    (ii) how she could acquire domicile in the UK under general law. **(4 marks)**

(b) Advise Ming as to the potential increase in her liability to UK IHT if she were to become domiciled in the UK. Your answer should include an explanation of why Ming's assets are or are not subject to UK IHT. **(12 marks)**

(c) (i) Calculate the UK income tax payable by Ming for 1999/2000.

    (ii) Calculate the additional UK income tax that would have been payable by Ming for 1999/2000 if she has been domiciled in the UK as from 6 April 1999. **(9 marks)**

(25 marks)

13 DOROTHY LAKE (6/97) *45 mins*

You are the tax adviser to Dorothy Lake, aged 75. Under the terms of her will, Dorothy has left her entire estate to her daughter Alice, since Dorothy's husband is wealthy in his own right. Dorothy does not expect to live past her eightieth birthday which is on 31 December 2004, and she therefore wants to know whether or not it would be beneficial for tax purposes to make a lifetime gift of assets to Alice. The gift will be made on 30 June 2000, and will consist of the following assets.

(a) 50,000 £1 ordinary shares in Windermere Ltd, an unquoted trading company. Dorothy owns a total of 100,000 shares in Windermere Ltd, and her husband also owns 100,000 shares in the company. Windermere Ltd has an issued share capital of 200,000 £1 ordinary shares. At present, the relevant values of Windermere Ltd's shares are as follows.

Shareholding	Value per share £
100%	4.50
75%	3.55
50%	2.95
25%	2.50

By 31 December 2004, these values are likely to have increased by 40%. Windermere Ltd owns investments in quoted shares that represent 12% of the value of its total assets.

Dorothy originally acquired 50,000 £1 ordinary shares in Coniston Ltd in March 1987 for £96,000. Coniston Ltd was taken over by Windermere Ltd on 15 October 1994, at which time Dorothy received two £1 ordinary shares in Windermere Ltd and £0.80 in cash for each share held in Coniston Ltd. On 15 October 1994 a 50% holding of Windermere Ltd's ordinary shares was worth £1.20 per share. Dorothy has never been a director or employee of either Coniston Ltd or Windermere Ltd.

Alice is a risk averse investor, and would therefore sell the shares in Windermere Ltd soon after receiving them.

(b) An antique painting worth £8,500. This was acquired in June 1987 for £1,400. The painting is not likely to change in value before 31 December 2004.

(c) A holiday cottage worth £165,000. Dorothy inherited the cottage on the death of her sister in May 1996 when it was worth £188,000. Because the cottage is situated on cliffs that are being eroded, it is only likely to be worth £90,000 on 31 December 2004. The cottage does not qualify to be treated as a furnished holiday letting.

Dorothy has other assets worth £350,000, has not made any previous lifetime transfers of assets, has not disposed of any assets during 2000/01, and is a higher rate taxpayer. Apart from the share in Windermere Ltd, it is likely that the assets gifted to Alice will still be owned by her at the end of Dorothy's death. Alice is also a 40% taxpayer.

Required

Advise Dorothy of whether or not it would be beneficial for tax purposes to make the gift of assets to Alice on 30 June 2000. Your answer should include a calculation of the inheritance tax and capital gains tax liabilities that would arise if Dorothy

(a) *Makes* the gift to Alice on 30 June 2000
(b) Does *not make* the gift to Alice on 30 June 2000.

You should assume that Dorothy dies on 31 December 2004, that wherever possible, beneficial elections or claims are made to postpone tax liabilities, and that the tax rates and allowances for 1999/00 apply throughout.

Your answer should show the due date of any IHT liabilities, and the amount of IHT that can be paid under the instalment option. You should include tax planning advice that you consider to be relevant. **(25 marks)**

14 MICHAEL EARL (12/95) *45 mins*

Michael Earl, aged 48, died on 30 June 1999. At the time of his death, Michael owned the following assets.

(a) 50,000 £1 ordinary shares in Compact Ltd, an unquoted UK resident trading company with an issued share capital of 1,000,000 shares. Michael originally bought 100,000 shares for £400,000 in May 1998. He made a gift of 50,000 shares to his daughter, Jade, on 10 July 1998. Michael's wife, Naomi, also owns 50,000 shares in Compact Ltd, which she also acquired in May 1998. The relevant values of Compact Ltd's shares, as agreed by the Inland Revenue, are as follows.

	Value per share	
Shareholding	at 10.7.98	at 30.6.99
	£	£
5%	5.00	6.00
10%	7.00	8.40
15%	10.00	12.00

(b) 50,000 £1 ordinary shares in Diverse Inc, a quoted trading company with an issued share capital of 10,000,000 shares. The company is resident in the country of

Gobolia. Michael originally bought 150,000 shares in March 1986. He made a gift of 100,000 shares into a discretionary trust for the benefit of his grandchildren on 19 August 1998. Michael paid the IHT arising as a result of the gift. Diverse Inc's shares were quoted on the Gobolian Stock Exchange at 308 - 316 on 19 August 1998, with recorded bargains of 296, 320 and 328 for that day. On 30 June 1999 they were quoted at 279 - 287, with recorded bargains of 275 and 285. All of the above figures are in pounds sterling.

(c) Other UK assets valued for IHT purposes at £850,000. This figure is after providing for any tax liabilities outstanding at 30 June 1999.

Under the terms of his will, Michael left £200,000 in cash to his wife Naomi, and the residue of his estate to his daughter Jade. Michael and Jade are domiciled in the UK, but Naomi is domiciled in Gobolia.

Following Michael's death, the following occurred:

(a) On 5 September 1999 the executors of Michael's estate sold the 50,000 shares in Compact Ltd for £260,000, and the 50,000 shares in Diverse Inc for £120,000.

(b) On 10 December 1999 Jade sold her 50,000 shares in Compact Ltd for £285,000.

Up to the date of his death Michael was a 40% taxpayer. Jade is also a 40% taxpayer. Neither Michael nor Jade has ever been a director or employee of either Compact Ltd or Diverse Inc.

Gobolian death duty of £35,000 was paid as a result of Michael's death. There is no double taxation treaty between the United Kingdom and Gobolia.

Required

(a) (i) Calculate the IHT liabilities arising as a result of Michael's death on 30 June 1999. Your answer should state who is liable for the payment of each liability, and should show the due date of payment. You should *ignore* the IHT annual exemption in your answer.

(ii) State what IHT reliefs will be available as a result of the disposals by the executors of Michael's estate on 5 September 1999, and advise them of whether or not a claim would be beneficial in each case. (16 marks)

You should assume that tax rates and allowances for 1999/00 apply throughout.

(b) (i) Assuming that holdover relief was *not claimed* in respect of the gift made by Michael to Jade on 10 July 1998, calculate Jade's CGT liability for 1999/00.

(ii) Advise Jade and the executors of Michael's estate as to the tax implications arising from making a claim for holdover relief in respect of the gift on 10 July 1998. You should assume that if a holdover relief claim is made, then the value of Michael's estate will increase by the amount of the CGT no longer payable.

You should *ignore* the CGT annual exemption in your answer. (9 marks)

(25 marks)

15 MAUD SMITH (6/95) *45 mins*

Maud Smith is a 71 year old pensioner who has been made a widow as a result of the death of her husband, aged 76, on 7 April 1999 (you should assume that today's date is 6 April 2000). Maud inherited all of her husband's estate upon his death, and now owns the following assets:

(a) Her main residence which is currently valued at £130,000.

(b) 20,000 50p ordinary shares in Sparks & Mincer plc, a 'blue chip' UK company currently quoted at 410 - 426. Sparks & Mincer plc regularly pays a dividend of 9 pence per share each year.

(c) 45,000 £1 ordinary shares in Bit-Part Ltd, an unquoted trading company with a share capital of 200,000 ordinary shares. The other shares in the company are held equally by Maud's three children. Bit-Part Ltd paid a dividend of 10 pence per share during 1999/00. Maud inherited all of these shares from her husband, who originally acquired them at their par value in March 1984. The shares were valued at £160,000 on 7 April 1999, and are currently worth £205,000. Maud is planning to make a gift of these shares to her children. Maud had never worked for Bit-Part Ltd.

(d) UK government stocks with an interest rate of 4%, and a nominal value of £100,000. These are currently quoted at 90-94, and are due for redemption in 2000. The interest on these gilts was paid to Maud net of tax.

(e) 25,000 units in Global Trust, a unit trust quoted in the UK at 210-218. The trust is aimed at capital growth, and therefore only paid a dividend of £450 (net) during 1999/00.

(f) Deposits of £86,000 in an instant access account with the Sprat & Minnow Building Society. This is a small building society, but is paying a high rate of interest of 9% gross pa.

(g) £10,000 in the National Savings Pensioners Guaranteed Income Bond, which pays a gross interest rate of 7%.

During 1999/00 Maud received income of £5,120 (net) as the life tenant of an interest in possession trust set up by her brother. The trust holds assets consisting of UK government stocks worth £65,200. Maud's only other income is the UK state pension of £3,471 pa, and a private pension of £2,500 pa (gross). Her husband did not have any taxable income for 1999/00.

Under the terms of her will, Maud has left all of her estate to her family. Her only previous lifetime gift of assets was a gift of £165,000 to a discretionary trust for the benefit of her children in June 1993. £165,000 was the gross gift before annual exemptions. Assume that the annual exemption has always been £3,000.

Maud considers herself to be a risk-averse investor. She wishes to maximise her income, whilst not risking the capital value of her assets.

Required:

(a) (i) Calculate the income tax refund that Maud will be entitled to for 1999/00.

  (ii) Calculate the IHT liability that would arise if Maud were to die during April 2000. Your answer should indicate who is liable for the tax, and by what date.

  (12 marks)

(b) Advise Maud of the tax implications that would arise from a gift of her 45,000 ordinary shares in Bit-Part Ltd to her children if the gift is made:

  (i) as a lifetime gift during April 2000, or

(ii) by varying the terms of her husband's will.

Your answer should include advice as to whether or not it might be beneficial for Maud to instead make the gifts to her grandchildren. (7 marks)

(c) Advise Maud as to the suitability of her present portfolio of investments as regards her stated investment criteria. Your answer should include brief suggestions as to how Maud's portfolio of investments might be improved upon in terms of making it more tax efficient or reducing risk. (6 marks)

You should assume that the tax rates and allowances for 1999/00 apply throughout.

(25 marks)

DO YOU KNOW - INVESTMENTS AND FINANCE; TRUSTS

- *Check that you can fill in the blanks in the statements below before you attempt any questions. If in doubt, you should go back to your BPP Study Text and revise first.*

- Unused personal pension relief can be carried forward for .... years. A premium paid can be related back for relief in ....

- An investor should consider not only any exemptions from income tax and/or CGT (for example those available for ISAs) but also .... and ....

- When a business is selecting a source of finance, its main choice is between debt and equity. Interest is tax-deductible, unlike dividends, but a high level of debt increases the risk of insolvency.

- Rental income is taxed on an .... basis under Schedule A.

- The special rules for furnished holiday lets apply if a property is available for commercial letting to the public for at least .... days, is actually let for at least .... of those days and is not normally in the same occupation for more than 31 days for at least seven months.

- Interest in possession trusts are taxed at ....% on non-savings income and at ....% on savings income. Dividends are received net of a tax credit of 10%. Discretionary trusts are taxed at ....%.

- The rate of capital gains tax for all trusts is .... Chargeable gains may arise when assets enter or leave a trust.

- There are special inheritance tax charges on property in discretionary trusts. As well as charges on every .... anniversary of the creation of the trust and on property ...., transfers into the trust are chargeable (at half the normal tax rates) when made.

TRY QUESTIONS 16 TO 19

DID YOU KNOW - INVESTMENTS AND FINANCE; TRUSTS

- *Could you fill in the blanks? The answers are in bold. Use this page for revision purposes as you approach the exam.*

- Unused personal pension relief can be carried forward for **six** years. A premium paid can be related back for relief in **the previous year**.

- An investor should consider not only any exemptions from income tax and/or CGT (for example those available for ISAs) but also **risk** and **liquidity**.

- When a business is selecting a source of finance, its main choice is between debt and equity. Interest is tax-deductible, unlike dividends, but a high level of debt increases the risk of insolvency.

- Rental income is taxed on an **accruals** basis un0der Schedule A.

- The special rules for furnished holiday lets apply if a property is available for commercial letting to the public for at least **140** days, is actually let for at least **70** of those days and is not normally in the same occupation for more than 31 days for at least seven months.

- Interest in possession trusts are taxed at **23%** on non-savings income and at **20%** on savings income. Dividends are received net of a tax credit of 10%. Discretionary trusts are taxed at **34%**.

- The rate of capital gains tax for all trusts is **34%**. Chargeable gains may arise when assets enter or leave a trust.

- There are special inheritance tax charges on property in discretionary trusts. As well as charges on every **tenth** anniversary of the creation of the trust and on property **leaving the trust**, transfers into the trust are chargeable (at half the normal tax rates) when made.

TRY QUESTIONS 16 TO 19

16 MING LEE (6/94) *45 mins*

Ming Lee, a UK resident who was born on 9 June 1947, is a self-employed management consultant. For 1999/00 she will have Schedule D Case II profits of £95,000, and this level of profits is expected to remain the same for the foreseeable future. Ming has had the following taxable profits since she commenced self-employment during 1992/93.

Tax Year	Schedule D Case II profits
	£
1992/93	26,000
1993/94	34,500
1994/95	47,000
1995/96	53,000
1996/97	63,500
1997/98	70,000
1998/99	90,000

Because she operates from rented office accommodation, Ming's only chargeable business asset is the goodwill of the business which is currently valued at £250,000. She plans to sell her business and retire in three or four years time. However, due to the high level of her profits, Ming is considering the incorporation of her business in the near future.

Ming has funds surplus to her requirements of £140,000, which are presently invested in an ordinary deposit account at a building society. She would like to invest these funds in a way that will reduce her overall liability to income tax. Apart from building society interest of £8,700 (net) pa, Ming, who is single, has no other income. Her only outgoing is interest of £12,000 pa (gross) on her mortgage of £120,000. Ming's only previous payment of a personal pension premium was one of £20,000 during 1996/97.

Required

(a) Calculate the maximum amount of tax deductible contributions that Ming could make into a personal pension scheme for 1999/00. Advise Ming of whether or not it would be beneficial for her to actually contribute this maximum amount, and whether or not this is a suitable investment for her. (7 marks)

(b) As an alternative to investing in a personal pension scheme, Ming is considering using her surplus funds as follows.

  (i) Repaying some, or all, of her mortgage.

  (ii) Purchasing National Savings Certificates.

  (iii) Investment in an enterprise zone trust which will itself invest in commercial properties situated in enterprise zones.

  Advise Ming of the suitability of each of these alternatives to her particular circumstances. Your answer should include an outline of the tax implications of each alternative. (8 marks)

(c) Outline the taxation factors that would have to be considered when deciding whether or not Ming should incorporate her business. You are *not* expected to include calculations in your answer, and you should *ignore* the implications arising from capital allowances and the private use of assets. (10 marks)

You should assume that the tax rates and allowances for 1999/00 apply throughout.

(25 marks)

Notes Question bank

17   MURIEL GRAND (6/96)   *45 mins*

On 31 December 1999 Muriel Grand aged 52, made a gift of a house in London to her brother Bertie, aged 45. Muriel had bought the house on 1 April 1985 for £60,000. Surplus land adjoining the house was sold for £24,000 to a neighbour in June 1986, at which date the market value of the property retained was £72,000. The market value at 31 December 1999 has been agreed by the Inland Revenue as £320,000. Muriel occupied the house as her main residence until 30 September 1992, and then moved on to another house that she owned in Glasgow. Muriel elected for the house in Glasgow to be treated as her main residence from 1 October 1992 onwards.

Bertie is to rent out the house in London, either unfurnished or as furnished holiday accommodation. In either case, the roof of the house must be repaired at a cost of £24,000 before it will be possible to let the house. The roof was badly damaged by a gale on 5 December 1999. If the house is let unfurnished, then Bertie will have to decorate it at a cost of £3,500. The forecast rental income is £28,000 pa. If the house is let as furnished holiday accommodation, then the house will be converted into two separate units at a cost of £42,000. The total cost of furnishing the two units will be £9,000. This expenditure will be financed by a £50,000 bank loan at an interest rate of 12% pa. The total forecast rental income is £45,000 pa, although 22.5% of this will be deducted by the letting agency. Other running costs, such as cleaning, will amount to £3,500 pa in total.

Bertie plans to sell the house when he retires on 31 December 2004 aged 50, and anticipates making a substantial capital gain. Both Muriel and Bertie are 40% taxpayers. Muriel has a portfolio of investments valued in excess of £1 million, and has already utilised her CGT annual exemption for 1999/00.

Required

(a) Calculate the CGT liability that will arise from Muriel's gift of the house in London to Bertie. (4 marks)

(b) Advise Muriel as to how it would be possible to roll-over the gain on the house in London by making an investment in EIS or VCT shares. State which of these investments will be the more risky and outline the other tax reliefs available. (6 marks)

(c) Advise Bertie of the tax implications of letting out the house in London either:

  (i) unfurnished; or

  (ii) as furnished holiday accommodation. Your answer should include details of the tax advantages of letting the house as furnished holiday accommodation. (13 marks)

(d) Advise Muriel as to where she could obtain independent financial advice. (2 marks)

(25 marks)

18   MARY MOLE (6/98)   *45 mins*

You are a Chartered Certified Accountant who is authorised to conduct investment business under the Financial Services Act 1986. Mary Mole, a client, inherited £25,000 on 15 December 1999, and has asked for your advice regarding a number of recommendations that she has received as to how this sum should be invested. The recommendations are as follows.

(a) Mary's bank manager has suggested that she invest the maximum amount possible in a maxi ISA, with the balance invested in a unit trust aimed at capital growth. The bank offers each of these investments.

(b) An insurance salesperson has suggested that Mary contribute the maximum tax deductible amount into a personal pension scheme. Mary was born on 1 December 1960, and has not previously made any provision for retirement. She is a partner in a business that writes computer software, and her recent Schedule D Case I assessments are as follows.

	£
1992/93	4,600
1993/94	46,200
1994/95	12,600
1995/96 and 1996/97	Nil (studying at university)
1997/98	8,100
1998/99	18,300
1999/00	57,400

(c) One of Mary's business partners has suggested that she make an investment in a venture capital trust. He believes that unquoted companies will offer an attractive investment return over the next five years, and that using a venture capital trust will diversify the risk of holding unquoted shares.

(d) Mary's post office manager has given her a leaflet on government stocks. She understands that these offer a competitive return, and has read that it is possible to purchase government stocks ex div and then to sell them cum div so that interest is effectively turned into a capital gain.

Mary's investment criteria are as follows:

(a) She would like to reduce her income tax and Class 4 NIC liability that you have advised her will be payable in respect of the 1999/00 partnership profits.

(b) Capital growth is more important that additional income.

(c) She is prepared to take a moderate amount of risk.

(d) Some or all of the capital may be needed in four years time when her daughter is expected to go to university.

Required

(a) In respect of each of the four recommendations:

　(i) explain the potential income tax and CGT implications. Your answer should include details of the maximum amount that can be invested in each case assuming that each investment will be made in 1999/00;

　(ii) advise Mary as to the suitability of each recommendation in relation to her investment criteria. **(21 marks)**

(b) (i) Explain the difference between a tied adviser and an independent adviser.

　(ii) The ACCA has issued Statements of Principle which cover the standards expected of an authorised person. State briefly what these principles are.

(4 marks)

(25 marks)

19 MR ROWE *45 mins*

At today's date (which you should assume is 1 July 1999), George Rowe, a single man aged 42, is expected to earn £63,000 from his employment as an oil company executive for the year ended 5 April 2000 (subject to PAYE of £19,400). During the year George expects to receive net dividends of £28,800 from his shareholdings.

On 6 April 1999, George had sold quoted shares in a multinational company Gong plc, which realised a capital gain of £90,000. He also intends to transfer further shares in

Gong plc, with a value of £245,000, into a trust for his brother Bob on 5 April 2000. This transfer will realise a further capital gain of £35,000. Bob is aged 12 and lives with George who has maintained him since the death of their parents in 1995. George is unsure whether the trust for Bob should be an accumulation and maintenance trust or a discretionary trust (of which George would not be a beneficiary). George has made no previous gratuitous transfers of any assets. He will pay any taxes or costs associated with setting up the trust. George is in excellent health.

George had acquired a house in Derby, together with grounds of 0.4 hectare on 1 August 1981 for £280,000. The house is subject to a mortgage (under MIRAS) from a building society of £100,000, bearing a fixed rate of interest of 10% pa gross. There was no change in the value of the house up to 31 March 1982. Unfortunately it has recently been decided that a motorway is to be built close to the house and as a result it is currently worth only £200,000. George's history of occupation of the house is as follows.

1.8.81 - 30.6.82	Occupied
1.7.82 - 31.12.83	Sent by employer to Saudi Arabia
1.1.84 - 30.9.92	Occupied
1.10.92 - date	Working in various parts of the UK on a four year tour of duty

George intends to sell the house on 31 December 1999 but is unsure whether or not he should reoccupy the house between 1 October 1999 (when his UK tour of duty ends) and 31 December 1999. He will rent a flat in Brighton from 1 January 2000 at a rent of £400 per month payable in advance.

Required

(a) Discuss the current and potential CGT and IHT implications for George of setting up:

    (i) an accumulation and maintenance trust for Bob;
    (ii) a discretionary trust for Bob. **(10 marks)**

(b) Compute George's income tax payable for 1999/00. **(8 marks)**

(c) Discuss whether George should occupy the house in Derby between 1 October 1999 and 31 December 1999. Show all supporting calculations. **(7 marks)**

(25 marks)

DO YOU KNOW – SELF ASSESSMENT AND PAYMENT OF TAX; SCHEDULE D CASES I AND II; PARTNERSHIPS; NATIONAL INSURANCE

- *Check that you can fill in the blanks in the statements below before you attempt any questions. If in doubt, you should go back to your BPP Study Text and revise first.*

- Under self assessment taxpayers must submit their tax return by the later of ......31.1...... following the tax year and ......3 months after issue......

- Payments on Account of income tax and Class 4 NICs are due on .... in the tax year and on the .... following. Final payments of income tax, Class 4 NICs and CGT are due on .... following the tax year.

- Interest may be charged on the late payment of tax.

- An initial surcharge of ...... is levied on unpaid income tax, CGT and Class 4 NICs which the taxpayer does not pay within ...... days of the 31 January following the tax year.

- There is a fixed penalty of .... for not making a tax return by the filing date when required to do so.

- The usual basis period for a tax year is the period of account ending ....
  - In the first tax year we tax profits arising from the .... to the following..........................
  - When an accounting date ends in the second tax year we tax the profits of .... or, if this is not possible, the profits of ....
  - When no accounting date ends in the second tax year we tax ....
  - In the third tax year we tax profits of the .... months to the accounting date ending in that year
  - In the final tax year we tax profits arising from the .... to ....

- .... arise when profits are taxed twice in the opening years of a business. These may either be relieved on .... or on ....

TRY QUESTIONS 20 TO 22, 24 TO 27

- A trading loss may be carried forward against ....

- A loss may be set against total income of .... and/or total income of ....

- Losses of the final twelve months of trading may be relieved against trading profits of the final tax year and the .... preceeding years, ... years first.

- Losses of the first four years of a business may be set against total income of the .... preceding years, ... year first.

TRY QUESTION 23

- Partners are taxed on their share of partnership profits. When a partner joins or leaves, commencement or cessation rules apply to ....

- The self-employed pay .... (flat rate) and .... (profit related) national insurance contributions.

TRY QUESTIONS 28 TO 30

DID YOU KNOW - SELF ASSESSMENT AND PAYMENT OF TAX; SCHEDULE D CASES I AND II; PARTNERSHIPS; NATIONAL INSURANCE

- *Could you fill in the blanks? The answers are in bold. Use this page for revision purposes as you approach the exam.*

- Under self assessment taxpayers must submit their tax return by the later of **31 January** following the tax year and **3 months after it was issued**.

- Payments on Account of income tax and Class 4 NICs are due on **31 January** in the tax year and on the **31 July** following. Final payments of income tax, Class 4 NICs and CGT are due on **31 January** following the tax year.

- Interest may be charged on the late payment of tax.

- An initial surcharge of **5%** is levied on unpaid income tax, CGT and Class 4 NICs which the taxpayer does not pay within **28** days of the 31 January following the tax year.

- There is a fixed penalty of **£100** for not making a tax return by the filing date when required to do so.

- The usual basis period for a tax year is the period of account ending **in the tax year.**

    o In the first tax year we tax profits arising from the **date of commencement** to the following **5 April**.

    o When an accounting date ends in the second tax year we tax the profits of **the twelve months to the accounting date ending in that year** or, if this is not possible, the profits of **the first twelve months**

    o When no accounting date ends in the second tax year we tax **the profits arising from 6 April to 5 April**

    o In the third tax year we tax profits of the **twelve** months to the accounting date ending in that year

    o In the final tax year we tax profits arising from the **end of the last accounting period** to **cessation**

- **Overlap** arise when profits are taxed twice in the opening years of a business. These may either be relieved on **change of accounting date** or on **cessation.**

TRY QUESTIONS 20 TO 22, 24 TO 27

- A trading loss may be carried forward against **future profits of the same trade.**

- A loss may be set against total income of **the year of the loss** and/or total income of **the preceeding year.**

- Losses of the final twelve months of trading may be relieved against trading profits of the final tax year and the **three** preceeding years, **later** years first.

- Losses of the first four years of a business may be set against total income of the **three** preceding years, **earliest** year first.

TRY QUESTION 23

- Partners are taxed on their share of partnership profits. When a partner joins or leaves, commencement or cessation rules apply to **that partner**.

- The self-employed pay **Class 2** (flat rate) and **Class 4** (profit related) national insurance contributions.

TRY QUESTIONS 28 TO 30

Question bank   Notes

20 TONY TORT (12/98)   45 mins

(a) Tony Tort commenced self-employment as a solicitor on 6 April 1998. His tax adjusted Schedule D Case II profit for the first year of trading to 5 April 1999 was £61,535, and the income tax and class 4 NIC liability for 1998/99 based on this figure was £19,275. The Inland Revenue issued a tax return for 1998/99 on 31 May 1999, but Tony did not submit this until 15 April 2000. He has made the following payments of income tax and class 4 NIC during 2000.

1998/99 Balancing payment	£19,275 paid 10 May 2000
1999/2000 First payment on account	£2,500 paid 15 June 2000
1999/2000 Second payment on account	£2,500 paid 31 July 2000

Because of cash flow problems, Tony claimed to reduce each of his payments on account for 1999/00 from £9,637.50 to £2,500.

Tony's tax adjusted Schedule D Case II profit for the year ended 5 April 2000 (before capital allowances) is £52,100. He purchased a new computer on 15 May 1999 for £5,200 and new photocopier on 20 January 2000 for £4,400. The tax written-down values of plant and machinery and Tony's motor car at 6 April 1999 were £13,600 and £17,800 respectively. The private use of the motor car is 10%.

Prior to 6 April 1998 Tony was employed by a firm of solicitor's. He is single, and has no other income or outgoings.

Required:

(i) Calculate the interest on overdue tax that Tony will be charged in respect of the late payments of income tax and class 4 NIC made during 2000. You should assume that the balancing payment for 1999/00 is made on the due date. Ignore leap years. Assume an interest rate of 10%.

(ii) Explain what surcharges and penalties Tony may be liable to.   (12 marks)

(b) On 10 September 2000 Tony received written notice from the Inland Revenue that they were to enquire into his tax return for 1998/99. The Inland Revenue gave written notice of the completion of the enquiry on 5 December 2000, stating that he has incorrectly claimed for entertaining expenditure of £4,500 in calculating his tax adjusted Schedule D Case II profit for the year ended 5 April 1999.

No adjustment is required to Tony's tax adjusted Schedule D Case II profit for the year ended 5 April 2000.

Required:

(i) State the possible reasons why the Inland Revenue has enquired into Tony's tax return for 1998/99.

(ii) Explain the options open to Tony following the completion of the Inland Revenue enquiry.

(iii) Advise Tony of the interest on overdue tax, surcharges and penalties that he may be liable to as a result of the Inland Revenue enquiry into his 1998/99 tax return.   (7 marks)

(c) Tony is planning to make a contribution of £20,000 into a personal pension scheme on 15 February 2001. A claim will then be made to relate the contribution back so that is it treated as paid during 1999/2000.

Tony is aged 43, and prior to 6 April 1998 was a member of the occupational pension scheme run by his employer.

Required:

Advise Tony of the implications of making the contribution into a personal pension scheme and claiming to relate is back to 1999/2000. Your answer should include a calculation on the maximum tax deductible contribution that Tony could make into a personal pension scheme for 1999/2000. **(6 marks)**

(25 marks)

21 TUTORIAL QUESTION: CHANGE OF ACCOUNTING DATE

Marie began trade on 1 January 1996 as a dressmaker. She prepared accounts to December each year until 2000 when she changed her accounting date by preparing accounts for the two months to 28 February 2000. Her schedule D case I results were:

	£
Year to 31.12.96	36,000
Year to 31.12.97	40,000
Year to 31.12.98	44,000
Year to 31.12.99	52,000
2 months to 28.2.00	14,000

Required

Show Marie's taxable profits for 1995/96 to 1999/00. Explain your treatment of overlap profits.

Guidance notes

1. The business commenced in 1995/96 so you must apply the opening year rules to the first three years.

2. There are two accounting periods ending during 1999/00 so the basis period runs from the end of the previous basis period to the new accounting date.

3. On a change of accounting date that results in more than 12 months worth of profits being taxed in a year, overlap relief is available to bring the number of months worth of profits that are being taxed down to 12.

22 CECILE GRAND (12/97) *45 mins*

(a) Cecile Grand has been a self-employed antiques dealer since 1989. Her income for 1999/00 was as follows.

	£
Adjusted Schedule DI profit	38,400
Dividends (net)	4,860
Schedule A profit	800
Capital gain before taper relief	7,800

The capital gain was in respect of a let property that was bought in 1986 and sold on 30 June 1999. The Schedule A profit is for the period 6 April 1999 to 30 June 1999. During 1999/00 Cecile paid a personal pension contribution of £3,500. Cecile's husband died on 15 June 1998, and she has not remarried.

Her forecast income for 2000/01 is as follows.

	£
Adjusted Schedule DI profit	21,750
Dividends (net)	4,320
Capital gain before taper relief	13,300

The capital gain is in respect of quoted shares bought in December 1999 and sold on 30 July 2000. Due to the fall in profits, Cecile will not pay a personal pension contribution during 2000/01.

Required

(i) Calculate Cecile's payments on account and balancing payment or repayment for 2000/01. You should assume that Cecile does not make a claim to reduce her payments on account. Assume 1999/00 rates and allowances apply throughout. (10 marks)

(ii) Based on the above figures, advise Cecile of the amount of the maximum claim that she could have made to reduce her payments on account for 2000/01. (2 marks)

(b) Cecile's adjusted Schedule D Case I profit for 2000/01 is an estimated figure based on her provisional accounts for the year ended 31 March 2001. The actual figures will not be available until 31 August 2001, because of the difficulty that Cecile has in separating antiques acquired for business purposes, from those acquired for private purposes.

Required

(i) Assuming that Cecile made the maximum claim to reduce the payments on account for 2000/01, explain the tax implications if her actual taxable income for 2000/01 is higher than the estimated figure. (2 marks)

(ii) Advise Cecile of the powers that the Inland Revenue have with regard to enquiring into her tax return for 2000/01. (2 marks)

(iii) Briefly advise Cecile of the tax implications if the Inland Revenue enquire into her tax return for 2000/01, and decide that the Schedule D Case I profits for the year ended 31 March 2001 are understated. (2 marks)

(c) Cecile is planning to change her accounting date from 31 March to 30 September by preparing her next accounts for the six month period to 30 September 2001. The forecast profit for this period is £18,000.

Required

(i) State the qualifying conditions that must be met for Cecile's change of accounting date to be valid. (2 marks)

(ii) Explain the tax implications of Cecile changing her accounting date from 31 March to 30 September. Your answer should include a calculation of the Schedule D Case I profits that Cecile will be assessed to for 2001/2002. (2 marks)

(iii) Briefly advise Cecile of the advantages and the disadvantages for tax purposes, of changing her accounting date from 31 March to 30 September. (3 marks)

(25 marks)

23 **CLARK KENT (6/94)** *45 mins*

(a) Clark Kent, aged 43, is to commence self-employment on 1 July 1999 running a business importing goods from the country of Guyani. Previously, Clark had worked in Guyani for five years, earning a salary of £26,000 pa, returning to the UK on 31 January 1998. During his period of employment in Guyani he was classed as non-resident in the UK. After returning to the UK, Clark immediately commenced employment with Krypton plc at a salary of £30,000 pa on a three year contract.

Unfortunately the company ran into financial difficulties and terminated his contract on 31 May 1999.

Under the terms of his contract, Clark was paid compensation of £10,500 in respect of its premature termination, and was also allowed to purchase his 1,800 cc company motor car for £5,000, despite its actual market value being £7,000. The car had been purchased new on 1 June 1998 for £9,700, and Clark will use the car in his new business. From 1 June 1998 to 31 May 1999, Clark drove 24,000 miles of which 80% were for business purposes, and was not required to reimburse Krypton plc for the use of private petrol. The proportion of business to private usage is likely to remain the same when he becomes self-employed.

Clark has forecast that for his first year of trading to 30 June 2000 he will make a tax adjusted trading loss of £14,000 plus any capital allowances. For the following year to 30 June 2001 he forecasts a profit of £20,000 less any capital allowances, with steadily increasing profits thereafter. On 1 September 1999 he is to purchase three machines costing £6,875 each. On 1 September 2000 he will purchase a delivery van for £12,375. He will claim the maximum capital allowances on all assets. Clark is single, and has no other income or outgoings.

Required

(i) Calculate Clark's taxable income for 1996/97 to 1999/00, *before* taking into account relief for his forecast Schedule D Case I trading loss for the year ended 30 June 2000. Your answer should include an explanation of your treatment of Clark's compensation package from Krypton plc.

(ii) Advise Clark of the possible ways of relieving his forecast Schedule D Case I trading loss for the year ended 30 June 2000. Your answer should state by what date each of the alternative loss relief claims should be made.

(iii) Advise Clark as to which loss relief claims would be the most beneficial for him. Your answer should include calculations of the tax refunds that will be due to Clark. You should ignore the possibility of any repayment supplement being due.

You should assume that the tax rates and allowances for 1999/00 apply throughout but that first year allowances do not continue beyond July 2000. (19 marks)

(b) Clark is to raise the necessary finance for his new business by borrowing £85,000 from a wealthy grandparent. The interest on this loan will be at a commercial rate, but no date has been agreed for the repayment of the loan. The grandparent has stated that she is prepared to write off £25,000 of the loan upon the date of Clark's marriage, which is planned to take place in 18 months time, and to make a gift of the balance of the loan under the terms of her will. The grandparent is 75 years old, and due to ill health is unlikely to survive beyond the age of 80. She has made substantial gifts of assets in recent years.

Required

Advise Clark and his grandparent of the taxation implications arising from the loan, and from its subsequent write off both at the date of Clark's marriage and upon the grandparent's death. (6 marks)

(25 marks)

24 BASIL NADIR (12/95) — 45 mins

Basil Nadir is a computer programmer. Until 5 April 1999, Basil was employed by Ace Computers Ltd, but since then has worked independently from home. Basil's income for his first 12 months of trading to 5 April 2000 is forecast to be £60,600, of which 50% will be in respect of work done for Ace Computers Ltd. His expenditure for the year will be as follows.

(a) Computer equipment costing £7,375 (inclusive of VAT) was purchased on 6 April 1999.

(b) Basil uses two rooms of his eight room private residence exclusively for business purposes. The cost of light, heat and insurance of the house for the year will amount to £1,800 (inclusive of VAT of £100).

(c) Basil's telephone bills currently amount to £250 per quarter. They were £100 per quarter up to 5 April 1999. Both figures are inclusive of VAT.

(d) Basil owns a two year old motor car which originally cost £15,000. It was worth £10,000 on 6 April 1999. His motor expenses for the year will amount to £3,500 (inclusive of VAT of £400). Although Basil works from home, he has to visit his clients on a regular basis. His mileage for the year ended 5 April 2000 will be as follows.

Visiting Ace Computers Ltd	10,000 miles
Visiting other clients	10,000 miles
Private use	5,000 miles

Basil spends 50% of his time working for Ace Computers Ltd, and since 6 April 1999 has been working for them on a 12 months contract to develop a taxation program for accountants. He visits the company's offices twice a week in respect of this contract. Apart from Ace Computers Ltd, Basil presently has five other clients.

On 8 August 1999, Ace Computers Ltd was the subject of an Inland Revenue PAYE compliance visit, and Basil's self-employed status in respect of his contract with the company was queried. The Inland Revenue have stated that they consider Basil to be an employee of Ace Computers Ltd for the purposes of both income tax and NIC. Basil has agreed to refund Ace Computers Ltd for any tax liability that the company suffers if the Inland Revenue's view is upheld.

Basil has not yet registered for VAT. He is single, and has no other income or outgoings. You should assume that today's date is 15 August 1999.

Required

(a) Briefly discuss the criteria that will be used in deciding whether Basil will be classified as employed or self-employed in respect of his contract with Ace Computers Ltd. You answer should include:

  (i) an explanation as to the likely reasons why the Inland Revenue have queried Basil's self-employed status; and

  (ii) advice to Basil and Ace Computers Ltd as to the criteria that they could put forward in order to justify Basil's self-employed status. (9 marks)

(b) Calculate Basil's liability to income tax and NIC for 1999/00 if he is treated as self-employed in respect of his contract with Ace Computers Ltd, and advise him of by how much this liability will increase if he is instead treated as employed.

You should *ignore* the implications of VAT, and should note that Basil's self-employed status in respect of his contracts with his other five clients is not in dispute. (10 marks)

(c) Assuming that Basil is classified as self-employed in respect of his contract with Ace Computers Ltd, state when he will have to compulsorily register for VAT. Explain the implications of being so registered, and advise him of whether or not it would be beneficial to voluntarily register before that date. You should assume that Basil's income accrued evenly throughout the year. Ignore leap years. (6 marks)

(25 marks)

25 GARDEN LTD (6/95) *45 mins*

(a) Garden Ltd is an unquoted company involved in the manufacture of gardening equipment. Due to a rapid expansion of its trade, the company requires an additional factory. Two alternative options have been identified as follows.

(i) A new factory can be constructed by a building company. This will cost £470,000 as follows.

	£
Land	80,000
Levelling the land	10,300
Architects' and legal fees	24,300
Ventilation and heating systems	12,500
Fire alarm and sprinkler system	6,400
Strengthened concrete floor to support machinery	16,500
General offices	62,500
Factory	187,500
VAT	70,000
	470,000

(ii) A suitable factory is available for rent. The owners of the factory are prepared to grant a 40 year lease for a premium of £470,000. The annual rent payable will be £35,250. The owners will exercise their option to tax the grant of the lease, and it will therefore be standard rated. Both figures are inclusive of VAT where applicable.

Whichever alternative is chosen, it will be financed as follows.

(i) A loan of £200,000 will be raised by an issue of 12% debentures.

(ii) A warehouse will be sold for £270,000 (including land of £90,000). The warehouse cost £120,000 (including land of £50,000) when it was acquired seven years ago. The warehouse was originally built 10 years ago at a cost of £102,000 (including land of £42,000). It has always been used to store raw materials. The relevant RPI factor in respect of this disposal is 0.360.

Garden Ltd is registered for VAT and makes only taxable supplies. None of the above buildings are situated in enterprise zones. Apart from the above no other expenditure will be incurred on buildings or on plant and machinery. The company is a small or medium sized company for capital allowance purposes.

Required

Advise Garden Ltd of the tax implications arising from the two alternatives, and from the financing of whichever alternative is chosen. (13 marks)

(b) In June 2000 Garden Ltd is to increase its share capital to 1,400,000 ordinary shares, by issuing 700,000 new ordinary shares at £1.00 per share. These will be subscribed for as follows.

Alex Bush	210,000
Carol Daisy	210,000
Edward Fern	210,000
Gary Hedge	70,000
	700,000

Garden Ltd's original share capital of 700,000 ordinary shares has been held by Alex Bush since 1988.

Alex and Gary have been directors of Garden Ltd since 1988, whilst Carol and Edward are going to be appointed as directors during 2000. Carol and Edward have not previously been employed by the company.

Alex is 57 years old, Gary is 51, whilst Carol and Edward are both 40. None of the shareholders are connected to each other. They are all 40% taxpayers. Carol will finance the cost of her shareholding by selling an investment property for £350,000, resulting in a chargeable gain of £175,000. This property had only been held for one year so taper relief is not due.

Due to its rapid expansion, Garden Ltd is planning to obtain a Stock Exchange listing within the next two or three years. This will be achieved by the company issuing 700,000 new ordinary shares on the Stock Exchange.

Required

Advise each of the shareholders of Garden Ltd of the tax implications arising from:

(i) their subscription for new ordinary share capital in Garden Ltd;

(ii) Garden Ltd's proposed listing on the Stock Exchange in two or three years time. **(12 marks)**

(25 marks)

26 ALEX ZONG (12/97) *45 mins*

(a) Alex Zong, aged 38, commenced self-employment as a builder on 1 October 1996. The business has been quite successful, and Alex is therefore going to incorporate his trade into a new limited company, Lexon Ltd, on 31 December 1999. The following information is available.

(i) Tax adjusted Schedule DI profits (before capital allowances) are as follows.

	£
Period ended 30.6.97	28,000
Year ended 30.6.98	44,000
Year ended 30.6.99	53,000
Period ended 31.12.99 (estimated)	29,000

The above figures are before capital allowances.

(ii) Alex has purchased the following assets.

		£
1.10.96	Freehold office premises	32,000
1.10.96	Lorry	8,800
15.6.97	Plant	6,400
30.11.98	Motor car	13,500

On 1 October 1996 Alex introduced his private motor car into the business at its market value of £4,000. This was sold on 30 November 1998 for £2,800, and replaced by the motor car bought on that date. Alex drives 12,000 miles per year, of which 4,800 are for private purposes.

On 10 December 1997 Alex extended the freehold premises using his own materials and labour at a cost of £6,700. The extension would have cost £10,000 if the work had been carried out externally.

(iii) The estimated market value of the business assets at 31 December 1999 is as follows.

	£
Goodwill	40,000
Freehold premises	75,000
Lorry	4,300
Plant	8,200
Motor car	11,500
Net current assets	21,000
	160,000

(iv) All of the business assets are to be transferred to Lexon Ltd. The consideration will consist of 1,000 £1 ordinary shares in Lexon Ltd, and a loan account balance of £10,000.

(v) Alex has capital losses of £12,500 resulting from the sale of investments in 1999/00.

(vi) Alex is registered for VAT.

Required

(i) Calculate Alex's Schedule D Case I assessment for 1999/00. You should ignore NIC. (11 marks)

(ii) Advise Alex of the capital gains tax implications of incorporating his business on 31 December 1999. (7 marks)

(iii) Advise Alex of the VAT implications of incorporating his business on 31 December 1999. (2 marks)

You should include any tax planning points that you consider relevant.

(b) Alex is in the process of completing his VAT return for the quarter ended 30 November 1999, and wants advice on how to deal with the following.

(i) On 20 May 1999 Alex completed a contract for a customer, and an invoice was raised for £9,400 (inclusive of VAT) on 15 June 1999. The customer paid £2,350 on 30 June 1999, but the balance of the amount owing is now considered to be a bad debt. The full debt was due to be paid within 10 days of the invoice date.

(ii) Alex has mistakenly not been claiming for the input VAT on plant which is leased for £475 (inclusive of VAT) per month. The same amount has been paid since the commencement of business on 1 October 1996.

(iii) A customer was invoiced for £3,400 (excluding VAT) on 30 September 1999. The customer was offered a 5% discount for payment within 30 days, but this was not taken and the customer paid the amount due on 28 November 1999.

Alex does not operate the cash accounting scheme.

Required

Advise Alex in respect of points raised. (5 marks)

(25 marks)

27 CHOW TONG (12/97) *45 mins*

(a) On 1 May 1999 Chow Tong, aged 35, bought a derelict property at an auction for £132,000. She paid cash of £42,000, and borrowed the remaining £90,000 from her bank at an interest rate of 8% per annum. On 15 July 1999 Chow obtained planning permission to convert the property into six holiday apartments, and entered into a contract with a builder to carry out the conversion. The work was completed on 30 September 1999 at a cost of £63,000, and Chow immediately put the six holiday apartments up for sale. Five of the holiday apartments were sold during November 1999 for £75,000 each. On 30 November 1999 Chow paid her builder and repaid the bank loan. She decided to keep the remaining holiday apartment, valued at £75,000, for her own use. Legal fees of £750 were paid in respect of each of the five holiday apartments sold, and advertising costs amounted to £1,200.

Since the sale of the holiday apartments is an isolated transaction, Chow believes that it should be treated as a capital gain rather than as an adventure in the nature of a trade. Chow is the director of an engineering company on an annual salary of £90,000, and has not disposed of any other assets during 1999/00.

Required

(i) Calculate Chow's tax liability arising from her property activities during 1999/00 if she is treated as (1) trading, and (2) not trading. You should ignore the implication's of NIC and VAT. (9 marks)

(ii) Advise Chow of whether or not you would agree with her belief that the property activities should be treated as a capital gain rather than an adventure in the nature of a trade.

Your answer should include a brief explanation of the criteria that would be used by the courts in determining whether or not an isolated sale transaction will be treated as an adventure in the nature of a trade. You are not expected to quote from decided cases. (8 marks)

(b) On 15 March 2000 Chow is to invest £200,000 of the proceeds from the sale of the holiday apartments by subscribing for 50,000 £1 ordinary shares in an unquoted trading company, Knife-Edge Ltd. The company, which is involved in computer technology, has an issued share capital of 1,000,000 £1 ordinary shares. Chow considers the investment in Knife-Edge Ltd to be quite risky, since the company's future is dependent upon a new computer microchip which is currently being developed. It will be at least two years before the outcome of the development is known. Chow is aware that tax relief under the enterprise investment scheme and EIS re-investment relief may be available as a result of making the investment, but wants advice on the following.

(i) The amount of tax relief that she will be entitled to as a result of making the investment, and whether this will be affected by the treatment of her property activities (as per (a) above) as either trading or non-trading. Chow also wants to know whether part of the investment should be postponed until 2000/01.

(ii) If the new microchip is successful, the Chow will become a director of Knife-Edge Ltd, and the company will obtain a listing on either the Alternative Investment Market or the Stock Exchange. Chow would probably take this opportunity to sell some of her shareholding at a substantial profit. She wants to know whether or not these events would lead to the withdrawal of any tax relief previously given.

(iii) If the new microchip is not successful, then Knife-Edge Ltd will go into liquidation. Chow's investment will become worthless, and she wants to know if any tax relief can be claimed as a result of this. (8 marks)

Required

Advise Chow in respect of the queries that she has raised. **(25 marks)**

28 MING KHAN AND NINA LEE (6/97)

45 mins

(a) Ming Khan and Nina Lee are in partnership running a music recording studio. The partnership commenced trading on 1 May 1998, and their first accounts for the 15 month period to 31 July 1999 show a tax adjusted Schedule D Case I trading loss (*before* capital allowances) of £71,250. On 12 May 1998 the partnership purchased a freehold building and converted it into a recording studio during May and June of 1998 at a cost of £211,500, made up as follows.

	£
Land and building	69,500
Recording equipment	70,300
Installation of electrical system for the recording equipment	19,400
Sound insulation	13,200
Replacement doors and windows	2,500
Heating system	5,100
VAT	31,500
	211,500

Ming and Nina decided not to claim first year allowances in respect of any or the above expenditure. They did, however, claim writing down allowances for the fifteen month period to 31.7.99.

Profits and losses are shared 60% to Ming and 40% to Nina. The partnership is registered for VAT, and all of its supplies are standard rated.

Required

(i) Show how the partnership's Schedule D Case I trading loss for the 15 month period to 31 July 1999 will be allocated between Ming and Nina for 1998/99 and 1999/00. Your calculations should be made on a monthly basis. (4 marks)

(ii) State the possible ways of relieving the Schedule D Case I trading loss. (3 marks)

(b) Ming was previously employed by a music company at an annual salary of £42,000. she was made redundant on 28 February 1998, and received an *ex gratia* redundancy payment of £60,000.

Nina was previously a student. She had inherited an investment property on the death of her parents, and sold this for £125,000 on 31 March 1998 in order to finance her partnership capital. The disposal resulted in a chargeable gain of £39,200. Until March 1998 Nina received Schedule A income of £6,250 pa.

Required

(i) Advise Ming and Nina as to which loss relief claims would be the most beneficial for them. (4 marks)

(ii) Calculate the tax refunds that will be due to Ming and Nina. You should ignore the possibility of any repayment supplement being due.

You should use the tax rates and allowances for 1999/00 throughout. Ignore taper relief. (7 marks)

(c) Ming and Nina are concerned about the partnership's financial position. They have asked for your advice on the following matters.

(i) One of the partnership's clients owes the partnership £23,500, and this amount is now four months overdue. Ming and Nina want to know how relief for bad debts can be obtained.

(ii) The partnership needs to purchase computer equipment costing £61,100, but does not have sufficient funds to do so outright. The computer equipment can either be leased for three years at a cost of £28,200 pa or can be bought on hire-purchase for an initial payment of £11,100 (including VAT of £9,100), followed by 35 monthly payments of £2,000.

The computer equipment will be replaced after three years use, at which time it will be worthless. Ming and Nina want to know the tax implications of each alternative method of financing the computer equipment.

All figures are inclusive of VAT where appropriate.

Required

Advise Ming and Nina in respect of the matters they have raised. Your answer should cover both the income tax and the VAT implications. You should ignore the implications of SSAP 21: *Accounting for leases and Hire-Purchase Contracts*.

(7 marks)

(25 marks)

29 SMART AND SHARP (6/96)   45 mins

You are the tax adviser to the partnership of Smart and Sharp, a firm of management consultants. There are currently two partners, Bob and Nick, who share profits equally after paying an annual salary of £180,000 to Bob and £80,000 to Nick. These salaries have not changed since commencement on 1 July 1997. You should assume that today's date is 15 November 1999.

(a) There have been no changes to the constitution of the partnership since commencement, but on 31 December 1999 a new partner, Justin, is to be admitted. From 1 January 2000 profits will be shared equally between the three partners. The tax adjusted Schedule D Case II trading profits have been as follows.

	£
Six months to 31 December 1997	280,000
Year ended 31 December 1998	710,000
Year ended 31 December 1999	640,000

The partners are planning to incorporate the partnership's business on 31 December 2002. Forecast profits to this date are as follows.

	£
Year ended 31 December 2000	750,000
Year ended 31 December 2001	750,000
Year ended 31 December 2002	750,000

Required

Calculate the amount of each partner's Schedule D Case II income where applicable, for the years 1997/98 to 2002/03 inclusive. You should assume that the partnership's business is incorporated on 31 December 2002. (10 marks)

(b) The partners would like advice as to whether or not it will be beneficial to incorporate the partnership's business. They are concerned that the current level of profits of £750,000 may not be high enough for incorporation to be beneficial.

Upon incorporation, the partnership's business will be transferred to a new company, Smash Ltd. The three partners will all become directors of Smash Ltd, and would each receive directors remuneration of £200,000 pa. Each of the partners has sufficient Schedule A investment income to utilise their personal allowances and basic rate income tax bands.

Required

Advise the partners as to whether or not it will be beneficial for the partnership's business to be incorporated. Base your answer solely on the current level of profits of £750,000, calculating:

(i) the annual tax liability of the three partners if the partnership is *not* incorporated; and

(ii) the annual tax liability of Smash Ltd and its directors if the partnership *is* incorporated.

Your answer should take into account the implications of NIC, and should use the tax rates for 1999/00. The figure for profits of £750,000 is *before* the deduction of directors remuneration. (8 marks)

(c) Explain the alternative ways in which the partners can obtain relief for any overlap profits. (3 marks)

(d) The partners have asked for your advice regarding the CGT and IHT implications on incorporating the partnership's business. All the partners are aged between 40 and 50.

Required

Draft a reply to the partners. (4 marks)

(25 marks)

30 SALLY AND TREVOR ACRE (12/98) *45 mins*

Sally and Trevor Acre, a married couple aged 53 and 48 respectively have been in partnership as estate agents since 1 October 1996. Due to Sally's ill health, they are to sell the business on 31 March 2000 to an unrelated third party. You should assume that today's date is 15 March 2000. The following information is available.

(1) Tax adjusted Schedule DII profits/(losses) are as follows:

	£
Period ended 31 March 1997	37,500
Year ended 31 March 1998	74,000
Year ended 31 March 1999	52,000
Year ended 31 March 2000 (estimated)	(68,000)

(2) Profits and losses, whether revenue or capital in nature, have always been shared 70% to Sally and 30% to Trevor.

(3) The market values of the partnership assets at 31 March 2000 are forecast to be as follows:

	£
Goodwill	100,000
Freehold property	230,000
Fixtures and fittings	140,000
Net current assets	80,000
	550,000

The freehold property and fixtures and fittings were purchased on 1 October 1996, and cost £170,000 and £155,000 respectively. Indexation on the property from October 1996 to April 1998 is £9,690. The fixtures and fittings qualify as plant and machinery for capital allowance purposes and no chargeable gain arises on disposal. The partnership assets will all be sold on 31 March 2000 for their market value.

(4) Sally personally owns a leasehold office building that is used rent-free by the partnership. She paid £85,000 for the grant of a 25-year lease on 1 July 1998. This property is to be sold on 31 March 2000 for £90,000.

(5) Sally has Schedule A profits of £5,835 p.a. Trevor has Schedule A profits of £2,000 pa. Neither of them plans to reinvest the proceeds from the sale of the business.

(6) Trevor realised other chargeable gains on the disposal of non business assets in 1999/00. These amounted to £38,000 before deducting taper relief and the annual exemption.

Required:

(a) Advise Sally and Trevor of the chargeable gains that will be assessed on them for 1999/00. Your answer should include an explanation as to the amount of retirement relief that will be available. **(9 marks)**

(b) (i) State the possible ways of relieving the partnership's Schedule D Case II trading loss of £68,000 for the year ended 31 March 2000.

(ii) Advise Sally and Trevor as to which loss relief claims would be the most beneficial for them.

(iii) After taking into account your advice in (ii), calculate Sally and Trevor's taxable income for the tax years 1996/97 to 1999/00, and their net chargeable gains for 1999/00.

You should assume that the tax rates and allowances for 1999/00 apply throughout.

(16 marks)

(25 marks)

DO YOU KNOW - CGT AND BUSINESSES; VALUE ADDED TAX

- *Check that you can fill in the blanks in the statements below before you attempt any questions. If in doubt, you should go back to your BPP Study Text and revise first.*

- Rollover relief .... gains on certain assets when the proceeds are reinvested. If proceeds are not completely reinvested the lower of .... and the .... is immediately chargeable.

- Retirement relief may permanently exempt a gain on the disposal of a .... or of shares in a .... company. EIS reinvestment relief may .... a gain.

  TRY QUESTIONS 31 TO 33

- VAT is charged on taxable supplies of goods and services by registered traders.

- Supplies may be taxable at 17½% (the VAT is 7/47 of the gross amount), taxable at 0% or exempt.

- A registered trader deducts VAT suffered on purchases from VAT charged on sales, and pays the net amount to HM Customs & Excise.

  o .... may restrict the recovery of VAT on purchases.

  o Most traders account for VAT ...., although monthly and annual accounting are also possible.

  o Returns and VAT are due ....

  o Traders must make monthly payments on account if their VAT liability exceeds .... a year.

- Traders must register when their turnover for the previous .... exceeds the registration limit.

  o Traders must also register when their anticipated turnover for the next .... exceeds the registration limit.

  o Trade within the .... may also give rise to a requirement to register.

  o Traders may register voluntarily.

- VAT invoices must contain prescribed details, and specified records must be kept.

  o Less detailed invoices may be issued for supplies worth .... including VAT.
  o Registered traders need VAT invoices for purchases in order to reclaim the VAT suffered.

- The .... determines in which VAT return a purchase or sale is dealt with.

- The cash accounting scheme allows businesses to account for VAT on the basis of .... The scheme can be used by a trader whose taxable turnover, excluding VAT, does not exceed ....

- The annual accounting scheme allows traders to make VAT returns .... The scheme can be used by traders whose taxable turnover, excluding VAT, does not exceed ....

- Bad debt relief is available if the debt is over .... old measured from ....

- A .... may arise when a VAT return is late.

- A misdeclaration penalty may apply if the VAT which would have been lost as a result of the misdeclaration is at least .... or is at least ......% of the .... (GAT ie Gross amount of tax).

  TRY QUESTIONS 34 AND 35

DID YOU KNOW - CGT AND BUSINESSES; VALUE ADDED TAX

- *Could you fill in the blanks? The answers are in bold. Use this page for revision purposes as you approach the exam.*

- Rollover relief **defers** gains on certain assets when the proceeds are reinvested. If proceeds are not completely reinvested the lower of **proceeds not reinvested** and the **gain** is immediately chargeable.

- Retirement relief may permanently exempt a gain on the disposal of a **business** or of shares in a **personal trading** company. EIS reinvestment relief may **defer** a gain.

TRY QUESTIONS 31 TO 33

- VAT is charged on taxable supplies of goods and services by registered traders.

- Supplies may be taxable at 17½% (the VAT is 7/47 of the gross amount), taxable at 0% or exempt.

- A registered trader deducts VAT suffered on purchases from VAT charged on sales, and pays the net amount to HM Customs & Excise.
  - **Exempt supplies** may restrict the recovery of VAT on purchases.
  - Most traders account for VAT **quarterly**, although monthly and annual accounting are also possible.
  - Returns and VAT are due **one month from the end of the VAT period**.
  - Traders must make monthly payments on account if their VAT liability exceeds **£2,000,000** a year.

- Traders must register when their turnover for the previous **12 months or less** exceeds the registration limit.
  - Traders must also register when their anticipated turnover for the next **30 days** exceeds the registration limit.
  - Trade within the **European Community** may also give rise to a requirement to register.
  - Traders may register voluntarily.

- VAT invoices must contain prescribed details, and specified records must be kept.
  - Less detailed invoices may be issued for supplies worth **£100 or less** including VAT.
  - Registered traders need VAT invoices for purchases in order to reclaim the VAT suffered.

- The **tax point** determines in which VAT return a purchase or sale is dealt with.

- The cash accounting scheme allows businesses to account for VAT on the basis of **cash paid and received.** The scheme can be used by a trader whose taxable turnover, excluding VAT, does not exceed **£350,000.**

- The annual accounting scheme allows traders to make VAT returns **once a year**. The scheme can be used by traders whose taxable turnover, excluding VAT, does not exceed **£300,000.**

- Bad debt relief is available if the debt is over **six months** old measured from **when payment is due.**

- A **default surcharge** may arise when a VAT return is late.

- A misdeclaration penalty may apply if the VAT which would have been lost as a result of the misdeclaration is at least **£1,000,000** or is at least **30%** of the **sum of the true input and the true output tax** (GAT ie Gross amount of tax).

TRY QUESTIONS 34 AND 35

31 TUTORIAL QUESTION: CHOOSING ASSETS TO SELL

Paris Ltd, a company with annual profits of approximately £10,000,000 and no associated companies, makes up accounts annually at 31 March.

(a) During the year to 31 March 2000 the company was experiencing cash flow difficulties and decided to sell, during February 2000, one of two areas of land it owns, each of which would realise £1,600,000. It is anxious to ensure that it sells that piece of land which will result in the lower taxation liability. Details concerning the two sites are as follows.

Site A

This had been purchased in February 1982 for £700,000 using the full proceeds of a sale, in the same month, of land which had been purchased in 1970 for £100,000. Rollover relief was claimed in respect of the gain arising in February 1982. The value of the land which might now be sold (in February 2000) at 31 March 1982 was £720,000.

Site B

This land was purchased in July 1982 for £900,000 using the full proceeds of a sale, in the same month, of land which had been purchased in 1971 for £150,000. Again, rollover relief was claimed in respect of the gain arising in July 1982.

Required

Compute the corporation tax charge which will arise as a result of each of the above proposed disposals. Assume the retail prices index for February 2000 is 171.0.

(b) One of the directors of the company, aged 62, intends to sell his holding of 8% of the ordinary shares on 31 March 2000. He acquired these shares and became a full-time director on 1 April 1991.

Draft a brief report to him outlining the rules which determine whether retirement relief will be available and how such relief would be computed.

Guidance notes

1. Site A's cost for capital gains purposes is affected by an earlier rollover claim. Site A was acquired before 31 March 1982. Why should the gain rolled over *not* be halved?

2. With site B, we again have to consider the effect of a rollover claim. Consider whether to halve the gain rolled over, and also consider what indexation allowance, if any, is due on the sale in 1982.

3. In part (b), ensure that your discussion of the rules on retirement relief is related to the particular circumstances of the director.

32 VELO LTD (6/98) *45 mins*

(a) Velo Ltd manufactures bicycles, making up its accounts to 31 March. The company is planning to move into new business premises during March 2000 (you should assume that today's date is 15 February 2000). The company's plans are as follows.

(i) On 25 March 2000 Velo Ltd is to sell its existing freehold factory for £920,000. The factory was purchased from a builder on 1 April 1989 for £326,000, and was immediately brought into use. The cost and selling price are made up as follows:

	Cost £	Selling price £
Land	95,000	180,000
Factory	160,000	575,000
General office	71,000	165,000
	326,000	920,000

(ii) On 1 March 2000 Velo Ltd is to purchase a freehold factory at a cost of £725,000, and this will be brought into use immediately. The factory was originally constructed between 1 January and 31 March 1991 at a cost of £640,000, and was bought into use on 1 July 1991. The original cost and purchase price are made up as follows:

	Original cost £	Purchase price £
Land	132,000	154,000
Factory	478,000	531,000
Drawing office	30,000	40,000
	640,000	725,000

Velo Ltd will immediately install a new overhead crane in the factory at a cost of £53,000. The crane is a long-life asset.

(iii) On 1 March 2000 Velo Ltd is to pay a premium of £80,000 for the grant of a 15 year lease on an office building. An annual rental of £16,200 will be payable quarterly in advance. The company will immediately install new computer equipment in the office building at a cost of £14,000. The computer equipment will probably be replaced in three years time.

The tax written down value of Velo Ltd's plant and machinery at 1 April 1999 is £38,000. The company is registered for VAT, and all of the above figures are net of VAT. Velo Ltd is a medium-sized company as defined by the Companies Acts.

Required

Advise Velo Ltd of the tax implications arising from each aspect of its proposed plan. Your answer should be supported by appropriate calculations. Assume the RPI figure for March 2000 is 171.5. **(17 marks)**

(b) Following further enquiries regarding Velo Ltd's proposed plan, the following additional information is now available in respect of the factory that is to be sold on 25 March 2000.

(i) On 10 March 1997 Velo Ltd installed heating and ventilation systems in the factory at a cost of £54,000. All of the expenditure qualified as plant and machinery. The tax written down value of these systems at 1 April 1999 is £28,000. This figure is included in the pool tax written down value of £38,000 above.

(ii) On 31 January 2000 Velo Ltd installed an overhead crane in the factory at a cost of £64,000. The crane is a long-life asset, and has a current market value equivalent to its cost.

The market value of each of these assets is included in the value of the factory of £575,000.

Required

Advise Velo Ltd of the tax implications arising from this additional information, and how it affects your answer to part (a) above. You should include tax planning advice in your answer as appropriate. **(8 marks)**

(25 marks)

33 SALLY JONES   *45 mins*

Sally Jones has been a shareholder and the managing director of Zen Ltd since its incorporation on 1 January 1994. Zen Ltd is a UK resident company manufacturing computer equipment. Sally is 58 years old and has been a widow since her husband died on 12 May 1998. Following her husband's death she has decided to retire as managing director of Zen Ltd on 31 December 1999, and plans to dispose of most of her shareholding on the same date.

Zen Ltd has a share capital of 60,000 £1 ordinary shares of which Sally holds 31,000. The remaining shares are held by the other directors who are not related to Sally. She would like to dispose of 20,000 of her shares but none of the other directors is in a position to purchase them. However, Zen Ltd currently has surplus funds and is prepared to purchase 20,000 of Sally's shares at their market value of £280,000. This will result in a chargeable gain for her, after indexation but before any reliefs, of £170,000.

Sally is paid director's remuneration of £24,000 pa, and she also receives an annual bonus based on Zen Ltd's annual results. For the year ended 31 March 1999 the bonus was £4,200, and for the year ended 31 March 2000 it is expected to be £5,700. The bonuses are agreed by the directors prior to the relevant year end, and then paid on the following 30 April. Sally will be entitled to her full bonus for the year to 31 March 2000 even though she will retire during the year. Zen Ltd is also to give Sally an *ex gratia* lump sum upon her retirement of £80,000, which she is not contractually entitled to. This is to be paid in two equal instalments on 31 March 2000 and 31 March 2001.

Sally has no other income or outgoings apart from a pension of £950 per month (payable at the end of each month) that will commence upon her retirement. She has an adopted child aged 17 who is currently studying full-time at college.

Required

(a) Outline the conditions to be met for the purchase of Sally's shares by Zen Ltd to qualify for the special treatment applying to a company's purchase of its own shares. Your answer should indicate whether or not these conditions are met.   (7 marks)

(b) Assuming that the purchase of Sally's shares qualifies for the special treatment:

   (i) calculate her income tax for 1999/00; and
   (ii) calculate her capital gains tax liability for 1999/00.

   Your answer should include an explanation of the treatment of Sally's annual bonuses and *ex gratia* payment.   (10 marks)

(c) What deductions will Zen Ltd be entitled to when calculating its corporation tax liability for the year ended 31 March 2000 in respect of the payments and emoluments provided to Sally? Your answer should include a consideration of NIC.
   (8 marks)

   (25 marks)

34 TUTORIAL QUESTION: REGISTRATION AND ACCOUNTING

You have recently received a request from the managing director of a newly-created business (which will make no exempt supplies and will have no dealings outside the UK) requesting your help with matters concerning value added tax. The following is an extract from the letter.

(a) We understand that some businesses are registered for VAT whilst others are not registered. We have only recently commenced trading and consider that it will take us about five years to reach full potential sales, which we envisage will rise from

£20,000 to £100,000 a year in that period. Could you please advise us of the position regarding registration?

(b) Once we are registered, how should the VAT content of our income and expenditure be reflected in our budgets and final accounts at the year end?

(c) When and how is VAT to be accounted for to HM Customs & Excise, and what is the position if we should pay out more VAT than we charge?

(d) What records must be kept by us in order to satisfy the regulations?

Required

Prepare a letter in response to the above requests.

Guidance notes

1   You are asked for a letter, so you should present your answer in letter format.

2   The company will clearly need to register at some stage. You should explain the rules on registration.

3   For part (b), remember that VAT on some items of expenditure is never recoverable.

4   You should consider the alternatives to quarterly accounting, both monthly and annual accounting. Also, might cash accounting be appropriate?

5   Several records must be kept. Most of these are records which a business would be likely to keep in any case, but you still need to list them because there are penalties for failure to keep the required records.

35 SCHOONER LTD (12/98)   *45 mins*

Schooner Ltd is an unquoted company that constructs yachts. The company has recently accepted a large contract to supply yachts to Highseas plc. The new contract will commence on 1 January 2000, and will have the following implications for Schooner Ltd.

(a) Each yacht will take three months to construct, and will be sold for £350,000. Highseas plc will pay a deposit of £50,000 at the beginning of the three-month period, and a further payment on account of £100,000 two months later. An invoice for the total price of £350,000 plus VAT will be raised 10 days after completion of each yacht, and the balance due will be paid within 60 days. The three-monthly construction periods will be coterminous with Schooner Ltd's quarterly VAT periods.

(b) Schooner Ltd will acquire new equipment costing £800,000 on 1 January 2000.

   (1) The company has sufficient funds to purchase £250,000 of the equipment outright, and all of this is to be imported into the UK. Equipment costing £160,000 will be imported from countries that are members of the European Union, with the remainder imported from countries that are outside the European Union.

   (2) Equipment costing £200,000 will be bought on hire purchase, with the company making 16 quarterly payments of £17,250 commencing on 1 January 2000. VAT will be paid with the first quarterly payment.

   (3) Equipment costing £350,000 will be leased at a cost of £145,000 pa. The lease will be treated as a finance lease, and the equipment will accordingly be capitalised as a fixed asset by Schooner Ltd.

All figures are exclusive of VAT where appropriate.

(c) Schooner Ltd will raise additional finance of £600,000 on 1 January 2000 in order to provide working capital.

　(1) The managing director of Schooner Ltd, Alex Barnacle, will borrow £100,000 at an interest rate of 8% using his main residence as security. This amount will be lent interest free to Schooner Ltd. At present, the main residence is not mortgaged. Alex owns 35% of Schooner Ltd's ordinary share capital.

　(2) An issue of 10% debentures will raise a loan of £300,000. The debentures will be issued at a 5% discount to their nominal value, and will be redeemable in five years time. Professional fees of £8,000 will be incurred in respect of the issue.

　(3) An issue of new ordinary £1.00 shares at £2.00 per share will raise £200,000. Chloe Dhow is to subscribe for 90,000 of the new shares. She presently has no connection with Schooner Ltd, but will be appointed a director following the share issue. Professional fees of £12,500 will be incurred in respect of the issue.

Schooner Ltd makes up its accounts to 31 December. It is a close company, currently has an issued share capital of 1,000,000 £1 ordinary shares, and is a small company as defined by the Companies Acts. The company's sales are all standard rated.

Required:

(a) Advise Schooner Ltd of the VAT rules relating to the time of supply for goods, and explain the output tax entries that will be made in respect of the new contract on its quarterly VAT returns. (5 marks)

(b) (i) Advise Schooner Ltd of the effect that the acquisition of the new equipment will have on its tax adjusted Schedule D Case I profits for the year ended 31 December 2000.

　(ii) Advise Schooner Ltd of the VAT implications of acquiring the new equipment. (9 marks)

(c) (i) Advise Schooner Ltd of the effect that raising the additional finance will have on its tax adjusted Schedule D Case I profits for the year ended 31 December 2000.

　(ii) Advise Alex and Chloe of the tax relief that will be available to them in respect of their investment in Schooner Ltd. (11 marks)

(25 marks)

DO YOU KNOW - CORPORATE TAXATION

- *Check that you can fill in the blanks in the statements below before you attempt any questions. If in doubt, you should go back to your BPP Study Text and revise first.*

- A company's Schedule D Case I profits are calculated in the same way as an individual's by taking the accounts profit and adding back .... items.

- Interest income on .... loan relationships is taxed under Schedule D Case III on an .... basis. Interest income on .... loan relationships is included within Schedule D Case I profits.

- Interest paid on .... loan relationships is a deduction in arriving at Schedule D Case I profits on an .... basis. Interest paid on a .... loan relationship is deducted in arriving at Schedule D Case III income on .... loan relationships.

- A company's profits are computed for *accounting periods*. If a period of account exceeds 12 months, the .... form one accounting period, and the .... forms another.

- Corporation tax is charged on a company's .... These include all of a company's income (except ....) and chargeable gains.

- The rate of corporation tax depends on the level of the company's 'profits'. 'Profits' are ……………………………………….. plus ……………………………..……..

- If 'profits' exceed the .... corporation tax is charged at the .... rate, 30% (FY99). If 'profits' are below the .... corporation tax is charged at .... rate, 20% (FY99). If 'profits' are between the .... corporation tax is charged at the .... rate less marginal relief.

- The marginal relief formula is ………………………………………………..

- Income tax is accounted for through quarterly returns.
    - Income tax is deducted from interest at ....%, and from charges at ....%.

- Trading losses and unrelieved trade charges may be carried forward against ………………………………………………….. Trading losses may also be set against ……………….. of the period of loss, and may then be carried back against …………….. of the preceding period(s), later periods first. The carry back period is normally .... but this is extended to .... in the case of a loss arising in the 12 months prior to the cessation of trade.

- A company controlled by .... participators is normally a close company.
    - Loans to participators give rise to a tax charge equal to ...., which can only be recovered when the loan is repaid.
    - Benefits in kind, if not taxed under Schedule E, are treated like .... received.

    TRY QUESTION 37

- One company's trading losses may be transferred to another company if they are in a group where there is a ....% effective interest of the holding company in each relevant subsidiary.
    - Companies in a group should be selected to benefit from group relief depending on their marginal tax rates (32.5% for companies with marginal relief, 30% at the full rate and 20% at the small companies rate).

- Companies in a 75% group (with over 50% effective interest) transfer assets between each other at .... Capital losses .... be surrendered.

- Companies that pay tax at the .... rate must pay 60% of their estimated corporation tax liability for the first accounting period ending after 30 June 1999 by .... instalments.

    TRY QUESTIONS 36 AND 38 TO 42

DID YOU KNOW – CORPORATE TAXATION

- *Could you fill in the blanks? The answers are in bold. Use this page for revision purposes as you approach the exam.*

- A company's schedule D Case I profits are calculated in the same way as an individual's by taking the accounts profit and adding back **disallowable** items.

- Interest income on **non-trading** loan relationships is taxed under Schedule D Case III on an **accruals** basis. Interest income on **trading** loan relationships is included within Schedule D Case I profits.

- Interest paid on **trading** loan relationships is a deduction in arriving at Schedule D Case I profits on an **accruals** basis. Interest paid on a **non-trading** loan relationship is deducted in arriving at Schedule D Case III income on **non-trading** loan relationships.

- A company's profits are computed for *accounting periods*. If a period of account exceeds 12 months, the **first 12 months** form one accounting period, and the **balance** forms another.

- Corporation tax is charged on a company's **profits chargeable to corporation tax**. These include all of a company's income (except **UK dividends**) and chargeable gains.

- The rate of corporation tax depends on the level of the company's 'profits'. 'Profits' are **profits chargeable to corporation tax** plus **grossed up dividends received (FII)**.

- If 'profits' exceed the **upper limit** corporation tax is charged at the **full** rate, 30% (FY99). If 'profits' are below the **lower limit** corporation tax is charged at **small companies** rate, 20% (FY99). If 'profits' are between the **upper and lower limits** corporation tax is charged at the **full** rate less marginal relief.

- The marginal relief formula is **(upper limit – 'profits')** × $\dfrac{\text{PCTCT}}{\text{'profits'}}$.

- Income tax is accounted for through quarterly returns.
    - Income tax is deducted from interest at **20%**, and from charges at **23%**.

- Trading losses and unrelieved trade charges may be carried forward against **future profits from the same trade**. Trading losses may also be set against **total profits** of the period of loss, and may then be carried back against **total profits** of the preceding period(s), later periods first. The carry back period is normally **12 months** but this is extended to **36 months** in the case of a loss arising in the 12 months prior to the cessation of trade.

- A company controlled by **five or fewer** participators is normally a close company.
    - Loans to participators give rise to a tax charge equal to **25% of the loan**, which can only be recovered when the loan is repaid.
    - Benefits in kind, if not taxed under Schedule E, are treated like **dividends** received.

    TRY QUESTION 37

- One company's trading losses may be transferred to another company if they are in a group where there is a **75%** effective interest of the holding company in each relevant subsidiary.
    - Companies in a group should be selected to benefit from group relief depending on their marginal tax rates (32.5% for companies with marginal relief, 30% at the full rate and 20% at the small companies rate).

- Companies in a 75% group (with over 50% effective interest) transfer assets between each other at **no gain and no loss**. Capital losses **may not** be surrendered.

- Companies that pay tax at the **full** rate must pay 60% of their estimated corporation tax liability for the first accounting period ending after 30 June 1999 by **quarterly** instalments.

    TRY QUESTIONS 36 AND 38 TO 42

36 HIGHRISE LTD (12/95) — 45 mins

(a) Highrise Ltd is an unquoted trading company. Highrise Ltd has always had an accounting date of 30 June, with its most recent accounts being prepared to 30 June 1998. However, the company now plans to change its accounting date to 31 December. Highrise Ltd has forecast that its results for the 18 month period to 31 December 1999 will be as follows.

(i) Tax adjusted Schedule DI trading profits before capital allowances, per six monthly period will be:

	£
Six months to 31.12.98	141,000
Six months to 30.6.99	126,000
Six months to 31.12.99	165,000

(ii) The tax written-down value of plant and machinery at 1 July 1998 is £20,000. On 31 May 1999 Highrise Ltd will purchase plant costing £75,000.

(iii) Highrise Ltd owns two freehold office buildings which have always been rented out unfurnished. These are both to be sold. The first building at Ampton will be sold on 31 December 1998 resulting in a chargeable gain of £42,000, whilst the second building at Bodford will be sold on 31 May 1999 resulting in an allowable capital loss of £38,000.

(iv) The building at Ampton is currently let at £48,000 pa rent being due quarterly in advance on 1 January, 1 April etc. The building at Bodford will be let for £1,000 per month until 30 April 1999, but will then be empty. It will be decorated at a cost of £12,000 during May 1999 prior to its disposal. Both lettings are at a full rent and Highrise Ltd is responsible for all repairs.

(v) Highrise Ltd has a 20% shareholding in Shortie Ltd, an unquoted trading company. A dividend of £11,250 (net) will be received from Shortie Ltd on 15 June 1999.

Required

Advise Highrise Ltd of whether it would be beneficial to:

(i) prepare one set of accounts for the 18 month period to 31 December 1999; or

(ii) prepare separate accounts for the six month period to 31 December 1998 and for the year ended 31 December 1999.

Your answer should include a calculation of Highrise Ltd's total mainstream corporation tax liability for the 18 month period to 31 December 1999 under each alternative. (17 marks)

(b) On 1 January 2000, Highrise Ltd is to purchase the 80% of Shortie Ltd's ordinary share capital that it does not already own. Shortie Ltd's results for the year ended 31 March 2000 are forecast to be:

	£
Schedule DI trading loss	155,000
Capital loss of sale of property - 1 September 1999	37,000

Shortie Ltd has a 10% shareholding in Minute Ltd. This investment is currently standing at a substantial capital loss.

Highrise Ltd has a 5% shareholding in Tiny Ltd. This investment is currently standing at a substantial capital gain.

Required

Briefly discuss how Highrise Ltd's acquisition of Shortie Ltd will affect the utilisation of Shortie Ltd's trading loss and capital loss that are forecast to arise in respect of the year ended 31 March 2000, and its unrealised capital loss in respect of its investment in Minute Ltd. You should assume that it is not possible for Shortie Ltd to carry back its trading loss to previous accounting periods. (8 marks)

(25 marks)

37 BARGAINS LTD *45 mins*

Bargains Ltd is a close company that buys and sells secondhand antiques. The company is under the control of the three Rotter brothers, Rodney, Reggie and Del, who each own one third of its ordinary share capital. However, only Rodney and Reggie are directors of the company, with Del being neither a director nor an employee.

Bargains Ltd was incorporated on 1 August 1998. On 1 January 1999 the company acquired business premises which were in a bad state of repair, and it immediately started to repair and refurbish them. On 1 February 1999 expenditure was incurred on an advertising campaign. The company commenced purchasing antiques for resale on 1 March 1999, but the business premises were not opened until 1 April 1999. On the same day the company registered for VAT and made its first sale. Accounts have been prepared for the period 1 August 1998 to 31 December 1999.

On 1 July 1999 Bargains Ltd bought three new 1,600 cc motor cars costing £10,575 each (including VAT), for the business and private use of Rodney, Reggie and Del. During 1999/00 the brothers' business mileage was Rodney 2,100 miles, Reggie 14,400 miles and Del nil miles. No private fuel is provided.

On 1 October 1999 Bargains Ltd made an interest free loan of £42,000 to Del, which he used to purchase a holiday villa in Spain. The loan has not yet been repaid.

Required

(a) (i) Set out the accounting periods for Bargains Ltd up to, and including, 31 December 1999.

(ii) How will Bargains Ltd's expenditure on its advertising campaign and the refurbishment of its business premises be treated for the purposes of corporation tax and VAT? (9 marks)

(b) What are the tax implications, for both Bargains Ltd and the Rotter brothers, arising from the provision of the three company motor cars? You should ignore the implications of NIC. (8 marks)

(c) Advise both Bargains Ltd and Del of the tax implications arising from the provision of the interest free loan. (4 marks)

(d) Outline the basis on which Bargains Ltd should account for VAT on the purchase and sale of its secondhand antiques. (4 marks)

(25 marks)

38 TARGET LTD (6/97) *45 mins*

You are the tax adviser to Expansion Ltd, a company involved in the computer business. Expansion Ltd wishes to acquire Target Ltd, and has made an offer to the shareholders of that company which it would like to finalise on 1 July 1999. At present, the ordinary share capital of Target Ltd is owned equally by Arc Ltd, Bend Ltd and Curve Ltd, and it is not known whether one, two or all three of these companies will accept the offer. You should assume that today's date is 15 May 1999. The forecast of results of Expansion Ltd and Target Ltd for the year ended 31 December 1999 are as follows.

	Expansion Ltd £	Target Ltd £
Adjusted Schedule DI profit/(loss)	214,000	(137,700)
Trading losses brought forward	-	(9,200)
Capital gain	-	51,300
Capital losses brought forward	(9,600)	-

Expansion Ltd purchased £120,000 of 8% Company Loan Stock on 1 May 1999 with interest received six monthly in arrears, on 31 October and 30 April. On 31 January 2000 the company is to purchase a new freehold factory for £118,000.

Target Ltd's capital gain is in respect of the proposed sale of a freehold office building for £140,000 on 15 October 1999. One of the building's four floors has never been used for the purposes of Target Ltd's trade.

Expansion Ltd has sufficient internal funds in order to finance the acquisition of either one third or two thirds of Target Ltd's share capital. However, if it acquires all of Target Ltd's share capital it will have to issue £250,000 of 10% debentures on 1 July 1999. The debentures will be issued at a 3% discount to their nominal value, and will be redeemable in five years time. Debenture interest will be paid on 1 July and 1 January, and professional fees of £15,250 will be incurred in respect of the issue. Expansion Ltd's adjusted Schedule DI profit for the year ended 31 December 1999 has been calculated *before* taking into account the issue of debentures. The company's accounting policy is to write off the cost of finance on a straight-line basis over the period of the loan.

Neither Expansion Ltd nor Target Ltd has any subsidiary companies. Arc Ltd, Bend Ltd and Curve Ltd are all profitable companies, and they are not connected to each other or to Expansion Ltd. All the companies are resident in the UK.

Required

Calculate the mainstream corporation tax liability for both Expansion Ltd and Target Ltd for the year ended 31 December 1999 if:

(a) Expansion Ltd acquires one third of Target Ltd's ordinary share capital from Arc Ltd on 1 July 1999. **(8 marks)**

(b) Expansion Ltd acquires two thirds of Target Ltd's ordinary share capital from Arc Ltd and Bend Ltd on 1 July 1999. **(5 marks)**

(c) Expansion Ltd acquires all of Target Ltd's ordinary share capital from Arc Ltd, Bend Ltd and Curve Ltd on 1 July 1999. **(12 marks)**

Your answer should include an explanation of your treatment of Target Ltd's losses, Target Ltd's capital gain, and Expansion Ltd's issue of debentures. You should assume that reliefs are claimed in the most favourable manner. **(25 marks)**

39 HYDRA LTD (6/96) *45 mins*

Hydra Ltd has owned 90% of the ordinary share capital of Boa Ltd and 80% of the ordinary share capital of Cobra Ltd since 1987. Cobra Ltd acquired 80% of the ordinary share capital of Mamba Ltd on 1 April 1999, the date of that company's incorporation. All of the companies are involved in the construction industry. The results of each company for the year ended 31 March 2000 are as follows.

	Tax adjusted Schedule D1 Profit/(loss) £	Capital gain (loss) £	Patent royalty paid £
Hydra Ltd	(45,000)	130,000	(20,000)
Boa Ltd	120,000	(15,000)	-
Cobra Ltd	85,000	-	-
Mamba Ltd	(10,000)	8,000	-

Hydra Ltd's capital gain arose from the sale of a factory for £350,000. As at 31 March 1999 the company had unused trading losses of £15,000. Boa Ltd purchased a new office building on 1 May 2000 for £280,000. Mamba Ltd's capital gain arose from the disposal of an investment.

Required

(a) Calculate the mainstream corporation tax liability for each of the four companies in the Hydra Ltd group for the year ended 31 March 2000. Your answer should include an explanation of your treatment of the trading losses of Hydra Ltd and Mamba Ltd. You should assume that reliefs are claimed in the most favourable manner. **(13 marks)**

(b) Explain why it would probably be beneficial to transfer the 80% shareholding in Mamba Ltd from Cobra Ltd to Hydra Ltd. **(3 marks)**

(c) Hydra Ltd, Boa Ltd and Cobra Ltd all make standard rated sales, and are registered as a group for VAT purposes. The sales of Mamba Ltd are zero-rated.

   (i) State the conditions that must be met for two companies to register as a group for VAT purposes, and the consequences of being so registered.

   (ii) Briefly discuss the factors that would have to be considered when deciding if Mamba Ltd should be included in the group VAT registration. **(9 marks)**

(25 marks)

40 ONGOING LTD (12/96) *45 mins*

Ongoing Ltd holds 80% of the ordinary share capital of Goodbye Ltd. Goodbye Ltd has faced deteriorating results in recent years, and therefore expects to cease trading on 31 December 2000. The company's expected results up to the date of its cessation are as follows.

	Adjusted D1 profit/ (loss) £	Schedule A £	Capital gain/ (loss) £	Franked investment income £	Patent royalty paid (gross) £	Deed of covenant paid to charity (gross) £
12 months to 30.6.96	88,500	6,000	(24,000)	-	(12,000)	-
12 months to 30.6.97	59,000	-	-	-	(12,000)	-
6 months to 31.12.97	62,500	1,500	-	17,500	(6,000)	(1,000)
12 months to 31.12.98	47,000	-	10,800	30,000	(12,000)	(1,000)
12 months to 31.12.99	(68,000)	-	-	-	(15,000)	(1,000)
12 months to 31.12.00	(140,000)	-	72,000	-	(11,250)	(1,000)

The rental income relates to one floor of Goodbye Ltd's office building that was let out until 31 December 1997.

The forecast results of Ongoing Ltd for the year ended 31 March 2001 are as follows.

	£
Adjusted trading profit (before deduction of debenture interest)	93,000
Bank interest accrued	3,500
Debenture interest payable (trade item)	(12,000)

As at 31 March 2000 Ongoing Ltd had unused trading losses of £14,500.

On 1 April 2000 Ongoing Ltd acquired 60% of the ordinary share capital of Forward Ltd. All of the other shareholders in Forward Ltd have holdings of less than 5%.

Required

(a) Assuming that reliefs for trading losses are claimed in the most favourable manner and that FY99 tax rates and allowances continue to apply after 6.4.99:

  (i) calculate Goodbye Ltd's mainstream corporation tax liabilities for all of the accounting periods from 1 July 1995 to 31 December 2000. Ignore group relief. *(10 marks)*

  (ii) calculate the tax refunds that will be due to Goodbye Ltd as a result of the loss relief claims in respect of its trading losses for the years ended 31 December 1999 and 31 December 2000. You should ignore the possibility of any repayment supplement being due. *(4 marks)*

  (iii) Calculate Ongoing Ltd's mainstream corporation tax liability for the year to 31 March 2001. You should assume that the maximum amount of group relief is claimed from Goodbye Ltd. *(4 marks)*

(b) Hazell Ltd, an unconnected company, has profits chargeable to corporation tax for the year to 30 June 2000 of £2,000,000. A notice to file its corporation tax return for this accounting period was received on 1 September 2000. The company has always paid corporation tax at the full rate.

  (i) Calculate the corporation tax liability due on these profits and explain when this will be due for payment. Assume that FY99 rates and allowances continue after 6.4.99. *(5 marks)*

  (ii) State the date by which Hazell Ltd's corporation tax return for the year must be filed and explain what rights the Revenue have to enquire into the return. *(2 marks)*

  (25 marks)

41 OCEAN PLC (6/95) *45 mins*

You are the tax adviser to Ocean plc, the holding company for a group of companies involved in the retail jewellery trade. For some time, Ocean plc has been trying to dispose of three loss making subsidiary companies. These subsidiaries are Tarn Ltd, Loch Ltd and Pool Ltd, all of which are 100% owned. Ocean plc has received an offer from Sea plc, an unconnected company also involved in the retail jewellery trade, who wishes to purchase the following.

(a) 80% of the ordinary share capital of Tarn Ltd
(b) 40% of the ordinary share capital of Loch Ltd
(c) All of the net assets of Pool Ltd

In each case, the consideration paid by Sea plc will be in the form of cash. Each of these subsidiary companies owns a number of freehold shops whose value is substantially in excess of their original cost. In the case of Tarn Ltd, these shops were acquired from Ocean plc. All three subsidiary companies have unused trading losses. However, it is likely that Sea plc's marketing expertise will result in them becoming profitable within two or three years. All of the above companies are registered for VAT.

Required:

Draft a report covering the tax implications arising from the disposals as they affect:

(a) Ocean plc;
(b) Tarn Ltd, Loch Ltd and Pool Ltd;
(c) Sea plc.

You should include tax planning advice as appropriate.

Your answer should be structured under the following headings as appropriate: 'capital gains', 'group status', 'VAT', 'trading losses' and 'capital allowances'. **(25 marks)**

42 STAR LTD (12/98) *45 mins*

(a) Star Ltd has two 100% subsidiaries, Zodiac Ltd and Exotic Ltd. All three companies are involved in the construction industry. The results of each company for the year ended 31 March 2000 are as follows:

	Star Ltd £	*Zodiac Ltd* £	*Exotic Ltd* £
Tax adjusted Schedule DI profit/(loss)	(125,000)	650,000	130,000
Capital gain/(loss)	130,000	(8,000)	-
Royalty paid (gross)	(10,000)	-	-
Franked investment income	-	-	15,000

Star Ltd's capital gain arose from the sale of a warehouse on 15 April 1999 for £380,000. As at 31 March 1999 Star Ltd had unused trading losses of £7,500.

Required:

Calculate the mainstream corporation tax liability for each of the group companies for the year ended 31 March 2000. You should assume that reliefs are claimed in the most favourable manner. State the amounts that remain to be carried forward at 31.3.00. **(9 marks)**

(b) Star Ltd is considering the following alternative ways of reinvesting the proceeds of £380,000 from the sale of its warehouse on 15 April 1999.

(1) A freehold office building can be purchased for £290,000.

(2) A leasehold office building on a 45-year lease can be purchased for a premium of £400,000.

(3) A loan could be made to Zodiac Ltd so that is can purchase a freehold warehouse for £425,000.

Regardless of which alternative is chosen, the reinvestment will take place during February 2001.

Required:

(i) Advise Star Ltd as to the 'rollover relief' that will be available in respect of each of the three alternative reinvestments.

(ii) Briefly explain how the claims for rollover relief will affect the way in which Star Ltd's Schedule DI loss for the year ended 31 March 2000 is relieved (as part (a)). **(10 marks)**

(c) Star Ltd and its two subsidiaries are registered as a group for VAT purposes, but the inclusion of Exotic Ltd is now being reconsidered. The relevant sales and purchases of the group companies for the year ended 31 March 2000 are as follows.

		Star Ltd £	Zodiac Ltd £	Exotic Ltd £
Sales:	Standard rated	1,900,000	-	-
	Zero-rated	-	1,800,000	-
	Exempt	-	-	950,000
Purchases		(600,000)	(700,000)	(200,000)
Overhead expenditure		(450,000)	-	-
Management fee		100,000	(50,000)	(50,000)

The purchases, overhead expenditure and management fees are all standard rated. Each of the company's purchases relate to its own sales. The overhead expenditure cannot be directly attributed to any of the three companies' sales. All of the above figures are exclusive of VAT where applicable.

Required

Explain why it would have been beneficial to exclude Exotic Ltd from the group VAT registration throughout the year ended 31 March 2000. Your answer should be supported by appropriate calculations. (6 marks)

(25 marks)

DO YOU KNOW - OVERSEAS ASPECTS AND TAX PLANNING

- *Check that you can fill in the blanks in the statements below before you attempt any questions. If in doubt, you should go back to your BPP Study Text and revise first.*

- The liability of an individual to UK taxation may be affected by their residence, their ordinary residence and their ………………….. In some cases, overseas income is only taxable if it is remitted to the UK.

- Individuals must include the gross amount of overseas income in their income tax computation. Individuals can gross income up for ……………………. tax only.

- Double tax relief for individuals is the lower of:

    o ……………………………………………………………..; and

    o ……………………………………………………………..

- The UK tax rate is computed by treating the overseas income as the ………………….. of the taxpayer's income.

TRY QUESTIONS 43 AND 45

- The ……………… amount of a company's foreign income must be included in calculating PCTCT.

- Double tax relief (DTR) is set against the company's corporation tax liability to arrive at its ……………….. . DTR on each source of income is the lower of

    …………………………………………………, and

    …………………………………………………

- Relief is available for underlying tax relating to a dividend received from a foreign company in which the UK company owns at least ……………………………………….., either directly or indirectly.

- The formula for calculating underlying tax is:

    ………………………………………………………………

TRY QUESTIONS 44 AND 46

- A company may be a controlled foreign company (CFC) if it is resident in a country where tax is payable at less that …………………………….. of the rate than it would have been on similar profits in the UK.

TRY QUESTIONS 47 AND 48

- Matters which may affect the choice between trading as a sole trader or through a company include tax rates, tax payment dates, the tax regimes for dividends and salaries, and the taxation of any capital gains on sales of assets.

TRY QUESTIONS 49 TO 52

DID YOU KNOW - OVERSEAS ASPECTS AND TAX PLANNING

- *Could you fill in the blanks? The answers are in bold. Use this page for revision purposes as you approach the exam.*

- The liability of an individual to UK taxation may be affected by their residence, their ordinary residence and their **domicile**. In some cases, overseas income is only taxable if it is remitted to the UK.

- Individuals must include the gross amount of overseas income in their income tax computation. Individuals can gross income up for **withholding** tax only.

- Double tax relief for individuals is the lower of:

    o **overseas withholding tax on the overseas income**; and
    o **UK tax on the overseas income**.

- The UK tax rate is computed by treating the overseas income as the **top slice** of the taxpayer's income.

TRY QUESTIONS 43 AND 45

- The **gross** amount of a company's foreign income must be included in calculating PCTCT.

- Double tax relief (DTR) is set against the company's corporation tax liability to arrive at its **MCT**.

    DTR on each source of income is the lower of

    UK tax on that income, and

    overseas tax on that income.

- Relief is available for underlying tax relating to a dividend received from a foreign company in which the UK company owns at least **10% of the voting power**, either directly or indirectly.

- The formula for calculating underlying tax is:

$$\text{Gross dividend income} \times \frac{\text{Foreign tax paid}}{\text{After tax accounting profit}}$$

TRY QUESTIONS 44 AND 46

- A company may be a controlled foreign company (CFC) if it is resident in a country where tax is payable at less that **three quarters** of the rate than it would have been on similar profits in the UK.

TRY QUESTIONS 47 AND 48

- Matters which may affect the choice between trading as a sole trader or through a company include tax rates, tax payment dates, the tax regimes for dividends and salaries, and the taxation of any capital gains on sales of assets.

TRY QUESTIONS 49 TO 52

43 TUTORIAL QUESTION: DOUBLE TAXATION RELIEF FOR INDIVIDUALS

(a) Mr Poirot is a Belgian oil engineer who is employed by a Belgian company and who maintains his house in Antwerp. From 1 March 1992 he has worked almost totally in the United Kingdom. His annual salary is paid in the United Kingdom and with benefits in kind totals £45,000. He opened a bank account in London on 7 April 1992: interest credited on 28 February 2000 was £800. Savings income arising in Belgium was £3,500 (when converted into sterling) and was paid into his account in Belgium: no remittance was made to him in the United Kingdom. His wife (who has no income) accompanies him to the United Kingdom: their only previous visits were three short holidays between 1975 and 1986.

Required

Compute Mr Poirot's liability to UK income tax for 1999/00. Ignore non-UK tax.

Outline his residence and domicile status for UK tax purposes.

(b) Mr Wain is a single man whose salary as a sales representative (including benefits in kind) is £31,644 a year. His National Savings Bank investment account interest paid on 31 December 1999 was £1,490. He also has dividends arising outside the United Kingdom of £2,400 a year (sterling equivalent) after the foreign tax withheld of 40%. He remits £2,000 a year to the United Kingdom, the remainder being used to maintain his invalid brother, aged 36, who lives in Spain.

Required

Compute Mr Wain's United Kingdom tax liability for 1999/00.

Guidance notes

1. Before computing Mr Poirot's UK income tax liability, you should consider his domicile. This will affect his liability to UK income tax on some of his income.

2. There is nothing to suggest that Mr Wain is anything other than UK resident, ordinarily resident and domiciled. This determines how much of his overseas income is taxable in the UK.

3. Double taxation relief is given because not all of the gross income from an overseas source is available to the UK taxpayer at the stage immediately before UK tax is imposed: some of the income has already been taken in overseas tax. If credit relief is to be claimed, the gross income must be subject to UK tax.

4. Do check for any restriction on double taxation relief. The UK government does not actually give away money or reduce the UK tax on UK income (as opposed to reducing the UK tax on overseas income) in order to compensate taxpayers for high rates of overseas tax.

44 TUTORIAL QUESTION: DOUBLE TAX RELIEF FOR COMPANIES

Stripe Ltd, is resident in the UK, and had the following results for the year ended 31 March 2000.

	Stripe Ltd £
UK trading profits	800,000
Utopia branch profits (gross)	600,000
UK capital gains	95,000
Dividend income (including withholding tax)	210,000
UK bank interest receivable	Nil
Trade charges paid (gross)	85,000

The Utopian branch profits were subject to overseas taxation at a rate of 37%.

The dividend income represents a dividend on a 20% shareholding in Lesslin Inc, a company resident in Erehwon. Erehwon has a rate of withholding tax of 12%.

The translated accounts of Lesslin Inc for the same period showed:

	£	£
Profit before tax		2,590,000
Less: provision for tax	510,000	
under-provision for previous years	230,000	
		740,000
Profit after tax		1,850,000
Less: dividend paid		1,050,000
Retained profit		800,000

The tax paid for the year was eventually agreed at £305,000.

Required

Calculate the mainstream corporation tax liability of Stripe Ltd for the year ended 31 March 2000.

Guidance notes

1. Start by grossing the dividend income up for underlying tax and then include the gross figure in computing Stripe Ltd's PCTCT.

2. Once you have arrived at PCTCT calculate corporation tax in the normal way and then deduct any double tax relief.

3. Double tax relief on each source of overseas income is the lower of the UK tax on the overseas income and the overseas tax on that income.

45 BARNEY HALL (6/98) *45 mins*

Barney Hall is employed by Sutol (UK) Ltd as a motor car designer, and he is currently (and has always been) resident, ordinary resident and domiciled in the UK. You should assume that today's date is 15 October 1999. On 1 November 1999 Barney is to be sent to the country of Yalam, where he will work on assignment for the parent company of Sutol (UK) Ltd. The assignment will be for a period of either fifteen months or eighteen months.

The company will pay for his travel expenses to Yalam costing £2,400, and subsistence expenses of £850 per month whilst working in Yalam. Barney's wife will visit him during January 2000, and he will pay for her travel expenses of £700. This amount will be reimbursed by Sutol (UK) Ltd. Barney is paid a salary of £33,600 pa by Sutol (UK) Ltd, and he will continue to be paid at the same rate whilst working overseas. Barney will not be subject to Yalamese tax in respect of his salary. He has the following other income:

(a) Schedule A profits of £2,600 pa from the rental of a property situated in the UK.

(b) Interest of £5,460 (net) pa from a bank deposit account in Yalam. The interest is subject to Yalamese tax at the rate of 30%.

Barney is to dispose of the following assets:

(a) On 15 December 1999 Barney is to sell a plot of land situated in Yalam for 180,000 Yalamese dollars. The exchange rate is currently $8 to £1. The plot of land was acquired as an investment on 1 January 1997 for 84,000 Yalamese dollars, when the exchange rate was $6 to £1. The disposal will not be subject to Yalamese tax.

(b) On 20 December 2000 Barney is to make a gift of 8,000 ordinary shares in ZYX plc to his daughter on her 21st birthday. The shares are currently quoted on the UK Stock Exchange at 210 - 218, and were acquired on 31 January 1997 for £9,450. He has made no previous gifts.

There is no double taxation agreement between the UK and Yalam. All of the above figures are in pounds sterling unless indicated otherwise.

Required

(a) Briefly explain the rules which determine whether a person is resident in the UK during a tax year. Your answer should include details of people leaving the UK and people coming to the UK. (6 marks)

(b) Advise Barney of the income tax and capital gains tax implications for 1999/00 if he works overseas for:

(i) a period of fifteen months, returning to the UK on 31 January 2001;

(ii) a period of eighteen months, returning to the UK on 30 April 2001.

Your answer should include a calculation of Barney's statutory total income and capital gains for 1999/00 in each case and explain how the gain made on 20 December 2000 will be charged to tax. You are not expected to calculate the tax liabilities. (15 marks)

(c) Comment on the IHT implications of his gift to his daughter in December 2000. Would it have made any difference if he gives her other shares of the same value which are quoted in Yalam instead? (4 marks)

(25 marks)

46 EYETAKI INC (6/97) *45 mins*

You are the tax adviser to Eyetaki Inc, a company resident in the country of Eyeland. Eyetaki Inc manufactures cameras in Eyeland, and has been selling these in the UK since 1 January 2000. Initially, Eyetaki Inc employed a UK based agent to sell their cameras and rented a warehouse in London in order to maintain a stock of goods. On 1 March 2000 Eyetaki Inc sent an office manager and two sales managers to the UK from their head office in Eyeland and rented an office building and showroom in London.

As the sale of cameras in the UK has been profitable, on 1 July 2000 Eyetaki Inc is to form a 10% subsidiary, Uktaki Ltd, which will be incorporated in the UK. The subsidiary will commence trading on 1 August 2000 and will make up its first accounts for the 18 month period to 31 December 2001. Uktaki Ltd is to initially sell cameras on a wholesale basis, but is to commence retail sales during 2001.

Uktaki Ltd is to purchase a new freehold building. The building will be used to:

(a) assemble cameras from components imported from Eyeland; and
(b) to store components prior to their assembly, and assembled cameras prior to sale.

The building will also contain a showroom and general offices. It is possible that the building will be situated in a designated enterprise zone.

Eyetaki Inc is to export the camera components to the UK at their normal trade selling price plus a markup of 25%. This is because the company wishes to maximise its own profits which are only subject to corporation tax at the rate of 15% in Eyeland.

Eyetaki Inc is to assign a director to the UK for a period of between two and three years in order to manage Uktaki Ltd. The director, who is currently resident and domiciled in Eyeland, will continue to be employed by Eyetaki Inc, and will perform duties both in the UK and Eyeland. The director has income from investments situated in Eyeland.

There is no double taxation treaty between the UK and Eyeland. Eyeland is not currently a member of the European Union, but is expected to become a member in the near future.

Required

(a) (i) Advise Eyetaki Inc of whether or not it will be liable to UK corporation tax during the period from 1 January 2000 to 31 December 2001, and, if so, how the corporation tax liability will be calculated.

(ii) Set out Uktaki Ltd's accounting periods for the period up to, and including, 31 December 2001. *(7 marks)*

(b) Explain as to what extent the new freehold building to be purchased by Uktaki Ltd will qualify for Industrial Buildings Allowance, and state the Industrial Buildings Allowance that will be available. *(6 marks)*

(c) Briefly advise Uktaki Ltd of the basis on which it will have to account for VAT on the components imported from Eyeland. Explain how this basis will alter if Eyeland becomes a member of the European Union. *(4 marks)*

(d) Advise Eyetaki Inc and Uktaki Ltd of the tax implications arising from the invoicing of camera components at their normal trade selling price plus a markup of 25%. *(3 marks)*

(e) Briefly state the circumstances in which the director of Eyetaki Inc will be liable to UK income tax in respect of:

(i) Emoluments for duties performed in the UK.
(ii) Emoluments for duties performed in Eyeland.
(iii) Investment income arising in Eyeland. *(5 marks)*

(25 marks)

47 MAGEE PLC (PILOT PAPER) *45 mins*

(a) Magee plc, a UK resident company with annual profits of £5,000,000, is planning to form a new 100% subsidiary, Gavin Ltd, that will carry out trading activities through a permanent establishment in Ruritania. There is no double taxation treaty between the UK and Ruritania. Magee plc does not want the company to be regarded as resident in the UK, and is considering three possible structures for Gavin Ltd, as follows.

(i) Incorporation in the UK, with directors' meetings being held in Ruritania.
(ii) Incorporation in Ruritania, with directors' meetings being held in the UK.
(iii) Incorporation in Ruritania, with directors' meetings being held in Ruritania.

Required

Advise Magee plc as to which of the above structures will meet its residence requirements for Gavin Ltd. You should give reasons for your conclusions in each case. *(4 marks)*

(b) The main reason why Magee plc does not want Gavin Ltd to be regarded as resident in the UK is the low corporation tax rate of 8% that is applicable to companies resident in Ruritania. The forecast results for Gavin Ltd's first year of trading to 31 March 2000 are as follows.

	£
Profits per accounts (before taxation)	400,000
Tax adjusted profits:	
under Ruritanian legislation	450,000
under UK legislation	420,000

There is no withholding tax imposed on dividends paid out of Ruritania.

Required

Assuming that Gavin Ltd is regarded as resident in Ruritania, and is classed as a controlled foreign company:

(i) explain what a controlled foreign company is. You are not expected to explain the various exclusion tests;

(ii) explain why it would be beneficial for Magee plc, if Gavin Ltd were to pay a dividend equivalent to at least 90% of its profits. Your answer should be supported by appropriate calculations. (10 marks)

(c) Magee plc is to send Alex Tower, one of its senior executives, to Ruritania in order to carry out strategic planning duties for Gavin Ltd. Alex will continue to be employed and paid by Magee plc. He will leave the UK on 1 December 2000, and will stay in Ruritania for either 14 or 18 months depending on circumstances. During that period he will return to the UK for holidays at least once every three months, for about two weeks at a time. Alex will not suffer any taxation in Ruritania.

Required

Explain Alex's potential liability to UK taxation whilst he is working in Ruritania.

(7 marks)

(d) Magee plc is to send another senior employee, Tony Smith, to work in Ruritania for a period of nine months. During this period, his wife and two children, aged 15 and 20, plan to visit him twice. Tony will initially pay for all travelling expenses himself, both for himself and his family, but will then be reimbursed by Magee plc.

Required

State whether these reimbursements will be taxable emoluments under Schedule E, and whether he will be able to deduct the travelling expenses under Schedule E.

(4 marks)

(25 marks)

48 PADDINGTON LTD (12/97) *45 mins*

Paddington Ltd, a UK resident company, has two 80% owned subsidiaries, Victoria Ltd and Waterloo Ltd. Victoria Ltd is a UK resident company, but Waterloo Ltd is resident in the country of Westoria. Paddington Ltd manufactures specialised medical equipment, and the equipment is then sold by its two subsidiaries. The forecast results of Paddington Ltd and Victoria Ltd for the year ended 31 March 2000 are as follows.

	Paddington Ltd £	*Victoria Ltd* £
Adjusted Schedule DI profit	79,000	245,000
Capital gain	6,000	-
Patent royalty paid (gross)	(12,000)	-

As at 1 April 1999 Paddington Ltd had unused trading losses of £7,000.

The forecast results of Waterloo Ltd for the year ended 31 March 2000 are as follows.

	£	£
Trading profit		420,000
Taxation:		
Corporation tax	117,600	
Deferred tax	8,400	
		126,000
Distributable profits		294,000
Dividends paid:		
Net	213,400	
withholding tax at 3%	6,600	
		220,000
Retained profit		74,000

Waterloo Ltd's dividends will all be paid during, and are in respect of, the year ended 31 March 2000. The figures are in pound sterling. Waterloo Ltd is controlled from Westoria, and is not classified as a controlled foreign company. The double taxation treaty between the UK and Westoria provides that taxes suffered in Westoria are relieved as a tax credit against UK corporation tax.

In order to encourage inward investment, the country of Westoria is to reduce its rate of corporation tax on 1 April 2000, from the present rate of 30% to 10%.

Required

(a) Calculate Paddington Ltd's mainstream corporation tax liability for the year ended 31 March 2000. (9 marks)

(b) Advise Paddington Ltd as to whether or not the reduction of the corporation tax rate in Westoria will result in Waterloo Ltd being classified as a controlled foreign company. Briefly explain the tax implications of Waterloo Ltd being so classified.

(6 marks)

(c) Open ended investment companies (OEICs) are an investment vehicle designed to replace unit trusts. Briefly compare OEICs with unit trusts and state how a dividend received from an OEIC is taxed. (3 marks)

(d) State who may open an Individual Savings Account, what the maximum investment limit is and what tax reliefs are available on an account. (7 marks)

(25 marks)

49 LUCY LEE (12/96) *45 mins*

(a) 'Every man is entitled if he can to order his affairs so that the tax attaching ... is less than it otherwise would be'. Duke of Westminster v CIR (1935)

Required

Briefly explain the difference between tax avoidance and tax evasion. (2 marks)

(b) You are the tax adviser to Lucy Lee, who has been a self-employed architect for the previous 20 years. You should assume that today's date is 20 April 2000. Lucy has asked for your advice on the following matters.

  (i) From 1 April 2000 Lucy has employed her husband, who was previously unemployed, as a personal assistant at a salary of £28,000 pa. This is more than Lucy's previous personal assistant was paid, but she considers this to be good tax planning. Lucy estimates that her Schedule D Case II profit for the year ended 31 March 2001 will be £180,000. Her husband has no other income.

Lucy wants to know if employing her husband at a salary of £28,000 will result in an overall tax savings and how such an arrangement will be viewed by the Inland Revenue.

(ii) On 1 April 2000 Lucy set up a new business venture in partnership with her brother. The partnership designs building extensions for the general public at a fixed fee of £1,000 (including VAT). The forecast fee income is £35,000 pa. A deposit of £500 is paid upon the commencement of each contract, which takes one month to complete. An invoice is then issued 21 days after the completion of the contract, with the balance of the contract price being due within a further 14 days. The partnership uses the office premises, equipment and employees of Lucy's architectural business.

(1) Lucy wants to know if the partnership will automatically have to account for VAT on its income as a result of her architectural business being registered for VAT

(2) Assuming that the new partnership *does* automatically have to account for VAT on its income, Lucy wants advice as to the basis that output VAT will have to be accounted for.

(iii) Lucy's daughter is to get married on 25 May 2000, and Lucy is to make her a wedding gift of £12,500. Lucy's husband does not have any capital of his own, so Lucy is to make a gift of £12,500 to him on 24 May 2000 in order that he can make a similar wedding gift to the daughter. Neither Lucy nor her husband have made any lifetime transfers of value within the previous three years. Lucy wants to know the tax implications of such an arrangement.

Required

Advise Lucy in respect of the matters that she has raised. You should assume that the tax rates and allowances for 1999/00 apply throughout. You should note that marks for this part of the question will be allocated on the basis of:

7 marks to (i)
6 marks to (ii)
4 marks to (iii)   (17 marks)

(c) A company, which is not a member of a group, incurs a schedule D Case I trading loss in its nine month accounting period ended 31.12.00. State the alternative ways in which relief may be given for this loss if

(i) the company continues trading
(ii) the company ceases trading on 31.12.00   (6 marks)

(25 marks)

50 LI AND KEN WONG

You are the tax adviser to Li and Ken Wong. Li (Ken's wife) has been a self-employed solicitor for a number of years, whilst Ken has recently commenced self-employment as a hairdresser. They are both aged 42, and have no other sources of income. They have a son aged 22 who is presently studying to be a solicitor. They have asked for your advice on the following matters.

(a) Li's fee income is £40,000 pa, all of which relates to work done for the general public in a highly competitive market. At present, she is not registered for VAT. Li's standard rated expenses amount to £2,600 pa, and her zero rated expenses amount to £1,800 pa. She has been offered a new contract from a VAT registered company worth £15,000 pa. In order to take on this contract, Li will have to employ a full-time secretary at a salary of £9,000 pa. Although the value of the contract may grow in the future, she wants to know if it will be profitable in the short term for her to accept it. All of the above figures are net of VAT. (5 marks)

(b) Assuming that the contract is accepted, Li wants to know whether the following alternatives to employing a full-time secretary would be beneficial. The alternatives are:

(i) employing two part-time secretaries on salaries of £4,650 each;
(ii) paying a self-employed secretary £9,200 pa. (3 marks)

(c) Li plans to bring her son into partnership as an equal partner as soon as he qualifies as a solicitor, which should be during 2000. The business has a number of assets, although her only chargeable asset is goodwill. The son will not introduce any capital or make any payment upon his admittance as a partner. Li would like to know the tax implications of bringing her son into partnership. (6 marks)

(d) Ken commenced trading on 6 April 1999, and estimates that his tax adjusted Schedule D Case I profits (before capital allowances) will be £1,600 per month for the first 12 months of trading, £2,000 per month for the following 12 months, and £2,500 per month thereafter. On 6 April 1999 he purchased a car at a cost of £6,000. The car was used entirely for business purposes. Ken wants to know the tax implications of making up his accounts either to 31 March or to 30 April, and the amounts of taxable profits for his first three tax years in each case. His first period of account will be 12 or 13 months long, not one month long. All calculations should be made to the nearest month. (7 marks)

(e) Li has provided legal services to Ken's business. She dealt with the legal aspects of Ken obtaining his business premises on a short lease during April 1999, and also acted for Ken during June 1999 when he was sued for compensation by a customer who lost all of her hair after having it cut at his shop. Li has made no charge yet for the work done. The couple want to know:

(i) if a charge must be made for the work done; and
(ii) if a charge is not necessary, whether it would in any case be beneficial to make a charge. (4 marks)

Required

Advise Ken and Li in respect of the matters that they have raised. **(25 marks)**

51 WHITE STALLION LTD (6/94) *45 mins*

White Stallion Ltd runs a nationwide chain of estate agencies, making up its accounts to 31 July. The company has suffered declining results in recent years, and is therefore planning to restructure its business operations during July 1999 (you should assume that today's date is 15 April 1999). The company's plans are as follows.

(i) Three branches of the business are to be closed, with the respective premises being sold. Details of the premises to be sold are as follows.

Branch	Purchased	Original cost £	Current market value £
Apton	May 1987	75,000	145,000
Bindle	October 1990	90,000	100,000
Cotter	May 1991	88,000	85,000

The premises at Apton and Cotter are owned freehold, whilst the premises at Bindle are owned leasehold. The lease had 40 years to run at the date of purchase. Surplus land adjoining the premises at Cotter was sold for £27,000 in June 1991, at which date the market value of the property retained was £70,000.

(ii) The employees from each branch to be closed will be made redundant, resulting in statutory and non-statutory redundancy payments totalling £45,800.

(iii) Ten motor cars, which were all purchased in December 1997, are to be sold. Six of the motor cars, which cost £7,500 each, are to be sold for £4,000 each, whilst the other four motor cars, which cost £14,000 each, are to be sold for £9,000 each. The tax written-down value of White Stallion Ltd's motor car pool at 1 August 1998 was £11,500.

(iv) The company is to sell its head office building, which cost £140,000 (including land of £50,000) in June 1987, for £285,000 (including land of £90,000). White Stallion Ltd is to relocate its head office to the Isle of Goats enterprise zone, where it is to purchase new premises for £140,000 (including land of £40,000).

(v) A review of White Stallion Ltd's trade debtors, which presently total £945,000, has identified specific doubtful debts of £56,500, of which £32,000 are over six months old. It has always been the company's policy to provide for a general bad debt provision of 5% on trade debtors.

Before taking into account the effect of the restructuring, White Stallion Ltd forecasts a tax adjusted Schedule D Case I trading loss of approximately £70,000 for the current year to 31 July 1999. A small trading profit is forecast for the following year to 31 July 2000, with steadily increasing profits thereafter. White Stallion Ltd's tax adjusted Schedule D Case I trading profits for recent years have been as follows.

	£
Year ended 31.7.96	1,150,000
Year ended 31.7.97	480,000
Year ended 31.7.98	280,000

The company has no other income or outgoings, has paid no dividends in recent years, and does not have any subsidiary companies.

Required

(a) Advise White Stallion Ltd of the tax implications arising from each aspect of its restructuring, and the effect that each will have on its forecast Schedule D Case I trading loss for the year ended 31 July 1999. (12 marks)

(b) (i) Advise White Stallion Ltd of the possible ways of relieving its forecast Schedule D Case I trading loss for the year ended 31 July 1999.

(ii) Advise White Stallion Ltd as to which loss relief claims would be the most beneficial.

(iii) Advise White Stallion Ltd as to whether or not it would be beneficial to delay some aspects of its restructuring until after 31 July 1999. Your answer should indicate which aspects, if any, it would be beneficial to delay.

(9 marks)

(c) Outline the principal differences between tax avoidance and tax evasion. Assuming that it is beneficial for White Stallion Ltd to delay certain aspects of its restructuring until after 31 July 1999, and does so, discuss how this strategy is likely to be viewed by the Inland Revenue. (4 marks)

(25 marks)

Assume tax rates and allowances remain unchanged after 1.4.99.

52 FRED BARLEY (12/95) *45 mins*

Fred Barley is a 68 year old farmer who has been in business as a sole trader since 1 June 1996. Due to ill health (you should assume that Fred will not live for more than five years), Fred plans to retire on 31 May 2000 and at that date he will sell the farm to his son, Simon, aged 37. The following information is available.

(a) Due to his ill health, Fred expects to make tax adjusted Schedule D1 trading loss of £36,000 for the five months to 31 May 2000. His tax adjusted profits (before capital allowances) are as follows.

	£
Seven months to 31.12.96	70,000
Year ended 31.12.97	122,000
Year ended 31.12.98	81,000
Year ended 31.12.99	34,000

(b) Simon forecasts that he will make an adjusted trading loss (before capital allowances) of £12,000 for his first year of trading to 31 May 2001, but thereafter expects the business to be profitable.

(c) Apart from the purchase of some items of plant and machinery for a total of £34,000 on 1 October 1996, Fred did not buy or dispose of any plant and machinery. Simon does not expect to acquire any plant, other than that taken over from Fred.

(d) The market value of the business at 31 May 2000 is forecast to be £1,000,000, made up as follows.

	£
Farm land and farm buildings	600,000
Investments	250,000
Plant and machinery	35,000
Net current assets	115,000
	1,000,000

The farm land and farm buildings were purchased on 1 June 1996 for £115,000. The agricultural value of the farm land and farm buildings at 31 May 2000 will be £375,000. The investments consist of shares in quoted companies, and were purchased in June 1997 for £35,000. No item of plant and machinery cost in excess of £6,000 or is currently valued in excess of £6,000.

(e) Simon is to take over all of the assets of the business. He will purchase the farm land and farm buildings at their agricultural value of £375,000, but no consideration is to be paid in respect of the other assets.

(f) Fred is a widower, who has no other sources of income, and has not made any lifetime gifts of assets within the previous seven years. The value of his estate (excluding the business and the consideration to be paid by Simon) is £350,000.

Simon is married, and is presently employed by Fred as the farm manager of the business at a salary of £52,500 pa.

Required

(a) Advise Fred and Simon of the income tax implications arising from the sale of the business to Simon on 31 May 2000. You should *ignore* NIC, agricultural buildings allowance, farmers averaging of profits, and the possibility of any repayment supplement being due. (12 marks)

(b) Advise Fred and Simon of the capital gains tax implications arising from the sale of the business to Simon on 31 May 2000. (7 marks)

(c) Advise Fred and Simon of the inheritance tax implications arising from the sale of the business to Simon on 31 May 2000. (6 marks)

Your answer should include any tax planning points that you consider relevant. You should assume that the tax rates and allowances for 1999/00 apply throughout.

(25 marks)

Answer bank

Answer bank Notes

1 TUTORIAL QUESTION: CAR AND TRAVEL

> **Tutor's hint**
>
> (a) **The first £500 of any benefit arising in respect of the private use of computer equipment is exempt.**
>
> (b) Where an employee is absent from the United Kingdom for a **continuous period of 60 days or more the travelling (but not accommodation) expenses of a spouse or child under 18 are allowable** if paid or reimbursed by an employer, in respect of up to two visits by the family in any tax year.
>
> (c) Tax **relief is available for all costs incurred in travelling to a temporary workplace** provided that the employee's attendance there is **necessary** rather than being for his personal convenience.
>
> (d) The loan to Mr Robb is at a low rate of interest. This leads to a taxable benefit, but because the loan is used to buy Mr Robb's house both the actual interest paid and the benefit of £625 will be tax reducers.
>
> (e) Foreign pensions and annuities which are **not taxed on the remittance basis** are charged to tax subject to a **deduction of 10%.**

TAXABLE INCOME

	Non-savings £
Salary	20,000
Less superannuation (4%)	800
	19,200
Benefits in kind (W)	9,005
Less deductible travel expenses (£1,600 + £800)	2,400
Schedule E	25,805
Schedule D Case V foreign pension £750 × 90%	675
STI	26,480
Less personal allowance	4,335
Taxable income	22,145

Working: benefits in kind

	£
Car £17,000 × 15%	2,550
Car fuel	2,270
Computer equipment (20% of market value when first provided as a benefit) (20% × £3,300) – £500 (exemption)	160
Reimbursed travel expenses (£1,600 + £800)	2,400
Foreign accommodation	1,000
Loan benefit £25,000 × (10 – 4)% × 5/12	625
Benefits in kind	9,005

2 TECHNO PLC

> **Tutor's hint.** It is important that you plan the structure of your answer to any written question. Here it was straightforward to follow the structure given to you in the question.
>
> **Examiner's comments.** Answers to this question were often badly laid out, with parts (a), (b)(i) and b(ii) not being separated.

(a) Income tax, NIC and CGT implications of the proposals

   (i) **Bonuses**

      Annual bonuses will be additional schedule E remuneration of the employees receiving them. This means that each recipient will suffer an additional income tax charge equal to 40% of the bonus received. Tax will be withheld at source from payments under the PAYE system.

No additional employee class 1 national insurance contributions will be due as the directors and key personnel are all already earning above the upper limit for class 1 purposes.

There will be no CGT implications.

(ii) **Profit sharing scheme**

Employees will have a **schedule E benefit equal to the market value of any shares received.**

There are **no NIC** implications.

A **CGT charge will arise when the shares are sold.** The base cost of the shares for CGT purposes will be equal to the market value of the shares when they were received.

(iii) **Company cars**

The **schedule E benefit arising in respect of a car** will be

$25\% \times £29,500$ (£27,500 + £2,000) = £7,375

This benefit is calculated on the assumption that all the optional accessories will be included in calculating the benefit. In fact, any optional accessory costing less than £100 will be excluded if it is fitted after the date that the car is provided.

There will be an **additional schedule E benefit in respect of the petrol** unless the employee concerned fully reimburses the company for any private usage. The benefit arising in 1999/00 will be £2,270.

The **provision of a parking space near an employee's workplace does not give rise to a benefit in kind. The provision of a mobile telephone does not give rise to a benefit in kind.**

There will be no NIC or CGT implications for the directors or key personnel.

(iv) **Interest free loan**

Whilst a loan is outstanding there will be an annual **schedule E benefit** equal to the amount of the loan multiplied by the official rate of interest. If a loan is written off there will be an additional schedule E benefit equal to the amount written off. If a loan is used for a qualifying purpose, such as the purchase of a main residence, then **income tax relief will be available in 1999/00 on the interest at the official rate** which the employee is effectively deemed to have paid.

There will be no NIC or CGT implications.

(v) **Share option schemes**

As the options have to be exercised within ten years, there will be no schedule E charge at the time of the grant. When an option is exercised there will be a schedule E charge on the difference between the market value of the shares and what the employee pays for them. This means that if the shares are worth £4.00 in five years time there will be a schedule E charge on £3.00 per share.

There are **no NIC** implications.

There will be a **CGT charge when the shares are sold**. The base cost of the shares for CGT purposes will be equal to the market value of the shares when the option is exercised.

(b) (i) **Profit sharing scheme**

To be approved, a profit sharing scheme must satisfy the following conditions.

(1) The scheme must be set up in the form of a trust and shares within the scheme must normally be **held by the trustees for at least two years.**

(2) The scheme must provide that the total of the **initial market values of the shares allocated to any participant in a tax year will not exceed £3,000 or, if greater, 10% of an employee's salary, up to a maximum of £8,000.** For this purpose, salary is defined as emoluments subject to PAYE, excluding benefits in kind.

(3) Although a scheme may allocate shares unequally depending on, say, length of service or salary, **all employees must participate on similar terms.**

(4) As the company is a **close company, employees who within the past 12 months have held over 25% of the shares must be excluded** from the scheme. This will apply to Martin Thatch.

(5) **All employees and full time directors must be eligible for the scheme** although a company can impose a minimum period of employment, **not exceeding five years**, that must be served before an individual becomes eligible for the scheme. Individuals must remain eligible for eighteen months after their employment ceases.

The proposed scheme will not qualify for approval because it is not extended to all employees.

(ii) **Share option scheme**

To be approved a share option scheme must satisfy the following conditions

(1) The shares must be **fully paid ordinary shares.**

(2) The **exercise price must not be less than the market value of the shares at the time of the grant** of the option.

(3) Participation in the scheme must be **limited to employees and full time directors**.

(4) The **total market values** of the shares over which an employee holds options **must not exceed £30,000**. The shares are valued at the time the options are granted.

(5) As the company is a **close company, employees who within the past 12 months have held over 10% of the shares must be excluded** from the scheme. This will apply to Martin Thatch.

(6) If the issuing company has more than one class of shares, **the majority of the class of shares in the scheme must not be held by, persons acquiring them through their positions as directors or employees** (unless the company is employee controlled) and/or the holding company (unless the scheme shares are quoted).

The proposed scheme will qualify for approval although the company will have to ensure that condition (4) is not breached.

(iii) If approval is obtained for the profit sharing scheme, there will **not be any schedule E charge in respect of shares allocated to employees under the scheme provided that the shares are held within the trust for at least three years.** This will result in an average maximum income tax saving of £8,000 × 40% = £3,200 for the directors and an average maximum tax saving of 40% × £4,000 = £1,600 for other key personnel.

If approval is obtained for the share option scheme there will be **no income tax charge on the grant of the option, or when it is exercised provided the exercise takes place between three and ten years after the grant. A capital gains tax charge will, however, arise on** the capital gain made when an employee eventually sells his shares. The maximum income tax saving per employee is £30,000 × 40% = £12,000.

Marking scheme (summarised)		Marks
(a) Bonuses		2
Profit sharing scheme		2
Company motor cars		4
Beneficial loans		3
Share option scheme		_3_
	Available	_14_
	Maximum	13
(b) (i) *Profit sharing scheme*		
Shares/trust fund		1
Retention of shares		1
Right to participate/allocation of shares		1
Employees with a material interest		1
Participating employees		1
Share option scheme		
Shares		2
Exercise price		1
Participation		1
Ineligible employees		_1_
	Available	_10_
	Maximum	7
(ii) Profit sharing scheme		3
Share option scheme		_3_
	Available	_6_
	Maximum	_5_
	Maximum	_25_

3 CLIFFORD JONES

Tutor's hint. On the facts given, there are several tax effects of marriage and tax planning opportunities. In questions like this one, you should look at each fact in turn to see what effect or opportunity it suggests.

Examiner's comment. Many candidates were confused about the relationship between the MCA and the APA.

(a) In 1999/00 the couple will be entitled to the **married couple's allowance**. This is a tax reducer, saving tax at 10%. The allowance for 1999/00 is £1,970. The tax reduction will be given to Clifford if no election is made. However, the couple can jointly elect to transfer all of it to Dinah. Alternatively, she can unilaterally elect to have half of it transferred to her.

In 1999/00, the year of marriage, Dinah will also be able to continue to claim the **additional personal allowance**. This is a tax reducer for single parents of £1,970 a year, saving tax at 10%. Clifford could also claim this for the year of marriage, instead of the married couple's allowance.

A married couple can have only one house eligible for mortgage interest relief. The house which qualifies will be the one which is in fact the couple's main residence. There will thus be an increase in the mortgage interest payable on one of the two houses following the marriage. The mortgage concerned will come out of the MIRAS system. The concessions on marriage which allow tax relief on two mortgages for 12 months will not apply, because they are only available when one spouse goes to live in the other's house or both go to live in a third house.

Where an income-yielding asset such as the holiday cottage is owned jointly by married couples, the Inland Revenue will **split the income between the spouses equally unless a declaration is made that the interests of the spouses are in fact in some other specified proportion.** If the 75:25 split is to be maintained, a declaration will have to be made.

(b) On the figures given, Dinah will have some unused basic rate band while Clifford will be a higher rate taxpayer. The main tax planning measure to take is therefore to **transfer income to Dinah, so as to use up her basic rate band.** This can be done by merging the two businesses into a partnership, and by transferring the holiday cottage and the building society account into Dinah's sole name. The 1999/00 tax computations without taking these suggested measures are as follows.

Clifford

	Non-savings £	Savings (excl dividend) £	Total £
Schedule D Case I	55,000		
Less personal pension contribution (20%)	11,000		
	44,000		
Schedule A (75: 25) (assumes declaration made)	3,750		
Building society interest		2,400	
	47,750	2,400	50,150
Less personal allowance	4,335		
Taxable income	43,415	2,400	45,815

	£
Income tax on non-savings income	
£1,500 × 10%	150
£26,500 × 23%	6,095
£15,415 × 40%	6,166
Income tax on savings (excl dividend) income	
£2,400 × 40%	960
	13,371
Less APA £1,970 × 10%	197
Tax liability	13,174
Class 2 NICs £6.55 × 52	£341
Class 4 NICs 6% × £(26,000 – 7,530)	£1,108

Dinah

	Non-savings £
Schedule D Case I	15,000
Less personal pension contribution (20%)	3,000
	12,000
Schedule A (75: 25) (assumes declaration made)	1,250
	13,250
Less personal allowance	4,335
Taxable income	8,915

	£
Tax on non-savings income	
£1,500 × 10%	150
£7,415 × 23%	1,705
	1,855
Less: APA (£1,970 × 10%)	(197)
Tax liability	1,658
Class 2 NICs (£6.55 × 52)	£341
Class 4 NICs (£15,000 – £7,530) × 6%	£448

Capital gains tax

The non-business assets do not qualify for taper relief, so the loss should be allocated against the gains made on these assets:

	£
Gains on non-business assets (£6,500 + £4,200)	10,700
Less loss	(2,400)
	8,300
Gain on business asset after taper relief (£9,000 × 85%)	7,650
	15,950
Less annual exemption	(7,100)
Chargeable gain	8,850

Tax at 20% = £1,770.

	Clifford	Dinah
Total liabilities (for couple £18,840)	£14,623	£4,217

The income to transfer to Dinah is:

(i) the £2,400 building society interest: it is assumed that the building society will not insist on crediting the interest to date at the time of transfer into Dinah's sole name;

(ii) the rental income from the cottage;

(iii) trading income so as to use up the balance of Dinah's basic rate band. The chargeable gain uses up £8,850 of the basic rate band so the amount remaining is:

	£
Basic rate band	26,500
Dinah's non-savings income	(7,415)
Transferred from Clifford (£3,750 + 2,400)	(6,150)
Chargeable gain	(8,850)
	4,085

However, additional trading income will allow additional personal pension contributions, so the unused basic rate band must therefore be grossed up at 20%. £4,085/(1 – 0.2) = £5,106. A partnership agreement should be drawn up to ensure that over the tax year as a whole, Dinah receives the right amount of trading income.

The revised computations are as follows.

Clifford

	Non-savings £
Schedule D Case I	49,894
Less personal pension contribution (20%)	9,979
	39,915
Less personal allowance	4,335
Taxable income	35,580

	£
Income tax on non-savings income	
£1,500 × 10%	150
£26,500 × 23%	6,095
£7,580 × 40%	3,032
	9,277
Less APA £1,970 × 10%	197
Tax liability	9,080
Class 2 NICs £6.55 × 52	£341
Class 4 NICs 6% of profits between £7,530 and £26,000	£1,108

Dinah

	Non savings £	Savings (excl dividend) £
Schedule D Case I	20,106	
Less personal pension contribution (20%)	4,021	
	16,085	
Schedule A	5,000	
Total non-savings income	21,085	
Building society interest × 100/80		2,400
Total income	21,085	2,400
Less personal allowance	4,335	
Taxable income	16,750	2,400

	£
Tax on non-savings income	
£1,500 × 10%	150
£15,250 × 23%	3,508
Tax on savings (excl dividend) income	
£2,400 × 20%	480
	4,138
Less: APA (£1,970 × 10%)	(197)
Tax liability	3,941
Class 2 NICs (£6.55 × 52)	£341
Class 4 NICs £(20,106 − 7,530) × 6%	£755
Capital gains tax liability (as before)	1,770

	Clifford	Dinah
Total liabilities (for couple £17,336)	£10,529	£6,807

The total tax saving is £(18,840 − 17,336) = £1,504.

(c) With the wills drafted as they are at present, only partial use will be made of the inheritance tax nil rate band of Clifford should he die first. The transfer to the surviving spouse will be exempt, and when the assets pass to the children on the death of that spouse, they will be subject to inheritance at 40% (possibly with the benefit of business property relief).

To ensure that the nil rate band of the first spouse to die is used in full, the wills should be re-written to leave each spouse's estate to the children, and not to the other spouse. If the spouses do not wish to do this because circumstances might change, the same effect could be achieved following the first death by the use of a deed of variation. Such a deed effectively re-writes the will.

(d) If the assets are put into an interest in possession trust, Dinah will have the use of them and the right to income from them during her lifetime, but will not be able to dispose of them: they will pass to the remainderman (Clifford's son) on Dinah's death.

Income tax

The trust will pay tax on its income at 20% (savings (excl dividend) income) or 23% (non-savings income), and will pay out income to Dinah net of the same tax rates. Dividends will be received by the trust net of a 10% tax credit and no further tax will be payable. Dinah will thus be in the same position as if she had received the income directly, except that there may be trust administration expenses (not tax-deductible) to pay.

CGT

The trust will take over the assets at their market values at Clifford's death, and will pass them on to Clifford's son at their market values at Dinah's death, but there will be no chargeable gains on either death. Gains on disposals by the trustees between the two deaths will be taxable at 34%, subject to an annual exemption of half of an individual's annual exemption.

IHT

The transfer into the trust on Clifford's death will be an exempt inter-spouse transfer because Dinah will have an interest in possession. The trust will not suffer the principal and exit charges, because they only apply to discretionary trusts, but if any property is transferred out of the trust it will be treated as a transfer by Dinah. On Dinah's death, the trust property will be taxed as part of Dinah's estate.

4 CHARLES CHOICE

Tutor's hint. This question has been amended to reflect syllabus changes. Part (c) is now extremely topical.

Examiner's comments. This was a reasonably popular question but not answered as well as would be expected given that the topics covered are examinable at Paper 7.

(a) **Accepting the company motor car**

The annual cost of accepting the company car is:

	£
Car benefit £14,400 × 25%	3,600
Less: contributions 12 × £35 (50 – 15)	420
	3,180
Fuel benefit (diesel)	1,540
	4,720

	£
Additional income tax liability at 23%	1,086
Contributions 12 × £50	600
Total annual cost to employee	1,686

Accepting the additional salary

The annual cost of accepting the additional salary is:

	£	£
Salary		2,800
Less: Income tax at 23%	644	
Class 1 NIC (Additional) £2,500 (£26,000 – £23,500) at 10%	250	
		894
		1,906
Mileage allowance (£8,000 at 23p)		1,840
Tax relief on expense claim £1,540 × 23% (see below)		354
Additional income		4,100
Running costs	1,650	
Leasing cost (12 × £285)	3,420	
		5,070
Total annual cost to employee		970

Based on purely financial criteria, the cash alternative appears to be the most beneficial as it results in a saving of £716 (£1,686 – £970).

Expense claim

Strictly, Charles' mileage allowance is a taxable benefit and Charles can make a claim to deduct the business proportion of his motoring expenses. This results in a net tax deduction as follows:

	£
Taxable mileage allowance (£8,000 × 23p)	1,840
Less: Business proportion of expenses (£5,070 × 8,000/12,000)	(3,380)
Net deduction	(1,540)

Alternatively, Charles can take advantage of the Fixed Profit Car Scheme (FPCS). The mileage allowance of £1,840 is less than the tax free amount laid down under the scheme:

	£
£4,000 × 35p	1,400
£4,000 × 23p	800
Tax free under scheme	2,200

This means the £1,840 Charles receives is tax free and an expense claim can be made by Charles to deduct the excess of £360 (£2,200 – £1,840).

Clearly Charles will obtain a larger net tax deduction under the former alternative.

(b) (i) (1) Charles' contributions to his personal pension scheme for 1999/00 were £5,875 (£23,500 at 25%). Under the company's occupational pension scheme, Charles' contributions for 2000/2001 will be £1,410 (£23,500 at 6%). The saving net of tax is £3,438 (£5,875 – £1,410 = £4,465 less 23%). Any unused personal pension relief brought forward from years prior to 1999/00 will be lost.

(2) With the occupational pension scheme, the Northwest Bank plc will also contribute £1,410 each year on Charles' behalf.

(3) A personal pension scheme is generally more flexible than an occupational pension scheme. This will be an important factor if Charles plans to leave the Northwest Bank plc in the foreseeable future.

(4) The pension payable under a personal pension scheme depends on the performance of the investment fund. The pension payable under an occupational pension scheme is based upon final salary and number of years' service. Thus the final pension received is predictable under the employer scheme and potentially less at risk than the pension receivable from a personal pension scheme.

(5) The normal earliest retirement age under an occupational pension scheme is 60 but under a personal pension scheme it is 50.

(6) The income tax implications are similar for both schemes.

(ii) The maximum tax deductible contributions that Charles could make into the occupational pension scheme are £3,525 pa (£23,500 at 15%).

Additional voluntary contributions of £2,115 pa (£3,525 – £1,410) could therefore, either be paid into the occupational scheme, or into a separate freestanding scheme. If Charles contributes into the company scheme then tax relief will be given as a deduction against Charles' Schedule E income. If he contributes into a freestanding scheme then tax relief will be given by making the payments net of basic rate tax. Any higher rate tax relief (if due in the future although not due on current salary levels) will be given through the PAYE coding system.

(c) As David Spence is leaving the UK for less than **five complete tax years** the gain on the sale of the holiday cottage will be subject to UK CGT. **Gains made during the year of departure are chargeable in that year.** If the cottage is sold during March 2000, the gain will, therefore, be subject to CGT in 1999/00. **Gains made in subsequent years are chargeable in the year that the individual resumes residence in the UK.** This means that if David delays the sale until September 2000 he will not be assessed on the gain until 2003/2004.

Marking guide	Marks	
(a)	*Accepting the company motor car*	
	Car benefit	1
	Contributions	1
	Fuel benefit	1
	Total annual cost	1
	Accepting the cash alternative	
	Income tax liability	1
	Class 1 NIC	1
	Mileage allowance	1
	Running and leasing costs	1
	Expense claim	
	Based on business expenditure	2
	Based on fixed profit car scheme	2
	Conclusion	1
	Maximum/Available	13
(b)	Contributions	2
	Company contributions	1
	Flexibility of personal pension scheme	1
	Pension payable	1
	Retirement age	1
	Income tax implications	1
	Additional voluntary contributions	1
	Schemes available	1
	Tax relief	1
	Available	10
	Maximum	7
(c)	Absent for 5 complete tax years	1
	Year departure	2
	Subsequent years	2
	Maximum/Available	5
		25

5 WILLIAM WILES

Tutor's hint. Tax relief is only available for maintenance payments made under a written agreement.

Examiner's comments. Many candidates did not appreciate that furnished holiday lets had to be dealt with separately from other properties.

(a) (i) The houses qualify to be treated as a trade under the furnished holiday letting rules, because they were:

(1) **let furnished on a commercial basis with a view to the realisation of profits.**

(2) **available for commercial letting to the public for at least 140 days** during 1999/00 (294 days and 224 days respectively).

(3) **on average let for at least 70 days.** House 2 satisfies this test since the average for the two houses is 77 days.

(4) **not occupied by the same person for more than 31 days for at least seven months** during 1999/00.

The tax advantages are that:

(1) **Relief for losses is available as if they were trading losses**, including the facility to set losses against other income. The usual Schedule A loss reliefs do not apply.

(2) **Capital allowances are available on furniture**.

(3) **The income qualifies as net relevant earnings for personal pension relief.**

(4) Capital gains tax **rollover relief, retirement relief, relief for gifts of business assets** and **relief for loans to traders** are all available.

(ii) The Schedule A loss on the furnished holiday lets must be calculated separately to the Schedule A loss arising on the other accommodation.

Schedule A loss on furnished holiday lets:

	£	£
Rental income		
House 1 (14 × £375)		5,250
House 2 (8 × £340)		2,720
		7,970
Expenses		
Business rates (£730 + £590)	1,320	
Insurance (£310 + £330)	640	
Advertising (£545 + £225)	770	
Repairs	6,250	
Capital allowances		
House 1 (£6,500 × 40% (FYA))	2,600	
House 2 (£6,500 × 40% (FYA))	2,600	
Private use (re house 1)		
(£730 + £310 + £2,600) × 10/52	(700)	
		13,480
Schedule A loss		5,510

Schedule A loss on other lettings:

	£	£
Rental income		
House 3 (£8,600 × 3/12)		2,150
Premium received (W)		448
Furnished room (£4,600 – £4,250)		350
		2,948
Expenses		
Rent	6,200	
Repairs	710	
Wear and tear allowance (£2,150 × 10%)	215	
		7,125
Schedule A loss		4,177

William should claim 'rent a room' relief in respect of the letting of the furnished room in his main residence, since this is more beneficial than the normal basis of assessment (£4,600 – £825 = £3,775).

Working

Premium

	£	£
Premium received		8,000
Less: £8,000 × 2% × (4 – 1)		480
		7,520
Less allowance for premium paid		
Premium paid	85,000	
Less: £85,000 × 2% × (25 – 1)	40,800	
	44,200	
Relief available £44,200 × 4/25		7,072
		448

William can claim under s 380 ICTA 1988 to have the Schedule A loss of £5,510 arising in respect of furnished holiday accommodation to be set off against his total income for 1999/00, and/or his total income for 1998/99.

The Schedule A loss of £4,177 will be carried forward and set against the first available Schedule A profits.

(b) (i) **Payments made between 1 July 1999 and 31 December 1999**

No tax relief will be due in respect of voluntary maintenance payments, school fees paid, or mortgage interest paid. The mortgage interest has not been paid for a qualifying purpose, as the property is not William's main residence. William's wife would have had to pay the mortgage interest on a home in her name for relief to be available.

Payments made under the divorce settlement from 1 January 2000 onwards

The lump sum payment of £25,000 will not attract any tax relief.

The maintenance payments made under written agreement will attract tax relief of £143 (£475 × 3 = £1,425 at 10%) in 1999/00.

No tax relief will be due in respect of mortgage interest paid.

Because the school fees are paid directly to the school (rather than to William's ex-wife) no tax relief is available in respect of them. If they had been channelled through the wife the maximum on which relief is available (£1,970 in 1999/00) means that relief would still have been unavailable for the full amount of maintenance and school fees paid.

(ii) In addition to his personal allowance, William will be entitled to a full **married couple's allowance of £1,970 for 1999/00,** unless a claim to transfer all or half of it to his wife has been made. He cannot claim the **additional personal allowance of £1,970 for 1999/00** because the additional personal allowance is not generally available at the same time as the MCA.

Marking guide		Marks
(a) (i) *Qualification as furnished holiday letting*		
Commercial basis		1
140 day rule		1
70 day rule		1
31 day test		1
Tax advantages		
Capital allowances/Net relevant earnings		1
Loss relief/CGT reliefs		<u>1</u>
	Available	<u>6</u>
	Maximum	5
(ii) *Furnished holiday accommodation*		
Separate identification		1
Rental income		1
Expenses		2
Capital allowances claim		1
Private adjustment		2
Other lettings		
Rental income/Premium received - house 3		3
Furnished room		1
Expenses		2
Relief for losses		
Furnished holiday lettings		1
Schedule A loss		<u>1</u>
	Available	<u>15</u>
	Maximum	14
(b) (i) *Voluntary payments*		
No tax relief		1
Mortgage interest		1
Divorce settlement		
Maintenance payments		2
Other payments		<u>1</u>
	Available	<u>5</u>
	Maximum	4
(ii) Married couple's allowance		1
Additional personal allowance		<u>1</u>
	Available/Maximum	<u>2</u>
	Maximum	<u>25</u>

6 DUNCAN MCBYTE

Tutor's hints. It is important to allocate your time carefully when answering written questions.

Examiner's comments. Many candidates wasted time by not carefully reading the requirements of the question.

(a) *Income tax*

The salary will be subject to income tax on a receipts basis. The contractual entitlement to the termination bonus means that it will also be subject to income tax. The termination bonus will only be taxable in the year that it is received so the amount assessable to income tax under schedule E in 1999/00 is £48,750 (£65,000 × 9/12).

The benefit in kind arising in respect of the accommodation will also be subject to income tax under Schedule E. The amount of the benefit in kind taxable in 1999/00 is:

	£
Rateable value (£6,700 × 9/12)	5,025
Additional benefit 10% (£170,000 – £75,000) × 9/12	7,125
Running costs (£6,200 × 9/12)	4,650
Furniture (20% × £21,000 × 9/12)	3,150
	19,950

A mileage allowance of up to the amount laid down by the fixed profit car scheme (FPCS) could be paid to Duncan tax free. If the amount paid by the company exceeds the amount laid down under the FPCS, the excess is taxable but if it is less than the amount laid down under the scheme, Duncan may claim to deduct the shortfall from his schedule E emoluments for the year. The position for 1999/00 is as follows:

FPCS amounts:	£
4,000 × 63p	2,520
5,000 × 36p	1,800
	4,320
Mileage allowance paid by company (9,000 × 40p)	(3,600)
Deductible from schedule E emoluments	720

As an alternative to using the FPCS Duncan could be taxed on the mileage allowance of £3,600 and claim a deduction for his actual business expenditure of £3,975 ((£1,800 × 9/12 + £380 × 9) × 1,000/1,200). Clearly this would be less beneficial for Duncan than using the FPCS.

The benefit in kind arising in respect of the loan is taxable under schedule E. The assessable benefit in kind for 1999/00 is

	£
$\dfrac{£60,000 + 50,000}{2} \times 10\% \times 9/12$	4,125
Less interest paid (£60,000 × 4% × 6/12) + (£50,000 × 4% × 3/12)	(1,700)
	2,425

The alternative method of calculating the interest benefit would give a benefit of £4,250 (£60,000 × 6/12 + £50,000 × 3/12) so it is assumed that this alternative method would not be used.

There will be no taxable benefit in respect of the subscription to the Institute of Chartered Computer Consultants, the liability insurance or the work related training. However, the £800 paid for the sports club membership will be a taxable benefit in kind in 1999/00. The full amount is taxable as it was all paid during January 2000.

As Duncan was granted options under an approved company share option scheme there is no income tax on the grant of the options or on the profit arising from the exercise of the options on 30 June 2002.

National insurance contributions

Employee Class 1 National insurance contributions (NIC) will be due in respect of both the salary and the termination bonus. The salary alone exceeds the Class 1 upper limit so the maximum amount of employee NICs will be due. Employer NICs will also be due on the salary and the termination bonus but no other NICs will be due.

(b) If the options had not been granted under an approved company share option scheme a schedule E charge would arise on the exercise of the options on 30 June 2002. If the market value of the shares on 30 June 2002 is £5 per share, the amount assessable under schedule E will be £48,750 (15,000 × £(5-1.75)). If the share option scheme was approved there would be no tax charge until the shares were disposed of and the amount subject to capital gains tax is likely to be lower than the amount that would have been taxable had the option been unapproved.

(c) As the residence is expected to be

(i) available for letting for at least 140 days in the tax year, and
(ii) actually let for at least 70 days of the year.

the letting can be treated as a furnished holiday let. This means that capital allowances can be claimed and the amount assessable under Schedule A will be:

	£
Rental income	21,000
Letting Agency (22.5%)	4,725
Running costs	900
First year allowances (£24,000 × 40%)	9,600
Interest (£5,400 × 9/12)	4,050
	1,725

Tutorial Note: It is assumed that a claim would be made to take the interest out of MIRAS. Such a claim would be beneficial as the full amount of interest would, as shown above, then be deducted in calculating schedule A profits.

Marking guide

		Marks
(a)	*Schedule E*	
	Salary	1
	Termination bonus	1
	Living accommodation:	
	Basic benefit	1
	Additional benefit	2
	Furniture/running costs	1
	Mileage allowance	
	Fixed profit car scheme	2
	Expense claim based on business expenditure	2
	Beneficial loan	
	Benefit in kind	3
	Alternative method	1
	Other payments	
	Sports club membership	1
	Other payments	1
	Share options	2
	National insurance contributions	2
	Available	20
	Maximum	17
(b)	No Schedule E charge on exercise	2
	Lower capital gains tax charge	1
	Maximum/Available	3
(c)	Qualification as furnished holiday letting	2
	Interest	1
	Rental income/Letting agency	1
	Running costs	1
	Capital allowances	1
	Available	6
	Maximum	5
	Maximum	25

7 TUTORIAL QUESTION: A CHATTEL, LAND AND SHARES

(a) (i) **The vase**

	£
Proceeds	10,900
Less cost	8,400
Unindexed gain	2,500
Less indexation allowance	
$\dfrac{162.6 - 79.4}{79.4} = 1.048 \times £8,400 = £8,803$, but limited to £2,500	2,500
Chargeable gain	0

(ii) **The land**

	Cost £	31.3.82 value £
Proceeds	54,000	54,000
Less incidental costs of sale	985	985
Net sale proceeds	53,015	53,015
Less: cost	(2,000)	
value on 31.3.82		(15,000)
enhancement expenditure 1.6.84	(3,000)	(3,000)
Unindexed gain	48,015	35,015
Less indexation allowance:		
on 31.3.82 value		
$\dfrac{162.6 - 79.4}{79.4} = 1.048 \times £15,000$	(15,720)	(15,720)
on 1.6.84 expenditure		
$\dfrac{162.6 - 89.2}{89.2} = 0.823 \times £3,000$	(2,469)	(2,469)
	29,826	16,826

The chargeable gain is £16,826.

Taper relief is not available in 1999/00 as this is a non-business asset.

(iii) **The Index plc shares**

The May 1998 shares

	£
Proceeds 2,000/12,000 × £42,000	7,000
Less cost	5,314
Chargeable gain	1,686

Tutorial note. There is no indexation after April 1998.

The 1982 holding

	No of shares	Cost £	31.3.82 value £
Acquisition 1.5.81	10,000	9,000	
Acquisition 1.3.82	2,000	2,000	
	12,000	11,000	16,800

	£
Proceeds 10,000/12,000 × £42,000	35,000
Less 31 March 1982 value	
(gives a lower gain than cost)	
10,000/12,000 × £16,800	14,000
Unindexed gain	21,000
Less indexation allowance	
$\dfrac{162.6 - 79.4}{79.4} = 1.048 \times £14,000 =$	14,672
Chargeable gain	6,328

Taper relief is not available in 1999/00 as the shares are non-business assets.

(iv) **The property**

	£
Proceeds	60,000
Less cost	25,000
Unindexed gain	35,000
Less indexation allowance	
$\dfrac{162.6-87.2}{87.2} = 0.865 \times £25,000$	21,625
Chargeable gain	13,375

This is a business asset so taper relief is available:

Gain after taper relief (£13,375 × 85%) £11,369

(v) **Tax liabilities**

Income tax position

	Non-savings £	Dividends £	Total £
Salary	6,000		
Dividends £16,875 × 100/90		18,750	
STI	6,000	18,750	24,750
Less personal allowance	4,335		
Taxable income	1,665	18,750	20,415

	£
Income tax on non-savings income	
£1,500 × 10%	150
£165 × 23%	38
Income tax on dividend income	
£18,750 × 10%	1,875
Income tax liability	2,063
Less tax credits on dividends £18,750 × 10%	1,875
Tax payable (subject to tax paid under PAYE)	188

Capital gains tax position

		£
Gain on vase		0
Gain on land		16,826
Gain on shares:	May 1998 acquisition	1,686
	the 1982 holding	6,328
Gain on tenanted property		11,369
		36,209
Less annual exemption		7,100
Taxable gains		29,109

	£
Capital gains tax	
£7,585 (£28,000 − £20,415) × 20%	1,517
£21,524 × 40%	8,610
Tax payable	10,127

(b) Capital gains tax for 1999/00 is due on 31 January 2001.

8 KEN SING

> **Tutor's hint.** In questions about people who are in the UK for limited periods, you will usually have to decide their residence and domicile status. In this question, it is clear that Ken is resident and ordinarily resident in the UK but domiciled in Pajan. In other questions, the position may not be so clear. You should also look out for cases where an individual is domiciled abroad, but is treated as domiciled in the UK for inheritance tax purposes under the '17 years out of the last 20' rule.
>
> **Examiner's comment.** In part (a), many candidates were unaware of the remittance basis.

(a) Ken is **not domiciled** in the UK, so his **foreign income and gains are only taxable in the UK** to the extent that they are remitted to the UK. Interest and dividends taxable on the remittance basis are non-savings income.

KEN SING: INCOME TAX COMPUTATION

	Non-savings £	Savings (excl dividend) £	Dividend £	Total £
Salary	75,000			
Car benefit £38,000 × 25%	9,500			
Fuel benefit	1,540			
Beneficial loan £90,000 × 10%	9,000			
Medical insurance	1,200			
Golf club subscription	1,500			
Schedule E	97,740			
Schedule D Case V				
Rents £3,500 × 100/70	5,000			
Interest £850 × 100/85	1,000			
UK dividends 100,000 × 9p × 100/90			10,000	
UK bank interest £2,240 × 100/80		2,800		
STI	103,740	2,800	10,000	116,540
Less personal allowance	4,335			
Taxable income	99,405	2,800	10,000	112,205

Income tax on non-savings income	
£1,500 × 10%	150
£26,500 × 23%	6,095
£71,405 × 40%	28,562
Income tax on savings (excl dividend) income	
£2,800 × 40%	1,120
Income tax on dividend income	
£10,000 × 32.5%	3,250
	39,177
Less mortgage interest relief	
£30,000 × 10% × 10%	300
	38,877
Less double taxation relief	
Rents £5,000 × 30%	1,500
Interest £1,000 × 15%	150
	1,650
Tax liability	37,227
Less tax paid and suffered	
PAYE	33,500
Dividends £10,000 × 10%	1,000
Interest £2,800 × 20%	560
	35,060
Tax payable	2,167

KEN SING: CGT COMPUTATION

	£
Sale of land in Pajan	
Proceeds	40,000
Less cost £50,000 × 40/(40 + 120)	12,500
	27,500
Less indexation allowance	
$\dfrac{162.6 - 92.8}{92.8} = 0.752 \times £12,500$	9,400
Chargeable gain	18,100
Less annual exemption	7,100
Taxable gain	11,000

CGT: £11,000 × 40% = £4,400.

Tutorial note. We ignore the sale of paintings because the proceeds have not been remitted to the UK.

(b) KEN SING: INHERITANCE TAX COMPUTATION

Because Ken Sing is **not UK domiciled, his overseas assets are excluded property. Land and buildings are situated at their physical location, shares where registered and bank accounts where the relevant branches are located.**

	£	£
House in London £(175,000 – 90,000)		85,000
Bank account in England		60,000
UK shares: 100,000 × £1.04		104,000
UK shares	65,000	
Less BPR £65,000 × 1,000/1,050 × 100%	61,905	
		3,095
		252,095

	£
Inheritance tax	
£231,000 × 0%	0
£21,095 × 40%	8,438
	8,438
Less quick succession relief (see below)	
£13,333 × $\dfrac{45,000}{58,333}$ × 40%	4,114
	4,324

Quick succession relief is computed as follows.

The estate rate on the death in September 1996 is £80,000/£350,000 = 22.857%.

The gift was a specific gift, and therefore did not bear its own tax. The gross gift was £45,000 × 100/(100 – 22.857) = £58,333, and the tax was therefore £(58,333 – 45,000) = £13,333.

These figures are then used in the usual formula:

Tax paid on first transfer × $\dfrac{\text{net transfer}}{\text{gross transfer}}$ × percentage

In cases such as this, where a specific legacy was grossed up, the quick succession relief can also be computed as net transfer × estate rate × percentage.

(c) KEN SING: CGT COMPUTATION

(i) The London house appears to have been Ken Sing's principal private residence throughout, so any gain or loss will be ignored.

The gain on the shares in High Growth plc is as follows.

	£
Proceeds 100,000 × £1.02 (the bid price because this is an actual sale)	102,000
Less cost	45,000
Unindexed gain	57,000
Less FA 1985 pool indexation to April 1998	
$\dfrac{162.6 - 153.8}{153.8} \times £45,000$	2,575
Chargeable gain	54,425
Gain after taper relief (£54,425 × 95%)	51,704

The gain on the shares in Small-time Ltd is as follows. Retirement relief is unavailable because Ken Sing has not worked full time for the company. Similarly, the shares do not qualify as a business asset for taper relief purposes because Ken Sing has not worked full time for the company and his percentage shareholding is only 8%.

	£
Proceeds	65,000
Less cost	20,000
Unindexed gain	45,000
Less FA 1985 pool indexation	
$\dfrac{162.6 - 141.9}{141.9} \times £20,000$	2,918
Chargeable gain	42,082
Gain after taper relief (£42,082 × 95%)	£39,978

The final computation is as follows.

	£
Gain on High-Growth plc shares	51,704
Gain on Small-time plc shares	39,978
Chargeable gains	91,682
Less annual exemption	7,100
Taxable gains	84,582
CGT £84,582 × 40%	£33,833

Both of the above assets have been owned for three complete years after 5.4.98 (including the bonus year) and they are non-business assets. This means 95% of the gain remains chargeable after taper relief.

(ii) Ken Sing is permanently leaving the UK. This means sales after returning to Pajan will be exempt from CGT, so long as the Revenue treat Ken Sing as no longer UK resident nor ordinary resident. The Revenue must so treat him from 6 April 2001 By concession, they will normally so treat him from the date of leaving the UK.

9 DESMOND AND MYRTLE COOK

> **Tutor's hint**. With regard to Myrtle's shares, note that the diminution in value principle applies for inheritance tax purposes but not for CGT purposes.
>
> **Examiner's comment**. Several candidates had problems with the seven year cumulation.

Notes *Answer bank*

(a) (i) DESMOND COOK: TAXABLE INCOME

	£	Non-savings £
Rental income		14,200
Less expenses: running costs	1,340	
repairs	1,600	
capital allowances (W)	1,420	
		4,360
Schedule A		9,840
Schedule E: pension		6,000
Statutory total income		15,840
Less personal allowance		4,335
Taxable income		11,505

MYRTLE COOK: TAXABLE INCOME

	Non-savings income £	Savings (excl dividend) £
Schedule E	40,000	
Savings income		10,000
Statutory total income	40,000	10,000
Less personal allowance (income too high for age allowance)	4,335	
Taxable income	35,665	10,000

Working

As the accommodation was let as furnished holiday accommodation capital allowances are available on the cost of the furniture:

	£
Year to 31.3.98	
Cost	10,098
WDA @ 25%	(2,525)
	7,573
Year to 31.3.99	
WDA @ 25%	(1,893)
	5,680
Year to 31.3.00	
WDA @ 25%	(1,420)
	4,260

DESMOND COOK: TAXABLE GAIN

	£
Deemed proceeds for cottage	115,000
Less cost	23,000
	92,000
Less indexation allowance	
$\dfrac{162.6 - 90.7}{90.7} = 0.793 \times £23,000$	18,239
Chargeable gain	73,761
Less retirement relief (*Note*)	14,276
	59,485

The gain arises on a non-business asset so no taper relief is available on a disposal in 1999/00.

	£
Gain after taper relief	59,485
Less annual exemption	7,100
Taxable gain	52,385

Tutorial note. The cottage has been owned for 15.5 years and has been let as furnished holiday accommodation for three years of that period. Therefore,

£14,276 (£73,761 × 3/15.5) of the gain is eligible for retirement relief. Retirement relief of 100% is available on gains up to £60,000 (£200,000 × 3/10), so the relief available is £14,276.

The full gain relating to the period of use as furnished holiday accommodation is eliminated by retirement relief. This means there is no remaining gain eligible for gift relief.

MYRTLE COOK: TAXABLE GAIN

	£
Deemed proceeds for shares 8,000 × £15	120,000
Less cost £78,000 × 8/20	31,200
	88,800
Less FA 1985 pool indexation	
$\dfrac{162.6 - 142.5}{142.5} \times £31,200$	4,401
Chargeable gain	84,399
Less annual exemption	7,100
Taxable gain	77,299

Non-business asset, so no taper relief in 1999/00.

(ii) DESMOND COOK: INHERITANCE TAX FOLLOWING DEATH

The gift in May 1993 was made more than seven years prior to death so it is a PET that does not become chargeable.

	£
March 2000 gift of cottage (no BPR on let property)	115,000
Less annual exemptions: 1999/00	(3,000)
1998/99	(3,000)
	109,000

None of the £Nil band was used in the previous seven years, so IHT is: £109,000 × 0% = £Nil

June 2001 estate at death £270,000/2	135,000

In the seven years before death, £109,000 of the £Nil band was used, so £122,000 remains.

IHT:

	£
£122,000 × 0%	Nil
£13,000 × 40%	5,200
	5,200

MYRTLE COOK: INHERITANCE TAX FOLLOWING DEATH

	£
March 2000 gift of shares	
Holding before gift 20,000 × £16.50	330,000
Holding after gift 12,000 × £15	180,000
	150,000
Less annual exemptions: 1999/00	(3,000)
1998/99	(3,000)
	144,000

In the seven years prior to March 2000 £108,000 (£114,000 − £3,000 − £3,000) of the £Nil band was used, leaving £123,000.

IHT:

	£
£123,000 × 0%	Nil
£21,000 × 40%	8,400
	8,400

	£
June 2001 estate at death	
Residence £270,000/2	135,000
Investments	125,000
Shares 12,000 × £15	180,000
	440,000

In the seven years prior to death, £144,000 of the £Nil band was used, leaving £87,000:

	£
£87,000 × 0%	Nil
£353,000 × 40%	141,200
	141,200

IHT on the 2000 gift (payable by Judy) is £8,400 and IHT on the estate is £141,200.

(b) TAX PLANNING MEASURES

Income tax

After the gift of the cottage, Desmond will remain a basic rate taxpayer. Myrtle is a higher rate taxpayer so Myrtle's investments should be transferred to Desmond, so that the income from them is taxed at 20%, instead of at 40%. This will increase Desmond's statutory total income to £16,000, so there will be no loss of age-related married couple's allowance.

Capital gains tax

Desmond could defer the payment of CGT by one year if he defers the gift of the cottage until after 5 April 2000. In addition the gain would be reduced as taper relief would be available on a disposal in 2000/01.

Myrtle could also give some shares before 6 April 2000 and some shares after 5 April, so as to benefit from two years' annual CGT exemptions (and three years' annual IHT exemptions). In 2000/01 she will also benefit from taper relief.

Inheritance tax

Desmond and Myrtle should equalise their estates so that both can make full use of their nil rate bands at death. (This is of course only relevant if, at death, they have nil rate bands which would be wasted: on death before April 2007, they would not have.)

Myrtle should wait until August 2000 to give away her shares, so that the July 1993 transfer drops out first. The gift of shares will then be within the nil rate band, should it become chargeable.

Answer bank Notes

Marking guide	Marks
(a) (i) Desmond Cook:	
Deductions	1½
Pension	½
Allowance	½
Chargeable gain	1
Retirement relief	3
Annual exemption	½
Gift relief	1
Myrtle Cook:	
Taxable income	1
Allowable cost (£31,200)	½
Chargeable gain	1
Annual exemption	½
	11
(ii) Desmond Cook:	
No BPR	1
Annual exemptions	1
Death estate	1
IHT	1
Myrtle Cook:	
Annual exemptions	1
Value shares	1
Death estate	1
IHT	2
Maximum	9
Available	7
(b) Income tax: transfer investments	2
CGT: Deferral of gifts	2
IHT: Equalise estates	2
Defer Myrtle's gift	1
	7
	25

10 BLUETONE LTD

Tutor's hint. It is important to be aware of the different share valuation rules for inheritance tax and capital gains tax.

Examiner's comments. In part (c) some candidates wasted time by explaining the conditions to be met for the purchase to be treated as a capital gain when this was clearly not a requirement of the question.

(a) *Melody's IHT liability*

The lifetime gifts made by her father will affect Melody's IHT liability as they will use up part of the available nil rate band. The amount of the lifetime gifts are:

		£
PET		30,000
Less:	Marriage exemption	(5,000)
	Annual exemption (95/96)	(3,000)
	Annual exemption (94/95)	(3,000)
		19,000

107 BPP Publishing

		£
Chargeable lifetime transfer		
Gift		161,000
Less: Annual exemption (96/97)		(3,000)
		158,000

The available nil band on death is therefore £(231,000 − 19,000 − 158,000) = £54,000:

Death estate	£	£
Personalty		
Bluetone Ltd Shares (Note 1)		
£11 × 50,000		550,000
Expanse plc shares		
Lower of		
¼ up $\frac{320-312}{4} + 312 = 314$		
and		
mid-bargain $\frac{324+282}{2} = 303$		
ie 303p × 42,000		127,260
World-Growth units (80p × 26,000)		20,800
Building society deposits (Note 2)		32,000
Life policy (proceeds)		61,000
		791,060
Less: income tax	6,600	
Gambling debts (Note 3)	Nil	
Funeral expenses	3,460	(10,060)
		781,000
Realty		
House	125,000	
Less: secured debt	(42,000)	83,000
Chargeable estate		864,000

Notes:

1 No BPR is available as Melody's father did not own the Bluetone shares for at least two years prior to his death.

2 No IHT relief is given to an ISA: only IT and CGT reliefs.

3 Gambling debts are not deductible.

IHT on estate

£(864,000 − 54,000) = £810,000 × 40% = £324,000

Melody's IHT

$\frac{550,000}{864,000}$ × £324,000 = £206,250

£206,250 is all due for payment on 31 August 2000 (or the delivery of the IHT account, if earlier).

Melody can elect to pay the tax in 10 equal annual interest-free instalments of £20,625. The first instalment is due on 31 August 2000.

(b) *CGT on Liam's gift*

	£
Deemed proceeds (£9 × 30,000)	270,000
Less: cost	(30,000)
Unindexed gain	240,000
Less: IA to April 1998 $\dfrac{162.6 - 130.3}{130.3} \times £30,000$	(7,437)
Indexed gain	232,563

Gain immediately chargeable to CGT (excess proceeds):

£(75,000 − 30,000) = £45,000

	£
Gain after taper relief (85% × £45,000)	38,250
Less: Annual exemption	(7,100)
Taxable gain	31,150
Tax @ 40%	12,460

Gift relief £(232,563 − 45,000) = £187,563

No taper relief is available to reduce the gain deferred. Liam's son's qualifying period for taper relief will run from 20 March 2000. Thus the remainder of Liam's taper relief will be lost.

IHT on Liam's gift

The value of the lifetime transfer will be:

		£
Before:	50,000 × £15 (part of 50% holding with Opal)	750,000
After:	20,000 × £12.50 (part of 35% holding with Opal)	(250,000)
		500,000
Less:	Proceeds paid	(75,000)
Gift		425,000

BPR will be available at 100% as these are unquoted trading company shares. However, the relief will be withdrawn if Liam dies within seven years and his son does not own the shares as business property at the date of Liam's death (unless the shares have been sold and replaced with other business property).

(c) *Noel*

If repurchase treated as distribution:

£(550,000 − 50,000) = £500,000 net

	£
Grossed up 100/90 × £500,000 =	555,556
Tax @ 32.5%	180,556
Less: credit	(55,556)
Tax to pay	125,000

If treated as CGT disposal:

	£
Proceeds	550,000
Less: cost	(50,000)
Unindexed gain	500,000
Less: IA to April 1998	
$\dfrac{162.6 - 130.3}{130.3} \times £50,000$	(12,394)
Indexed gain	487,606
Less: retirement relief (9½ years)	
95% × £200,000 in full	
(Upper limit 95% × £800,000 = £760,000)	(190,000)
£(487,606 – 190,000) × 50%	(148,803)
Gain after retirement relief	148,803
Gain after taper relief (85% × £148,803)	126,483
Less Annual exemption	(7,100)
Taxable gain	119,383
Tax @ 40%	£47,753

Therefore it is better to use the CGT route (which is mandatory if the relevant conditions are satisfied in any case). Neither option has any effect for Bluetone Ltd.

Marking guide

			Marks
(a)	Wedding gift		1
	Chargeable lifetime transfer		1
	Shares in Expanse plc		1
	Shares in Bluetone Ltd/units in Word-Growth		1
	BPR not available		1
	Building society deposits/life policy		1
	Income tax/funeral expenses		1
	House		1
	IHT liability/IHT due by Melody		2
	Due date/instalments		1
		Available	11
		Maximum	10
(b)	CGT:		
	Gift relief		2
	Deemed consideration		1
	Cost/Indexation		1
	Taper relief		1
	Annual exemption/CGT		1
	IHT Value transferred		2
	BPR		1
		Available/Maximum	9
(c)	Retirement relief		2
	Capital gain		1
	Taper relief		1
	Additional income tax liability on distribution		1
	Conclusion		1
		Available/Maximum	6
		Maximum	25

11 MONTY NOBLE

> **Tutor's hint.** It was necessary to consider the IHT position with and without the plan.
>
> **Examiner's comments.** This was a popular question but the majority of candidates answered it quite badly.

(a) (i) **IHT position prior to the implementation of the plan**

No IHT liability will arise at the date of Monty's death since his entire estate is left to his wife.

Upon Olive's death on 31 December 2002, the IHT liability will be as follows.

	£	£
Personalty		
Building society deposits		285,000
Ordinary shares in Congo Ltd 20,000 at £3.50 (note 1)	70,000	
Business property relief £70,000 × $\frac{80(100-20)}{100}$ × 100%	56,000	
		14,000
Agricultural land and buildings	225,000	
Agricultural property relief (note 2)	180,000	
		45,000
		344,000
Realty		
Main residence		330,000
Holiday cottages (£47,500 + £58,100 + £54,400)		160,000
Chargeable estate		834,000
IHT liability £231,000 at nil %		nil
£603,000 at 40%		241,200
£834,000		241,200

IHT of £241,200 will be payable by the executors of Olive's estate by 30 June 2003 (or delivery of account if earlier).

Notes

1. BPR is only given in respect of assets used wholly or mainly for the purposes of the business. Property being let out is not being used for the business so BPR will not be due on that proportion of the asset.

2. APR is available since the property is let out for the purposes of agriculture, and has been owned for at least seven years. Olive is deemed to own the property for the period that Monty owned it. APR of 100% is thus available against the agricultural value of the asset.

IHT position following the implementation of the plan:

Monty's estate

	£	£
Personalty		
Building society deposits		285,000
Ordinary shares in Congo Ltd (W1)		70,000
Agricultural land and buildings	225,000	
Agricultural property relief	180,000	
		45,000
		400,000
Realty		
Main residence		255,000
Holiday cottages (3 × £55,000)	165,000	
Relief for reduction in value (W2)	3,300	
		161,700
		816,700
Exempt legacy – Olive (£255,000 + £270,000)		525,000
Chargeable estate		291,700
IHT liability £231,000 at nil %		nil
£60,700 at 40%		24,280
£291,700		24,280

£24,280 will be payable by the executors of the estate by 31 January 2000 (or delivery of account, if earlier).

Gift of main residence

The gift of the main residence by Olive to Peter will be a PET. It is unlikely to be treated as a gift with reservation since Olive is paying a commercial rent for the use of the two rooms. As a result of Olive's death within seven years, the PET will become chargeable as follows.

		£	£
Main residence			255,000
Annual exemptions	1999/00	3,000	
	1998/99	3,000	
			6,000
			249,000

	£
IHT liability £231,000 at nil%	nil
£18,000 at 40%	7,200
	7,200

IHT after taper relief £7,200 × 80% = £5,760

£5,760 must be paid by Peter by 30 June 2003.

Olive's estate

IHT on Olive's estate will be as follows.

	£
Cash	270,000
IHT liability £270,000 at 40%	108,000

£108,000 will be payable by the executor's of Olives estate by 30 June 2003.

IHT payable

	£
No plan	241,200
With plan (£24,280 + £5,760 + £108,000)	138,040
IHT saving	103,160

Workings

1 **BPR**. BPR is not available to offset against the value of the Congo Ltd shares since Monty has not owned the shares for at least two years.

2 Land and buildings sold within four years after death

A claim can be made to reduce the value of the holiday cottages to the **gross sale proceeds**. The relief is restricted because of the reinvestment in farm land.

	£
Cottage 1 (£55,000 – £47,500)	7,500
Cottage 2 (£55,000 – £58,100)	(3,100)
	4,400
Restriction £4,400 × $\frac{£27,000 - £600}{£47,500 + £58,100}$	1,100
	3,300

The loss on cottage 3 of £600 (£55,000 – £54,400) is ignored as it is less than £1,000.

(ii) A deed of variation must be made within **two years** of Monty's death. The deed must be **in writing**, and must be **signed by the beneficiaries under the original will** (in this case only Olive) and **the new beneficiaries under the revised terms of the will. A written election must then be made to the Inland Revenue within six months**, so that the will is treated as rewritten for IHT purposes.

(iii) The shares in Congo Ltd should be left to Olive. By the time of Olive's death the joint ownership period will be sufficient to ensure that 100% BPR will be available, resulting in an IHT saving of £22,400 (£56,000 at 40%). The shares will be included in Olive's death estate computation so the IHT of £5,600 (£14,000 at 40%) will be postponed until Olive's death.

Under the plan the full fall in value of cottage 1 is not taken into account due to the profit made on cottage number 2 and the reinvestment in land by the estate. The full £7,500 fall in value of cottage 1 would be available if cottage 2 is left to Peter or Penny (who could subsequently sell it), and the trust purchased the field itself by being left additional cash. This would save IHT of £1,680 (£7,500 – £3,300 = £4,200 at 40%).

(b) An **accumulation and maintenance trust** is one where the beneficiary or beneficiaries become **entitled to the trust assets or to interests in possession therein on or before attaining the age of 25**.

The proposed trust will not qualify as an accumulation and maintenance trust because the elder two children will be over the age of 25 when the youngest reaches 18.

The advantages of being treated as an accumulation and maintenance trust rather than a discretionary trust are:

(i) there is **no exit charge** when assets leave the trust;
(ii) there is **no principal charge** on every 10th anniversary of the trust's creation.

12 MING WONG

> **Tutor's hints.** In part (b) it was important to include an explanation of why assets were or were not subject to IHT. If you merely calculated the increase in the IHT liability, you would have lost many easy marks.
>
> **Examiner's comments.** The majority of candidates answered this question very well and there were a number of near perfect answers.

(a) (i) **Ming will be treated as domiciled in the UK if she has been resident in the UK for at least 17 out of the 20 tax years ending with the year in which any chargeable transfer is made.**

As Ming has been resident in the UK since 1985/86, she will become domiciled here for IHT purposes in respect of any chargeable transfers made in 2001/02 and later years.

(ii) **Ming could acquire a domicile of choice in the UK under general law by severing all her ties with Yanga and settling in the UK with the clear intention of making her permanent home here.**

(b) If Ming is non-UK domiciled only her UK assets are subject to UK IHT. However, once she becomes UK domiciled all of Ming's assets will be subject to IHT. The following rules apply in deciding which of Ming's assets are UK assets.

(i) **Property is situated where it is physically located.** This means the residence is a UK asset but the house in Yanga is not.

(ii) **The shares are not UK assets because they are not registered or normally dealt with in the ordinary course of business in the UK.**

(iii) **The antiques are a UK asset because they are physically located in the UK.**

(iv) **Bank deposits are situated at the branch that maintains the account** so the £30,000 at the London branch is a UK asset but the other £20,000 is not.

(v) **A debt is situated where the debtor resides** so the loan is not a UK asset.

(vi) **Government stocks are situated at the place of registration** so the UK government stocks are a UK asset. This makes the trust a UK asset.

Ming's IHT liability if she is domiciled and she is non-UK domiciled is, therefore, as follows:

	UK Domiciled £	Non-UK domiciled £
Residence	245,000	245,000
House in Yanga	60,000	-
Ganyan Inc shares	124,000	-
Antiques	35,000	35,000
Bank deposits	50,000	30,000
Loan	15,000	-
Trust	18,500	18,500
	547,500	328,500

	£	£
IHT:		
£231,000 × 0%	-	-
£316,500/£97,500 × 40%	126,600	39,000
Less: DTR		
Lower of (i) £48,000		
(ii) £126,600 × $\frac{184,000}{547,500}$	(42,547)	
IHT liability	84,053	39,000

Answer bank   Notes

The potential increase in Ming's IHT liability if she were to become UK domiciled is £45,053.

(c) (i) Whilst non-UK domiciled Ming is not liable to UK income tax on income arising in Yanga unless it is remitted to the UK. This means her income tax liability for 1999/00 is

	Non-savings income £	Savings (excl dividend) income £	Total £
Schedule E	29,000		
Bank deposit interest		2,100	
	29,000	2,100	31,100
Less: personal allowance	(4,335)		
Taxable income	24,665	2,100	26,765

Non-savings income

	£
£1,500 × 10%	150
£23,165 × 23%	5,328
Savings (excl dividend) income	
£2,100 × 20%	420
	5,898
Less: tax suffered on bank interest	(420)
Income tax payable	5,478

(ii) If Ming had been UK domiciled her UK income tax position would have been:

	Non-savings £	Savings (excl dividend) £	Dividend £	Total £
Schedule E	29,000			
Schedule D Case V:				
Rents	7,500			
Dividends (× 100/85)			7,000	
Bank interest (× 100/85)		1,800		
UK bank interest (× 100/80)		2,100		
	36,500	3,900	7,000	47,400
Less: personal allowance	(4,335)			
Taxable income	32,165	3,900	7,000	43,065

Tax on non-savings income: £
£1,500 × 10%   150
£26,500 × 23%   6,095
£4,165 × 40%   1,666

Tax on savings (excl. dividend) income:
£3,900 × 40%   1,560

Tax on dividend income:
£7,000 × 32.5%   2,275
    11,746

Less: Double tax relief (W)
    Rental income   (2,625)
    Dividends (£7,000 × 15%)   (1,050)
    Bank interest (£1,800 × 15%)   (270)
    7,801
Less: tax suffered on bank interest   (420)
Income tax payable   7,381

Ming's additional income tax payable if she had been UK domiciled during 1999/00 would have been £1,903 (£7,381 - £5,478).

Working

1 Double tax relief

As the rents are taxed most highly overseas, they are treated as the top slice of income: taxable non savings income excluding the rents is, therefore, £24,665 and the UK tax liability is:

	£
On non-savings income	
£1,500 × 10%	150
£23,165 × 23%	5,328
On savings (excl dividend) income:	
£3,335 × 20%	667
£565 × 40%	226
On dividend income	
£7,000 × 32.5%	2,275
	8,646

The UK tax on the overseas rental income is therefore £3,100 (£11,746 – £8,646 and DTR is the lower of:

(i) UK tax £3,100
(ii) Overseas tax £2,625

ie £2,625

Marking guide

			Marks
(a)	17 out of last 20 years		1
	Application to Ming		1
	Domicile of choice		1
	Procedure involved		<u>1</u>
		Maximum/Available	4
(b)	*Location of assets*		
	Land and buildings		1
	Registered shares and securities		1
	Bank accounts		1
	Chattels/Debtor		1
	Property held in trust		1
	Chargeable estate – Not domiciled in UK		2
	– Domiciled in UK		2
	IHT liability		1
	Double taxation relief		2
	Endowment mortgage (not deducted)		1
	Additional IHT liability		<u>1</u>
		Available	14
		Maximum	12
(c)	*Income tax liability – Not domiciled in the UK*		
	Taxable income		1
	Income tax		1
	Remittance basis		1
	Income tax liability - Domiciled in the UK		
	Taxable income		2
	Income tax		2
	Double taxation relief		3
	Additional income tax liability		<u>1</u>
		Available	11
		Maximum	<u>9</u>
		Maximum	<u>25</u>

13 DOROTHY LAKE

> **Tutor's hint.** Capital losses are set against capital gains before taper relief. You can choose how to allocate losses which means you should always choose to allocate them against gains on non-business assets first.
>
> **Examiner's comments.** The answers of some candidates were badly presented and it was difficult to know which part of the question was being answered.

Tax implications if Dorothy makes the gift.

Inheritance tax

The gift will be a PET that will become chargeable as a result of Dorothy's death within seven years:

	£
Value of gift (W1)	371,000
Less: A/E 2000/01	(3,000)
1999/00	(3,000)
	365,000

None of the £Nil band had been used in the previous seven years, so IHT due at death rates is:

	£
£231,000 × 0%	Nil
£134,000 × 40%	53,600
365,000	53,600

IHT due after tapering relief £53,600 × 60% = £32,160.

£32,160 will be payable by Alice on 30 June 2005. It will be possible to pay IHT of £7,802 (£32,160 × 90,000/371,000) in respect of the holiday cottage in ten equal instalments commencing on 30 June 2005. The IHT payable by instalments could be increased if the gift of the holiday cottage was made subsequent to the other gifts, since the nil rate band of £231,000 would be allocated to the earlier gifts.

Dorothy's estate

	£
Shares in Windermere	
50,000 at £4.97 (£3.55 plus 40%)	248,500
Business property relief £248,500 × $\frac{88(100-12)}{100}$ × 100%	218,680
	29,820
Other assets	350,000
Chargeable estate	379,820
IHT liability £379,820 at 40%	151,928

£151,928 will be payable by the executors of Dorothy's estate on 30 June 2005.

Capital gains tax

Shares in Windermere Ltd

	£
Deemed consideration (25% holding) (50,000 at £2.50)	125,000
Cost (£72,000 (W2) × $\frac{50,000}{100,000}$)	36,000
	89,000
Indexation to April 1998 £36,000 × $\frac{162.6-100.6}{100.6}$	22,187
Gain before taper relief (see below)	66,813

Antique painting

	£
Deemed consideration	8,500
Cost	1,400
	7,100
Indexation $\frac{162.6-101.9}{101.9}$ = £1,400 × 0.596	834
Gain before taper relief (see below)	6,266
Limited to: (£8,500 – £6,000) × 5/3 =	4,167

Holiday cottage

	£
Deemed consideration	165,000
Cost	188,000
Loss	(23,000)

For taper relief purposes the assets have been held for 3 years (this includes the bonus year). The painting is a non-business asset so 95% of the gain remains chargeable after taper relief. Dorothy's holding of Windermere Ltd shares is a business asset and so 77.5% of this gain remains chargeable after taper relief.

Losses are set against gains before taper relief as follows.

	£	£
Non-business asset	4,167	
Less: current loss	(4,167)	
		-
Business asset	66,813	
Balance of current loss (£23,000 – £4,167)	(18,833)	
		47,980
		47,980

	£
Gain after taper relief (£47,980 × 77.5%)	37,185
Less: annual exemption	(7,100)
	30,085

CGT @ 40% = £12,034

The gain before taper relief of £66,813 in respect of the shares in Windermere Ltd could be held over if Dorothy and Alice make a joint election. However, a claim does not appear to be beneficial since Alice is to sell the shares soon after receiving them (thus crystallising the gain), and Dorothy's capital loss would then be wasted. In addition, as the gain to be heldover is before taper relief, the benefit of the above taper relief is wasted. Dorothy could consider postponing the gift of the painting until 2001/2002 so as to partly utilise that year's annual exemption. This would give £4,167 more loss to the gain on the shares resulting in an overall chargeable gain of £26,855 (66,813 – 23,000 = 43,813 × 77.5% – 7,100) and a CGT bill for £10,742.

Tax liabilities arising if Dorothy does not make the gift

Inheritance tax

Dorothy's estate at death will be:

	£
Personalty	
Shares in Windermere Ltd (based on a 100% holding)	
100,000 at £6.30 (4.50 plus 40%)	630,000
Business property relief £630,000 × $\frac{88(100-12)}{100}$ × 100%	554,400
	75,600
Antique painting	8,500
Other assets	350,000
	434,100
Realty	
Holiday cottage	90,000
	524,100
IHT liability £231,000 at nil%	nil
£293,100 at 40%	117,240
	117,240

Rate of IHT on estate = 22.3698% (117,240/524,100)

£117,240 will be payable by Dorothy's executors by 30 June 2005. It will be possible to pay the IHT of £20,133 (£90,000 at 22.3698%) in respect of the holiday cottage in 10 equal instalments commencing on 30 June 2005. It will not be possible to pay the IHT in respect of the shares in Windermere Ltd by instalments if they are immediately sold by Alice.

Capital gains tax

No CGT liability arises in respect of transfers on death, and Alice will take over the assets with a base cost based on their market values at the date of death.

Summary

Tax due if gift made to Alice.

	£
IHT (£32,160 + £151,928)	184,088
CGT	12,034
Total	196,122

Tax due if no gift made

	£
IHT	117,240
CGT	-
	117,240

Difference £78,882

Conclusion

It appears to be beneficial for Dorothy to not make the gift to Alice.

Workings

1 Value of gift

   Shares in Windermere Ltd (Note 1)

	£	£
Value shares held before gift (100,000 × £4.50)	450,000	
Value of shares held after gift (50,000 × £3.55)	(177,500)	
		272,500
Painting		8,500
Cottage	165,000	
Fall in value	(75,000)	
		90,000
		371,000

   Note 1: The values of the shares must take the related property into account. BPR is not available because Alice would sell the shares before Dorothy's death.

2 Takeover

	£
50,000 × 2 Ordinary shares × £1.20	120,000
50,000 × 0.8 Cash	40,000
	160,000

   Allocate original cost to 100,000 ordinary shares

   $$\frac{120,000}{160,000} \times £96,000 = £72,000$$

Answer bank   Notes

Marking guide		Marks
Gift made		
Inheritance tax - PET		
Shares in Windermere Ltd - value		2
Business property relief		2
Antique painting/Holiday cottage		1
Annual exemptions		1
Fall in value of lifetime gift		1
IHT liability		1
Due date/Instalment option		2
Inheritance tax - Estate		
Shares in Windermere Ltd		1
Business property relief		1
IHT liability/Due date		1
Capital gains tax		
Shares in Windermere Ltd		2
Antique painting		1
Holiday cottage		1
Taper relief/offset of loss		2
CGT liability		1
Holdover relief		1
Gift not made		
Shares in Windermere Ltd		1
Business property relief		1
Other assets		1
IHT liability/Estate rate		1
Instalment option		1
CGT implications		1
Conclusion		2
	Available	29
	Maximum	25

14 MICHAEL EARL

Tutor's hint. As Michael Earl died on 30.6.99, IHT at death rates is due on all gifts made after 30.6.92 and on the value of his chargeable estate at death. Before calculating the tax due on death, you should calculate any lifetime tax which was paid on the gifts Michael made after 30.6.92.

Examiner's comments. In part (a) the calculation of the related property valuation of the unquoted shares caused problems, and business property relief was often overlooked.

(a) (i) **Lifetime tax**

10 July 1998 - Gift to daughter

This was a PET so no IHT was due when the gift was made.

19 August 1998 - Transfer to discretionary trust

This transfer was a CLT in August 1998. As Michael paid the tax, the gift made was a net gift and the IHT payable was (£310,000 (W1) − £231,000) × 1/4 = £19,750. The gross gift was £329,750.

IHT arising as a result of Michael's death on 30.6.99

PET on 10.7.98

The value of Michael's shareholdings must take into account Naomi's shares as Naomi's shares are related property.

	£
Value of Michael's holding before the gift 100,000 × £10	1,000,000
Value of Michael's holding after gift 50,000 × £7	(350,000)
PET	650,000

Business property relief is not available as the shares had not been owned for two years.

None of the £nil band had been used in the seven years prior to this PET. So IHT due is:

£		£
231,000 × 0%		Nil
419,000 × 40%		167,600
650,000		167,600

IHT of £167,600 must be paid by Michael's daughter, Jade, by 31.12.99.

CLT on 19.8.98

These shares have fallen in value by 30.6.99 (W2) so the IHT payable by the trustees by 31.12.99 is calculated as:

	£
CLT on 19.8.98	329,750
Less: Fall in value (W2)	(30,000)
	299,750

All of the £nil band had been used in the seven years prior to 19.8.98 so IHT due is:

	£
£299,750 × 40%	119,900
Less: Lifetime tax already paid	(19,750)
Additional tax payable by trustees by 31.12.99	100,150

Chargeable estate on 30.6.99

	£
Compact Ltd shares (W3) 50,000 × £8.40	420,000
Diverse Inc shares	
Lower of (i) 1/4 up principle (281p)	
(ii) average of highest/lowest marked bargains (280p)	140,000
Other assets	850,000
	1,410,000
Less: Exempt legacy to non domiciled spouse	(55,000)
Chargeable estate	1,355,000

The IHT on the chargeable estate at death is calculated ignoring the fall in value of the Diverse Inc shares.

In the seven years before death, the £nil band had been fully utilised, so IHT on death estate is £1,355,000 × 40% = £542,000.

The IHT payable by the executor's of Michael's estate on the earlier of 31.12.99 and the date of delivery of their account is:

	£
IHT due	542,000
Less: DTR	
Lower of UK tax (£140,000 × 40% = £56,000)	
Overseas tax (£35,000)	(35,000)
	507,000

(ii) **Relief for related property**

The valuation of the Compact Ltd shares in Michael's death estate took into account Naomi's share as these were related property. However, as Michael's shares were sold within three years of his death for less than their related property valuation, the executor's of Michael's estate can claim relief based on the unrelated valuation of the shares.

	£
Original valuation	420,000
Less: unrelated valuation 50,000 × £6.00	(300,000)
	120,000

Reduction in IHT liability £120,000 × 40% = £48,000. Clearly such a claim is beneficial.

Relief on sale of quoted investments within twelve months of death

As the quoted shares in Diverse Inc were sold within 12 months of death for less than their probate value the executor's can claim relief for the loss.

	£
Probate value	140,000
Sale proceeds	(120,000)
Loss	20,000

Reduction in IHT liability = £20,000 × 40% = £8,000. Clearly such a claim is beneficial.

(b) (i) **Jade - CGT liability**

	£
Sale proceeds	285,000
Deemed cost	250,000
Gain before taper relief	35,000

There is no taper relief as this non-business asset has been owned for one year only.

Capital gains tax £35,000 × 40%   £14,000

(ii) If Jade and the executors of Michael's estate make a claim for holdover relief in respect of the gift on 10 July 1998, then Jade will be able to deduct the IHT payable as a result of the PET becoming chargeable, when calculating her chargeable gain. Her CGT liability would be as follows.

	£	£
Sale proceeds		285,000
Deemed cost	250,000	
Gain held over (W4)	(50,000)	
		(200,000)
		85,000
Less: IHT liability		(167,600)
		Nil

	£
Capital gains tax	Nil

The 1998/99 CGT liability of £20,000 (£50,000 at 40%) due out of Michael's estate will no longer be payable. This will increase Michael's estate by £20,000, and additional IHT of £8,000 (£20,000 at 40%) will be due. Claiming holdover relief would therefore result in an overall tax decrease.

	No claim	Holdover relief claim
	£	£
CGT liability - Jade	14,000	0
- Michael's estate	20,000	0
Additional IHT liability	0	8,000
	34,000	8,000

Workings

1   **CLT August 1998**

    The transfer is valued at the lower of

    (a) ¼ up principle (308p + ¼ (316p– 308p) = 310p
    (b) average of highest and lowest marked bargains ½ (296 + 328) = 312p.

    That is 100,000 × 310p = £310,000

2   **Diverse Inc**

    The value of the shares on 30.6.99 was the lower of:

    (a) 279 + 1/4 (287 – 279) = 281p
    (b) 1/2 (275 + 285) = 280p

    The shares have fallen in value since the date of the CLT and the trustees can make a claim for the fall in value of £30,000 (£310,000 – £280,000) to be taken into account in calculating the additional IHT due. However, the cumulative total of gifts is not reduced by this fall in value.

3   **Shares in Compact Ltd**

    These shares must be valued taking into account the shares held by Naomi as Naomi's shares are related property. There is no BPR as the shares have not been owned for two years

4   **Gain on gift 10.7.98**

	£
Deemed proceeds	250,000
Less: cost	(200,000)
Gain	50,000

    No indexation or taper relief due.

15 MAUD SMITH

> **Tutor's hint**. Heirs have two years from a death to make a deed of variation which will be effective for tax purposes. Thus there is still time for Maud to vary her husband's will.
>
> **Examiner's comment**. In part (c), the stated requirements for high income and low risk were often ignored.

(a) (i) MAUD SMITH: INCOME TAX COMPUTATION

	Non-savings £	Savings (excl dividend) £	Dividend £	Total £
Pension: state	3,471			
Pensions: private	2,500			
Dividends				
Sparks & Mincer plc 20,000 × £0.09 × 100/90			2,000	
Bit-Part Ltd 45,000 × £0.10 × 100/90			5,000	
Global Trust £450 × 100/90			500	
Gilts interest £100,000 × 4%		4,000		
Building Society interest £86,000 × 9%		7,740		
National Savings bond interest £10,000 × 7%		700		
Trust income £5,120 × 100/80		6,400		
STI	5,971	18,840	7,500	32,311
Less personal allowance (income too high for age allowance)	(4,335)	–		
	1,636	18,840	7,500	27,976

	£	£
Income tax on non-savings income		
£1,500 × 10%		150
£136 × 23%		31
Income tax on savings (excl dividend) income		
£18,840 × 20%		3,768
Income tax on dividend income		
£7,500 × 10%		750
		4,699
Less tax reductions		
Married couple's allowance £5,195 × 10%	520	
Widow's bereavement allowance £1,970 × 10%	197	
		(717)
Tax liability		3,982
Less: tax credit on dividend income		(750)
Less tax suffered £(18,840 – 700) × 20%		(3,628)
Repayment due		(396)

The full married couple's allowance for the over-75s is available because Maud's husband had no income for 1999/00. However, Maud is not entitled to the personal age allowance because her STI is too high.

(ii) MAUD SMITH: INHERITANCE TAX COMPUTATION

The gift in June 1993, £165,000 – £6,000 (two annual exemptions) = £159,000, will not suffer further tax because it falls within the nil rate band. It will however leave only £72,000 (£231,000 – £159,000) of the nil rate band available for the estate.

	£	£
Free estate		
Residence		130,000
Shares in Sparks & Mincer plc 20,000 × £4.14 (£4.10 + 1/4 (4.26 − 4.10))		82,800
Shares in Bit-Part Ltd	205,000	
Less 100% BPR	205,000	
		0
Gilts £100,000 × 0.91 (90 + 1/4 (94 − 90))		91,000
Global Trust 25,000 × £2.10 (use lowest value)		52,500
Building Society deposit		86,000
National Savings bond		10,000
		452,300
Settled property		65,200
Estate		517,500

IHT:

£		£
72,000 × 0%		Nil
445,500 × 40%		178,200
517,500		178,200

Business property relief is available because Maud's husband had owned the shares in Bit-Part Ltd for at least two years.

The executors can pay IHT on the building (£178,200 × 130,000/517,500 = £44,765) in ten equal annual instalments starting on 31 October 2000.

The executors must pay £178,200 × 322,300/517,500 = £110,983 when they apply for probate and in any case by 30 April 2001, but interest will run on the tax from 31 October 2000.

The trustees must pay £178,200 × 65,200/517,500 = £22,451 by 31 October 2000.

(b) A lifetime gift will result in a chargeable gain as follows.

	£
Deemed proceeds	205,000
Less cost	160,000
	45,000

There is no indexation as the shares were inherited after 6 April 1998.

This could be held over by gift relief, reducing the base cost for the children to £(205,000 − 45,000) = £160,000.

There would be a PET for inheritance tax purposes of £205,000. Should this become chargeable, 100% business property relief will be available so long as the recipients have retained the shares and they remain relevant business property.

A transfer by **variation of Maud's husband's will would avoid a chargeable gain. It would also avoid making a PET which would be at risk of becoming chargeable on Maud's death.**

A **direct transfer to the grandchildren would have the advantage of skipping a generation, reducing the risk of further inheritance tax charges in the next 40 years or so** on the deaths of Maud's children.

(c) The shares in Sparks & Mincer plc are probably a sound investment as a component of a low-risk equity portfolio, but should not be held as the single equity in an undiversified portfolio. Maud should consider selling them and investing in a high-income unit trust or investment trust to achieve diversification at low cost.

The shares in Bit-Part Ltd, an unquoted company, are clearly unsuitable for a low-risk portfolio. Maud is planning to give them away in any case.

The government stock is highly suitable: its price will not fluctuate much so close to redemption.

The Global Trust is oriented to capital growth. Maud should transfer her investment to a high-income unit trust.

The building society deposit is a reasonable investment, but there is some risk in having so much with one small society. Maud should spread her deposit among several societies. She should consider an Individual Savings Account (ISA).

The National Savings bond is appropriate for Maud.

16 MING LEE

> **Tutor's hint.** You were given taxable profits for tax years so you did not need to apply basis period rules.
>
> **Examiner's comment.** In part (a), many candidates forgot about the earnings cap.

(a) PERSONAL PENSION PREMIUM

The maximum percentages of net relevant earnings for all years are as follows.

Year	Earnings £	Percentage %	Amount £
1992/93	26,000	20	5,200
1993/94	34,500	20	6,900
1994/95	47,000	25	11,750
1995/96	53,000	25	13,250
1996/97	63,500	25	15,875
1997/98	70,000	25	17,500
1998/99	90,000	25	22,500
1999/00	90,600 (cap)	30	27,180

The 1996/97 premium will have used up the 1996/97 relief and £(20,000 − 15,875) = £4,125 of the 1992/93 relief.

The maximum 1999/00 premium is as follows.

	£
To relate back to 1998/99 to use the 1998/99 relief	22,500
To relate back to 1998/99 and use the remaining 1992/93 relief of £(5,200 − 4,125)	1,075
	23,575
To relate back to 1998/99 and/or claim in 1999/00: £(6,900 + 11,750 + 13,250 + 17,500)	49,400
To claim in 1999/00	27,180
	100,155

Ming should pay this maximum amount, but should divide it between 1999/00 and 1998/99 so as to get tax relief at 40% on the whole amount. A split such as £31,615 claimed in 1999/00 and £68,540 related back to 1998/99 would achieve this.

This is likely to be a suitable investment, because of the tax relief and because on retirement 25% of the fund's value can be taken as a tax-free lump sum. However, the pension obtained may not be high because the fund may only be invested for a few years.

Nevertheless the tax deductibility of premiums paid and the tax exempt status of most income makes a pension fund attractive.

(b) OTHER INVESTMENTS

(i) **Repayment of the mortgage**

Ming currently obtains tax relief at 10% on interest on 30/120 = 0.25 of her mortgage, so her net interest is £12,000 × (0.75 + 0.25 × 0.9) = £11,700. If she were to pay off her mortgage using some of her building society deposit, she would therefore save considerably more net interest than she would lose (£8,700 × 120/140 × 100/80 × 60% = £5,593). There would also be no investment risk, although there would be some loss of flexibility because Ming would no longer be able to invest her savings to take advantage of any good opportunities which might arise.

(ii) **National Savings Certificates**

These offer a modest return, but it is guaranteed and is also tax-free. This last point is particularly valuable to a higher rate taxpayer such as Ming: a 6% tax-free return is as good as a 10% taxable return. This investment may well be suitable for Ming. The two main disadvantages are the need to invest for five years in order to obtain the best rate of return, and the limit on the investment, usually £10,000 per issue of certificates.

(iii) **Enterprise zone trusts**

In an enterprise zone trust, investors pool their funds to buy commercial buildings in enterprise zones. Each investor gets an appropriate share of the 100% initial allowance, and in Ming's case this would save her tax at 40% (though her marginal rate will be less than this beyond the point where her taxable income is reduced below the top of the basic rate band). The tax saving may well make this investment suitable for Ming, but she should consider the following disadvantages.

(1) The sale proceeds of buildings will be taxable income up to the original cost, and may give rise to chargeable gains if they exceed this amount.

(2) There is a considerable risk: the value of property, and the rental income from it, can fall.

(c) INCORPORATION

Ming should consider the following factors when deciding whether or not to incorporate her business.

(i) **Adjustments to basis periods**

On the cessation of a sole trade (which includes incorporation) the basis period for the final tax year runs from the end of the previous basis period to the date of cessation. Relief will be available for any unrelieved overlap profits. The long basis period may lead to higher taxable profits than had been anticipated. The extent of the problem will depend on the time of incorporation.

(ii) **Capital gains**

A capital gain will arise on incorporation in respect of the goodwill, but if the consideration is shares this gain will be rolled over against the cost of the shares.

Incorporation will not affect Ming's entitlement to retirement relief, because the pre-incorporation and post-incorporation periods of trading can be aggregated. However, the eligible gain would be less than the full gain if the company were to acquire any chargeable non-business assets.

Retirement relief is to be abolished on 6 April 2003 so it may be worth Ming crystallising a gain on incorporation in order to take advantage of the relief while it is still available. Ming will need to weigh up the benefits of the retirement relief that is available now with the decreased rates of taper relief that are available on an early sale.

(iii) **The taxation of profits**

At present, Ming's profits are subject to income tax, with a marginal rate of 40%. If her business were incorporated, profits would only be taxed at 20% and Ming could limit her total income (salary, dividends and sources from outside the business) so as to avoid higher rate tax. The retention of profits in the company would increase Ming's gain on its eventual disposal, but until 2002/03 retirement relief should limit the effect of this.

For a small company, corporation tax is due nine months after the end of the accounting period. Income tax on an unincorporated business's profits is due on 31 January following the tax year, but with payments on account 12 months and six months earlier.

(iv) **National Insurance contributions**

The combined burden of NICs on a company and on Ming as a director will be much higher than the burden on Ming as a sole trader, unless Ming draws a very low salary. She could also draw dividends (which do not attract NICs).

(v) **Pension contributions**

Ming could continue to make personal pension contributions following incorporation, but based only on her remuneration, not on dividends.

If the business is incorporated, the company could alternatively set up an approved occupational scheme for her. She could contribute up to 15% of her remuneration, and the company's contributions would not be subject to any percentage limit. However, benefits would be limited, based on Ming's (fairly short) period of service, and the effective limit on contributions would be the rule that such schemes must not be over-funded. On balance, Ming could probably obtain a better pension by putting 30% of her earnings into her personal pension fund.

(vi) **Value added tax**

The transfer of Ming's business to a company as a going concern will be outside the scope of VAT, so there will be no VAT consequences of incorporation.

17 MURIEL GRAND

> **Tutor's hint**. Many topics in this question were new when the question was set. This demonstrates how important the examiner considers current developments to be.
>
> **Examiner's comment**. A considerable number of candidates were unaware of the new schedule A rules, despite this topic being included in the examiner's newsletter article on the most recent Finance Act.

(a) MURIEL'S CAPITAL GAINS TAX LIABILITY

	£
Deemed proceeds	320,000
Less: cost (W1)	(45,000)
Unindexed gain	275,000
Less: Indexation to April 1998 £45,000 × $\frac{162.6 - 94.8}{94.8}$ (0.715)	(32,175)
	242,825
Less: PPR exemption (W2) £242,825 × $\left(\frac{126}{177}\right)$	(172,858)
	69,967

This is a non-business asset so there is no taper relief.

CGT liability £27,987 (£69,967 × 40%)

(b) **EIS: Capital gains tax relief**

It may be possible for Muriel to defer the gain on the house if she invests in newly issued EIS shares. The company issuing the shares must be unquoted. It could be on the AIM, but not on the USM. An amount equal to at least the full amount of the gain of £69,967 must be invested if Muriel wishes to defer the full gain. Any amount of the gain not invested will be chargeable immediately.

The deferred gain becomes chargeable on the disposal of the new shares or on a breach of any of the various conditions within a five year period.

Reinvestment in qualifying EIS shares must be made in the period from 1 January 1999 to 31 December 2002.

EIS: Income tax relief

In addition to rollover relief Muriel will be entitled to 20% income tax relief in respect of any amount (up to £150,000) invested in EIS shares. This income tax relief is withdrawn if the shares are disposed on within five years.

Venture capital trusts (VCT): Capital gains tax

Alternatively, Muriel will be entitled to rollover relief and 20% income tax relief in respect of any amount (up to £100,000) invested in VCT shares.

Investment in a VCT must be made in the period from 1 January 1999 to 31 December 2000. The VCT is itself quoted but 70% of its investments must be in unquoted trading companies. 30% of the investments must be in new ordinary shares.

VCT: Income tax relief

The income tax relief is again withdrawn if the shares are disposed of within five years. Any gain on the disposal of VCT shares is exempt. Any loss will not be allowable in any circumstances. Dividend income from a VCT is exempt from income tax.

Investment in a VCT is less risky than investment under the EIS as a spread of unquoted shares are invested in.

(c) The rental income from Bertie's letting business will be taxed on an **accruals basis under Schedule A** whether the house is let unfurnished or as furnished holiday accommodation. In either case **revenue expenses will be deductible if they are incurred wholly and exclusively for the letting business.**

The cost of repairing the roof will not be deductible in calculating Schedule A profits in either case. **The repairs must be done before the house can be let and so, following the decision in *Law Shipping Co Ltd v CIR (1923)*, the repairs are** capital rather than revenue expenses. The capital expenditure will, however, be deductible in calculating any gain or loss arising on the disposal of the house.

The other tax implications depend on whether the house is let unfurnished or as furnished holiday accommodation.

Unfurnished letting

Decorating costs will normally be deductible revenue expenses. Revenue expenses incurred before the letting business begins will be treated as a deductible expense on the day the business begins. However, if the house was in a bad state of repair when it was acquired some of the £3,500 may be classified as capital rather than revenue expenditure.

Any capital gain arising on the disposal of the property will be subject to capital gains tax.

Furnished letting

It is likely that the £42,000 spent on converting the house into two separate units will be capital expenditure which can be deducted from any chargeable gain arising on the disposal of the property. Any items of revenue expenditure that are included in the £42,000 will be deductible in calculating schedule A profits.

The £9,000 spent on furniture will be a capital expense. However, Bertie will either be able to claim a wear and tear allowance or he will be able to claim for capital expenditure on furniture to be deductible on a renewals basis. **The wear and tear allowance will equal 10% of, rent less any water rates or council tax** paid by Bertie.

Bertie will also be able to deduct the following expenses from his annual gross rents of £45,000:

(i) Loan interest of £6,000 (£50,000 × 12%)
(ii) Letting agency fees of £10,125 (£45,000 × 22.5%)
(iii) Other running costs of £3,500

The amount of the deductible expenses will be restricted if Bertie occupies the house for his own use.

If, in any tax year, the house is available for **commercial letting to the public for at least 140 days, is actually let for at least 70 of those days, and is not normally in the same occupation for more than 31 days for at least seven months (including the 70 days), the special rules applicable to furnished holiday lettings will apply.** This means

(i) **Capital allowances will be available for expenditure on plant and machinery** such as the furniture. This will almost certainly be more beneficial than the wear and tear allowance or the renewals basis.

(ii) **The Schedule A profits will be net relevant earnings** for personal pension purposes.

(iii) **Relief for any losses will be available as if they were trading losses**, including the facility to set losses against other income. The schedule A loss rules will not apply.

(iv) **CGT rollover relief, gift relief and relief on loans to traders will also be available.** The property will be treated as a business asset for taper relief purposes.

(v) **VAT registration will be required if rental income in any twelve month period exceeds the VAT registration threshold.** The letting of holiday accommodation is standard rated.

Conclusion

Letting the house as a furnished holiday letting will produce annual income of approximately £25,375 (£45,000 – £6,000 – £10,125 – £3,500), compared to £28,000 if the house is let unfurnished. It will also be necessary to incur additional expenditure of £47,500 (£42,000 + £9,000 – £3,500). This must be compared the benefits available if the house is let as furnished holiday accommodation.

(d) **Independent financial advice**

Independent advice could be obtained from accountants, solicitors and stockbrokers. In addition some banks and building societies (if they are not tied advisers) may provide independent advice.

Workings

1   **Cost relating to land disposed of in 1986**

$$£60,000 \times \frac{24,000}{24,000 + 72,000} = £15,000$$

∴ cost relating to land given to brother £45,000 (£60,000 – £15,000)

2   **PPR exemption**

	Actual or deemed occupation	Other
1.4.85-30.9.92	90	
1.10.92-31.12.96		51
1.1.97-31.12.99 (last 36 months)	36	
	126	51

18   MARY MOLE

> **Tutor's hint.** ISAs are a new investment product and therefore must be considered extremely topical for exam purposes.
>
> *Prizewinners point.* It is generally not possible to avoid income tax by buying stocks 'ex-interest' and selling them 'cum interest'. This is because there is an anti-avoidance scheme called the accrued income scheme. The interest included in the buying and selling prices will be taxed in the same way as if the interest was actually received.
>
> **Examiner's comments.** There was a lack of depth in many answers with many candidates showing poor exam technique by repeating the same point several times.

(a) *Investments*

Option 1

The maximum amount that Mary could invest in a maxi-ISA for 1999/00 is £7,000. This must comprise a stocks and shares element (up to £7,000). It can also include a cash element (maximum £3,000) and a life assurance element (maximum £1,000), in which case the stocks and shares element limit is reduced appropriately. In view of the possibility of the investment being needed in 4 years time, a shares only investment or a shares and cash investment would seem appropriate, as the life assurance element can only be on the life of the investor.

The stocks and shares that can comprise this element include gilt edged stocks (at least 5 years from redemption), shares listed on a recognised stock exchange, securities (not short dated) issued by a company listed on a recognised stock exchange and shares and securities in certain investment trusts, companies and funds. In general, therefore, the stocks and shares investments would not be considered high risk.

Investments in an ISA are exempt from both income and capital gains tax. In addition, up to and including 2003/04, the 10% tax credit is repayable on dividends from UK companies. There is no statutory minimum period for holding the ISA, so the investments could easily be liquidated in four years time if needed, without any adverse tax consequences. However, the investment would not reduce Mary's tax liability in 1999/00.

Mary should look at a wide range of ISAs, not just those being offered by the bank and should in particular look at the charges levied.

The balance of the inheritance £(25,000 − 7,000) = £18,000 invested in a unit trust will not gain any tax relief. Income received from a unit trust is usually taxed as if it were dividend income (ie. with a 10% non-repayable tax credit). Capital gains tax will be chargeable on any gains made when units are sold, in the same way as shares. Again, unit trusts are not considered a high risk investment.

Option 2

Mary's maximum personal pension premium deductible in 1999/00 is £27,050:

	Age at start of tax year	%	Net relevant earnings £	Maximum premium £
1993/94	32	17.5	46,200	8,085
1994/95	33	17.5	12,600	2,205
1997/98	36	20	8,100	1,620
1998/99	37	20	18,300	3,660
1999/00	38	20	57,400	11,480
				27,050

Mary could therefore invest all of her inheritance in a personal pension and obtain tax relief in 1999/00. This would save Mary tax at her marginal rate of 40% in 1999/00 and therefore meet her first investment criteria.

Benefits under a personal pension can be taken when Mary reaches 50 and at that date she can withdraw 25% of the accumulated income as a tax-free lump sum. The pension itself will be taxable as non-savings income under Schedule E.

This option should provide reasonable capital growth and is not considered high risk. However, the capital will not be available in four years time.

Option 3

A VCT allows an investor to invest indirectly in unquoted companies, thus spreading the risk of investment. The VCT itself is a quoted company. However, although there may be capital growth, a VCT investment is still relatively high risk.

An investor in a VCT obtains a tax reduction of 20% of the amount invested in the year that the investment is made ie. if Mary invests £25,000 (maximum investment per tax year is £100,000) she will be entitled to a tax reducer of £5,000. If Mary disposes of the shares within five years, the relief will be subject to a claw-back.

Dividends from a VCT are generally tax-free income. Capital gains are also exempt from CGT, but, again, the shares must be retained for five years to qualify for this relief. It is also possible to claim a 'reinvestment relief' if Mary has a gain within 12 months before and 12 months after the investment. Again, a claw-back charge will arise on the disposal of the VCT shares.

As disposal in four years time will result in the withdrawal of tax relief, this investment may not be suitable for Mary.

Option 4

Interest on government stocks is normally paid gross but Mary will be liable to income tax at 40% on the interest received. Any chargeable gains arising on government stocks are exempt. Losses are not allowable.

It is generally not possible to avoid income tax by buying stocks 'ex-interest' and selling stocks 'cum interest'. This is because there is an anti-avoidance scheme called the accrued income scheme. The interest included in the buying and selling prices will be taxed in the same way as if the interest was actually received.

This option would not reduce Mary's income tax liability for 1999/00. Mary could buy short dated stocks for redemption in four years time. This would ensure that her capital is intact and government stocks are not high risk. However, she would not obtain capital growth.

(b) (i) Tied advisers only recommend the investment products of the financial institution to which they are tied. An independent adviser is able to give recommendations about investment products from any source.

(ii) The statements of principle are that an authorised person should:

(1) Act with high standards of integrity and market conduct.

(2) Act with due skill, care and diligence.

(3) Obtain relevant information about, and provide appropriate information to, clients.

(4) Avoid conflicts of interest.

(5) Safeguard assets held on behalf of clients.

(6) Maintain adequate financial resources and internal organisation.

(7) Deal with the regulator (ACCA in this case) in an open and co-operative manner.

Marking guide

		Marks
(a)	*Option 1*	
	Maxi-ISA CGT/IT exemptions	2
	Limits on investment	2
	Risks	1
	Liquidity	1
	Suitability for Mary	1
	Unit trusts	1
	Other providers	1
	Option 2	
	Tax deductible amount in 1999/00	2
	Benefits on retirement	1
	Suitability given Mary's investment criteria	2
	Option 3	
	Tax relief/5 year period	1
	Dividends/disposal	1
	Re-investment relief	1
	Suitability for Mary	1
	Option 4	
	Paid gross	1
	Income tax	1
	Chargeable gains exempt/losses not allowable	1
	Accrued income scheme	1
	Suitability for Mary	2
	Available	24
	Maximum	21
(b) (i)	Tied advisers/independent advisers	1
(ii)	*Statements of principle*	
	Integrity/skill etc	1
	Information	1
	Conflicts of interest/safeguard assets	1
	Financial resources/regulator	1
	Available	5
	Maximum	4
	Maximum	25

19 MR ROWE

Tutor's hint. You might well have found part (b) of this question the most straightforward. In such cases, and provided you are satisfied that the answer to an easy part does not depend on the answer to earlier parts, there is no harm in answering the easy part first, so as to start earning marks and at the same time improve your grasp of the question as a whole. However, you must make it absolutely clear to the examiner which part of your answer relates to which part of the question.

Examiner's comment. This question was well done. However, many candidates did not appreciate the interaction between chargeability to inheritance tax and the availability of CGT gift relief.

(a) (i) **An accumulation and maintenance trust**

Such a trust may only be set up if **all the beneficiaries will become beneficially entitled to the trust assets, or to interests in possession therein, on reaching specified ages which are not greater than 25.**

George's transfer of property into such a trust would be a potentially exempt transfer. It would be exempt if he were to survive for seven years after the transfer. If he did not, inheritance tax would be payable as follows (assuming that the rates applicable to transfers on or after 6 April 1999 continue to apply).

	£
Transfer of value	245,000
Less annual exemptions: 1999/00	(3,000)
1998/99	(3,000)
Chargeable transfer	239,000
Less nil rate band	231,000
Taxable at 40%	8,000
IHT at 40%	£3,200

In addition, if George were to die more than three years after the transfer, the tax would be reduced by tapering relief of between 20% (for death up to four years after the transfer) and 80% (for death over six years after the transfer).

Additional capital gains tax of £35,000 × 40% = £14,000 would arise. The transfer would not be immediately chargeable to inheritance tax, so gift relief would be unavailable.

(ii) **A discretionary trust**

There would be an **immediate liability to inheritance tax**, based on half scale rates and applying grossing-up (because George is to bear the tax). This liability would be £8,000 × 1/4 = £2,000, giving a gross chargeable transfer of £239,000 + £2,000 = £241,000.

If George were to die within seven years, tax at the full rates would be computed on this gross chargeable transfer. The tax would be reduced by tapering relief as above, and by the tax of £2,000 already paid, and only the balance of tax would be payable. However, none of the £2,000 tax already paid could be refunded.

A capital gains tax liability of £14,000 would normally arise. However, because the transfer would be immediately chargeable to inheritance tax George could elect for gift relief. The trustees would then have a deemed acquisition cost equal to George's acquisition cost plus indexation allowance up to April 1998.

(b) INCOME TAX COMPUTATION

	Non-savings £	Dividend £	Total £
Salary	63,000		
Dividends £28,800 × 100/90		32,000	
Statutory total income	63,000	32,000	95,000
Less personal allowance	4,335		
Taxable income	58,665	32,000	90,665

	£	£
Income tax on non-savings income		
£1,500 × 10%		150
£26,500 × 23%		6,095
£30,665 × 40%		12,266
Income tax on dividend income		
£32,000 × 32.5%		10,400
		28,911
Less tax reductions		
Interest under MIRAS: ignore		
Additional personal allowance		
£1,970 × 10%		197
Tax liability		28,714
Less: tax credits on dividends	3,200	
PAYE tax deducted	19,400	
		22,600
Tax payable		6,114

(c) If George were to live in the house at any time in the period between the end of his period of employment elsewhere in the UK and the date of sale, up to four years of that period of employment elsewhere in the UK would, like his previous absence, be treated as a period of occupation. The consequence would be that the principal private residence exemption would increase, and George's allowable loss would be smaller. He should, therefore, not re-occupy the house. The allowable loss which will arise if he follows this advice is as follows.

	£
Proceeds	200,000
Less cost (31 March 1982 value identical)	280,000
Loss (indexation allowance cannot increase a loss)	80,000
Less exemption (W) £80,000 × $\frac{162}{213}$	60,845
Allowable loss	19,155

This loss would be set against the chargeable gains of £90,000 which have already been realised.

Working: PPR exemption

	Exempt Months	Chargeable Months
1. 4.82 - 30. 6.82 (occupation)	3	
1. 7.82 - 31.12.83 (overseas duties)	18	
1. 1.84 - 30. 9.92 (occupied)	105	
1.10.92 - 31.12.96		51
1. 1.97 - 31.12.99 (last 36 months)	36	
	162	51

The last 36 months of ownership must be treated as exempt. Periods of ownership before 31 March 1982 are ignored.

20 TONY TORT

> **Tutor's hints.** It was important to realise in part (a) that you needed to calculate the 1999/00 income tax and Class 4 NIC liability in order to work out the amount by which payments on account were underpaid.
>
> **Examiner's comments.** This question was answered badly which was disappointing given that self assessment had been covered in my newsletter articles.

(a) (i) Payments due during 2000:

	Amount due £	Due date	Date paid	Days late	Interest at 10% £
1998/99 balancing payment	19,275	31.1.00	10.5.00	99	522.80
1999/00 First payment on account	2,500	31.1.00	15.6.00	135	92.47
	3,141.50 (W)	31.1.00	31.1.01	365	314.15
	5,641.50				
1999/00 Second payment on account	2,500	31.7.00	31.7.00	0	-
	3,141.50 (W)	31.7.00	31.1.01	184	158.37
	5,641.50				

(ii) *Surcharge*

A surcharge of 5% may be levied on the late payment of the 1998/99 balancing payment because it was not paid within 28 days or the due date. Tony may, therefore, be liable to a surcharge of £963.75 (£19,275 × 5%). However, the Revenue may mitigate this if there is reasonable excuse for the late payment. Surcharges are not levied in respect of payments on account.

Penalties

Unless he has a reasonable excuse, Tony will be subject to a £100 penalty for the late filing of his tax return. In addition a daily penalty of £60 could have been imposed if leave to do so was given by the Commissioners.

A penalty could also be charged if Tony made the claim to reduce his payments on account fraudulently or negligently. Since Tony made his claim for cash flow reasons it was negligently made and the Revenue could impose a penalty of £6,283 (£3,141.50 × 2).

(b) (i) The Revenue may have randomly selected Tony's tax return for an enquiry or they may have made the enquiry because of a suspected tax risk.

(ii) Tony has 30 days from the end of the enquiry to amend his self assessment in accordance with the Revenue's conclusions. Tony can appeal at the end of the enquiry if he does not accept the Revenue's conclusions.

(iii) Tony's additional income tax liability as a result of the enquiry is £1,800 (£4,500 × 40%). Interest will run on this amount from 31.1.00. There will be no surcharge unless the tax is paid later than 28 days after the due date (which is 30 days from the date of the amendment to the assessment). A penalty of up to £1,800 could be imposed if Tony's tax return was fraudulently or negligently submitted.

However, the Revenue can at their discretion mitigate this penalty.

(c) The maximum tax deductible pension premium in 1999/00 is 20% of:

	£
1999/00 net relevant earnings	42,160
1998/99 net relevant earnings b/f to 1999/00 (£61,535 + 4,500)	66,035
	108,195

20% × £108,195 = £21,639

Therefore relate the whole of the £20,000 contribution back to 1999/00 to reduce his income tax liability by:

£		£
9,825 (W1) (£37,825 - £28,000) × 40%		3,930
10,175 × 23%		2,340
20,000		6,270

The income tax reduction will not affect the payments on account that were due for 1999/00 or the interest on them. The tax reduction will either be set against Tony's 2000/01 tax liability or will be given by way of a refund in respect of 1999/00.

Working

1 1999/00 income tax liability

	£
Profits	52,100
Less: capital allowances	
Computer (FYA @ 40%)	(2,080)
Photocopier (FYA @ 40%)	(1,760)
Plant and machinery (WDA @ 25%)	(3,400)
Private use car (£3,000 × 90%)	(2,700)
Schedule D Case II	42,160
Less: personal allowance	(4,335)
Taxable income	37,825

	£
Tax on non-savings income	
£1,500 × 10%	150
£26,500 × 23%	6,095
£9,825 × 40%	3,930
Income tax liability	10,175
Class 4 NICs: (£26,000 – 7,530) × 6%	1,108
Total tax	11,283

Payments on account should therefore have been reduced to £5,641.50 rather than £2,500. Interest will run on the underpaid £3,141.50 (£5,641.50 – £2,500) from the due dates for the payments on account.

Notes   **Answer bank**

Marking guide

				Marks
(a)	(i)	Calculation of taxable income		2
		Income tax		1
		Class 4 NIC		1
		Underpayment of payments on account		1
		Calculation of interest on payments		2
	(ii)	*Tax return for 1998/99:*		
		Fixed penalty		1
		Daily penalty		1
		Surcharge		2
		Penalty for fraudulent or negligent reduction of payments on account		2
			Available	14
			Maximum	12
(b)		*Reasons for enquiry*		
		Inland Revenue suspicions		1
		Random enquiry		1
		Completion of the enquiry		
		Amendment of self assessment		1
		Right of appeal		1
		Interest, surcharges and penalties		
		Interest		1
		Surcharge		1
		Penalty		1
			Available/Maximum	7
(c)		Calculation of maximum tax deductible premium		2
		Conclusion		1
		Income tax reduction		2
		Set off in 2000/2001/claim for refund		1
		Interest/Payments on account		1
			Available	7
			Maximum	6
			Maximum	25

21 TUTORIAL QUESTION: CHANGE OF ACCOUNTING DATE

Tutor's hint. When two accounting periods end in a tax year, the basis period for the year ends on the new accounting date. It begins immediately following the previous basis period.

TAXABLE PROFITS FOR 1995/96 TO 1999/00

Tax year	*Basis period*		*Profits* £
1995/96	(1.1.96 – 31.3.96) 3/12 × £36,000		9,000
1996/97	(1.1.96 – 31.12.96)		36,000
1997/98	(1.1.97 – 31.12.97)		40,000
1998/99	(1.1.98 – 31.12.98)		44,000
1999/00	(1.1.99 – 28.2.00)		
	£52,000 + £14,000	66,000	
	Less: relief for overlap profits	(6,000)	
			60,000

Profits of the fourteen months to 28.2.00 are taxed in 1999/00, so overlap relief is available for 2 months worth of any unrelieved overlap profits. Overlap profits of £9,000 arose on commencement in respect of the three months to 31.3.96. This means 2/3 of these profits may be relieved in 1999/00. Overlap relief is available to bring the number of months worth of profits taxed in the year down to 12.

The unrelieved overlap profits of £3,000 are carried forward for relief either on a future change of accounting date or on the cessation of the business.

22 CECILE GRAND

> **Tutor's hint.** This was a straightforward question if you had learnt the rules.
>
> **Examiner's comments.** The failure to give due dates lost several easy marks.

(a) (i) Cecile's payments on account for 2000/01 will be based on her income tax and class 4 NIC liability for 1999/00 as follows.

	Non-savings £	Dividends £	Total £
Schedule D Case I	38,400		
Pension contribution	3,500		
	34,900		
Schedule A	800		
Dividends (£4,860 × 100/90)		5,400	
	35,700	5,400	41,100
Personal allowance	4,335		
Taxable income	31,365	5,400	36,765

	£
Income tax on non-savings income	
£1,500 at 10%	150
£26,500 at 23%	6,095
£3,365 at 40%	1,346
Income tax on dividend income	
£5,400 × 32.5%	1,755
	9,346
Widow's bereavement allowance (£1,970 at 10%)	(197)
	9,149
Tax credit - dividends (£5,400 at 10%)	(540)
	8,609
Class 4 NIC (£26,000 – £7,530) × 6%	1,108
	9,717
Payment on account due 31.1.01 – 50%	£4,858.50
Payment on account due 31.7.01 – 50%	£4,858.50

Cecile's forecast actual tax liability for 2000/01 is as follows.

	Non-savings £	Dividends £	£
Schedule D Case I	21,750		
Dividends (£4,320 × 100/90)	-	4,800	
	21,750	4,800	26,550
Personal allowance	4,335	-	
Taxable income	17,415	4,800	22,215

Income tax on non-savings income
		£
£1,500 at 10%		150
£15,915 at 23%		3,660

Income tax on dividend income

£4,800 at 10%		480
		4,290
Tax credit on dividends (£4,800 at 10%)		(480)
		3,810
Class 4 NIC (£21,750 – £7,530) × 6%		853
		4,663

	£	
Capital gain (**no taper relief due**)	13,300	
Annual exemption	(7,100)	
Chargeable gain	6,200	

Capital gains tax
£5,785 (28,000 – 22,215) at 20%	1,157	
£415 at 40%	166	
		1,323
		5,986
Paid on account		(9,717)
Balancing refund		(3,731)

Cecile is due a tax refund of £3,731 since the payments on account made by her exceed the actual tax payable for 2000/01.

(ii) The forecast actual income tax and Class 4 NIC payable (not CGT) for 2000/01 is £4,663. Cecile could reduce her payments on account to this amount resulting in the following payment schedule.

31.1.2001	£2,331.50	(£4,663/2)
31.7.2001	£2,331.50	(£4,663/2)
31.1.2002	CGT only due of £1,323	

(b) (i) If Cecile's payments on account are too low, then she will be charged interest. This will run from the due dates for each payment on account of 31 January 2001 and 31 July 2001 respectively, until the date of payment, which will presumably be 31 January 2002. A penalty will also be charged if a claim to reduce payments on account is made fraudulently or negligently.

(ii) The Inland Revenue can enquire into Cecile's tax return, provided they give written notice. The time limit for giving notice of an enquiry is 31 January 2003 assuming that the return was filed on time (later enquiry notification dates apply to returns filed late). If the return was filed on time and the Inland Revenue do not give notification of an enquiry by 31 January 2003 then an enquiry after that date can normally only be made where the taxpayer has been fraudulent or negligent.

(iii) Following the completion of an enquiry, the Inland Revenue will inform Cecile of their findings. Cecile would then normally amend her tax return to take account of the Inland Revenue's conclusions. A new self-assessment of tax would be calculated by Cecile and the additional tax liability will be due 30 days from the date of the notice of amendment. Interest will be charged on the additional tax liability from 31 January 2002 (the due date for the tax return). No surcharge will be due provided that the additional tax liability is paid by the due date. A penalty will only be charged where a tax return is filed incorrectly due to fraud or negligence.

(c) (i) For Cecile's change of accounting date to be valid:

- The change must be notified to the Inland Revenue by 31 January 2003; and

- There must have been no previous change of accounting date in the last five tax years. This condition will not apply if the present change is to be made for genuine commercial reasons.

(ii) Following Cecile's change of accounting date, the basis period for 2001/02 will be the twelve months to 30 September 2001. The profits of this period will be:

	£
Year ended 31.3.01 (£21,750 × 6/12)	10,875
Period ended 30.9.01	18,000
	28,875

The profits of £10,875 for the period 1 October 2000 to 31 March 2001 are overlap profits, having already been assessed in 2000/01. These overlap profits may be relieved when Cecile ceases trading.

(iii) **Advantages**

The main advantage of Cecile changing her accounting date to 30 September is that she should have actual Schedule D Case I profits available before the first payment on account for a tax year is due on 31 January in the tax year. Also, the time between earning profits and paying the related tax liability will be six months later than it was with a 31 March year end.

Disadvantages

The disadvantages are that the final assessment upon cessation may be for a longer period with a 30 September year end. Also the change of accounting date creates overlap profits which will not be relieved until the business ceases.

23 CLARK KENT

> **Tutor's hint**. When losses arise in opening years, you must take great care not to double-count a loss.
>
> **Examiner's comment**. Some candidates wasted time by discussing loss relief against capital gains.

(a) (i) TAXABLE INCOME

(1) **1996/97**

Clark has no taxable income, because he is non-resident and his only income is from his job in Guyani.

(2) **1997/98**

Again, Clark's income from Guyani is not taxable.

Clark's taxable income is as follows.

	£
Schedule E: £30,000 × 2/12	5,000
Less personal allowance	4,335
Taxable income	665

(3) **1998/99**

	£
Salary	30,000
Car £9,700 × 15% = £1,455 × 10/12	1,212
Fuel £1,540 × 10/12	1,283
Schedule E	32,495
Less personal allowance	4,335
Taxable income	28,160

(4) **1999/00**

	£
Salary £30,000 × 2/12	5,000
Car £1,455 × 2/12	242
Fuel £1,540 × 2/12	256
Compensation	10,500
Purchase of car £(7,000 − 5,000)	2,000
Schedule E	17,998
Less personal allowance	4,335
Taxable income	13,663

The compensation payment is fully taxable because Clark is contractually entitled to it. The purchase of the car at an undervalue has been treated in the same way on the basis that it appears to form part of the same compensation package.

(ii) **LOSS RELIEF CLAIMS**

To work out the losses, we must first calculate the capital allowances.

	Pool £	Car (80%) £	Allowances £
1.7.99 - 30.6.00			
Acquisition		7,000	
WDA @ 25%		(1,750)	1,400
		5,250	
Acquisitions qualifying for FYA	20,625		
FYA @ 40%	(8,250)		8,250
	12,375		9,650
	12,375		
1.7.00 - 30.6.01			
Acquisition	12,375	−	
	24,750	5,250	
WDA	(6,188)	(1,313)	7,238
	18,562	3,937	

The adjusted loss for the first period is £(14,000 + 9,650) = £23,650, and the adjusted profit for the second period is £(20,000 − 7,238) = £12,762.

The losses and taxable profits are as follows.

Year	Basis period	Working	Profit/(loss) £
1999/00	1.7.99 - 5.4.00	£(23,650) × 9/12	(17,738)
2000/01	1.7.99 - 30.6.00	£(23,650) − £(17,738)	(5,912)
2001/02	1.7.00 - 30.6.01		12,762

The possible loss relief claims for the two losses are as follows.

(1) **Relief against the first future profits of the same trade under s 385 ICTA 1988.** A claim to establish the amount of each loss must be made by 31 January 2006 (for the 1999/00 loss) and by 31 January 2007 (for the 2000/01 loss). Relief will be given without any further claim.

(2) **Relief against the total income of the tax year of loss and/or the preceding tax year under s 380 ICTA 1988.** A claim must be made by 31 January 2002 for the 1999/00 loss, and by 31 January 2003 for the 2000/01 loss.

(3) **Relief against the total income of the three tax years preceding the tax year of loss, earlier years first, under s 381 ICTA 1988.** A claim must be made by 31 January 2002 for the 1999/00 loss, and by 31 January 2003 for the 2000/01 loss.

(iii) THE CHOICE OF CLAIM

Relying on s 385 will delay relief, and a s 381 claim would lead to a waste of the personal allowance for 1997/98. The best claims, which will ensure that relief is obtained at 40% and 23% for all losses, are s 380 relief in 1998/99 for the 1999/00 loss and s 380 relief in 1999/00 for the 2000/01 loss. With the top of the basic rate band being £28,000 of taxable income, tax repayments will be as follows.

	£
1998/99	
£(28,160 – 28,000) = £160 × 40%	64
£(17,738 – 160) = £17,578 × 23%	4,043
	4,107
1999/00	
£5,912 × 23%	1,360
	5,467

(b) THE LOAN

The **making of the loan will not be a transfer of value, because the loan is repayable and is at a commercial rate of interest**.

The first write-off will be a potentially exempt transfer. If the grandparent's annual exemptions for both the year of write-off and the preceding year are available, the PET will be £25,000 – £2,500 (marriage exemption) – 2 × £3,000 = £16,500. If the grandparent survives for the following seven years, there will be no inheritance tax. On death within three years, the tax will be £16,500 × 40% = £6,600 (assuming that none of the nil rate band is available). On death between three and seven years after the write-off, this tax would be reduced by tapering relief.

The final write-off of £60,000 will be a chargeable specific gift on death. The inheritance tax liability of up to £60,000 × 40/60 = £40,000 will be paid out of the residue of the estate (so that Clark will get the full benefit of the write-off) unless the will provides otherwise.

The interest on the loan will be a deductible expense for Schedule D Case I purposes provided that the loan is used for business purposes.

24 BASIL NADIR

> **Tutor's hint**. It is important to carefully plan your answer to a written question like this in order to ensure you answer all parts of the question in the allotted time.
>
> **Examiner's comments**. In part (a) a number of candidates wasted time by repeating the same point several times.

(a) The distinction between employment and self-employment is a fine one. It has been held that **employment involves a contract of service, whereas self employment involves a contract for services**. There is no single test that is conclusive in deciding whether a person is employed or self-employed and each case must be decided on its own facts. The criteria that will be used in deciding whether Basil will be classified as employed or self employed in respect of his contract with Ace Computers Ltd include:

(i) the degree of control exercised over him;
(ii) whether he must accept further work;
(iii) whether Ace Computers Ltd must provide further work;
(iv) whether he provides his own equipment;
(v) whether he hires his own helpers;

(vi) what degree of financial risk he takes;
(vii) what degree of responsibility for investment and management he has;
(viii) whether he can profit from sound management;
(ix) whether he can work when he chooses;
(x) the wording of the contract between Basil and Ace Computers Ltd.

The fact that Basil does a large amount of work for Ace Computers Ltd and the fact that he was previously employed by the company are likely to have led the Revenue to have queried Basil's self employed status.

The following factors could be put forward to justify Basil's self employed status.

(i) He has bought his own equipment.

(ii) He has his own office at home.

(iii) He has five other clients.

(iv) The change in his rights since being an employee. For instance he may no longer be entitled to holiday pay or sick pay.

In addition it may be possible to use the terms of the twelve month contract with Ace Computers Ltd to help justify Basil's status. For instance, if the contract is to be done for a fixed fee, self employment rather than employment is indicated. If, however, the contract requires Basil to work two specific days a week, then it is likely that Basil is an employee.

(b) If Basil is classified as self-employed, all of his income will be taxed under Schedule D case II. The costs of running an office from home and the costs of travelling between home and the offices of Ace Computers Ltd should be deductible. Basil's income tax and NIC liabilities for 1999/00 will therefore be as follows.

	£	£
Income		60,600
Expenses		
Use of office (£1,800 × 2/8)	450	
Telephone (£150 × 4)	600	
Motor expenses (£3,500 × 20,000/25,000)	2,800	
Capital allowances		
Computer equipment (£7,375 × 40% (FYA))	2,950	
Motor car (£10,000 × 25% × 20,000/25,000)	2,000	
		8,800
Schedule D case II		51,800
Personal allowance		4,335
Taxable income		47,465

		£
Income tax:	£1,500 at 10%	150
	£26,500 at 23%	6,095
	£19,465 at 40%	7,786
		14,031

	£
Class 2 NIC (52 × £6.55)	341
Class 4 NIC (£26,000 − £7,530) × 6%	1,108
	1,449

The total income tax and NIC liability is £15,480 (£14,031 + £1,449)

If Basil is classified as employed in respect of his contract with Ace Computers Ltd, then his tax liabilities will increase as a result of the following.

(i) Basil's travelling costs between home and the offices of Ace Computers Ltd of £1,400 (£3,500 × 10,000/25,000) will not be deductible. The capital allowances in respect of Basil's motor car will be reduced by £1,000 (£10,000 × 25% ×

10,000/25,000). As a result Basil's income tax liability will increase by £960 (£2,400 × 40%).

(ii) Basil will be liable to the maximum employee's class 1 NIC in respect of his £30,300 Schedule E earnings from Ace Computers Ltd. These will be £22,568 (£26,000 – £3,432) × 10% = £2,257.

Thus the increase in national insurance contributions will be £808 (£2,257 – £1,449).

(c) **Basil will become liable to register for VAT if at the end of any period of up to twelve consecutive calendar months, the value of his taxable supplies (excluding VAT) exceeds the registration limit.** The registration limit is £51,000.

The registration limit will be exceeded on 28 February 2000 as the value of Basil's taxable supplies in the eleven months to 28 February 2000 will be £55,550 (£60,600 × 11/12). Basil will have to notify HM Customs and Excise that he is required to be registered within 30 days, that is by 30 March 2000. He will be registered from 1 April 2000.

Implications of VAT registration

From the date of registration, Basil will have to account for output tax on his income. Since Ace Computers Ltd and his other clients are presumably VAT registered, Basil will be able to charge VAT on top of his fees charged. His output tax will amount to £10,605 pa (£60,600 × 17.5%). Basil will be able to recover the input tax on the business use of light and heat of £25 pa (£100 × 2/8), the business use of his telephone of £89 pa (£150 × 7/47 × 4), and motor expenses of £400. **He will have to account for output tax based on the fuel scale charge, since fuel is being provided for private use.** This can be avoided by not reclaiming any input tax in respect of fuel, although due to Basil's high business mileage this is unlikely to be beneficial.

Voluntary registration

Upon registering for VAT, **Basil will also be able to recover pre-registration input tax of £1,098 (£7,375 × 7/47) in respect of his computer equipment, provided that it is still owned at the date of VAT registration. He will only be able to recover input tax on the business use of light and heat, the business use of his telephone, and motor expenses, incurred within the six months prior to VAT registration.** Basil would therefore be advised to voluntarily register for VAT on or before 5 October 1999, in order to maximise the recovery of input tax.

25 GARDEN LTD

> **Tutor's hint.** This question neatly illustrated the fact that substantial business investments have several tax ramifications. We have to ask where the money is coming from, as well as what it is being spent on.
>
> **Examiner's comment.** Candidates had problems with the deductible element of the lease premium.

(a) (i) **The new factory**

IBAs will be available on the following cost.

	£
Levelling the land	10,300
Architects' and legal fees	24,300
Strengthening the floor	16,500
Factory	187,500
General offices	62,500
	301,100

IBAs each year for 25 years will be £301,100 × 4% = £12,044.

Plant and machinery capital allowances will be available on £(12,500 + 6,400) = £18,900. Depending on the date of expenditure first year allowances may be available in the accounting period of purchase. If the plant and machinery is purchased in the two years to 2 July 2000 first year allowances are available at the rate of 40%. In subsequent periods writing down allowances of 25% per annum on a reducing balance basis will be available. If the plant and machinery is not purchased before the above dates writing down allowances at 25% per annum on a reducing balance basis will, in any event, be available.

(ii) **The leased factory**

The effective premium and annual rental will be £470,000 × 40/47 = £400,000 and £35,250 × 40/47 = £30,000, because Garden Ltd will reclaim the VAT.

The rent deductible each year for corporation tax purposes will be as follows.

	£
Rent	30,000
Premium £400,000 × (50 – (40 – 1)) × 2% × 1/40	2,200
	32,200

(iii) **The debenture loan**

Interest of £200,000 × 12% = £24,000 will be deductible in calculating Schedule D Case 1 profits each year as a trading expense.

Garden Ltd will have to deduct 20% income tax from interest payments and account for that income tax quarterly.

(iv) **The sale of the warehouse**

There will be a balancing charge of the IBAs obtained: £60,000 × 7/22 = £19,091.

There will be a chargeable gain as follows.

	£
Proceeds	270,000
Less cost	120,000
	150,000
Less indexation allowance 0.360 × £120,000	43,200
Gain before taper relief	106,800

If the new factory is chosen, this gain can be rolled over. If the leased factory is chosen, it can only be held over for up to ten years.

(b) (i) **The subscription for new shares**

Alex Bush is connected with the company (over 30% shareholding) and cannot claim enterprise investment scheme (EIS) relief. Gary Hedge is also excluded from EIS relief because he is a paid director who has not subscribed for EIS shares in the company while unconnected with it.

If shares are issued under the EIS Carol Daisy and Edward Fern can obtain EIS relief, each getting tax reductions of £150,000 × 20% = £30,000 in 2000/01 and £25,000 × 20% = £5,000 by carry-back to 1999/00. However, the tax reduction is limited to the actual tax for the year available to reduce.

Carol Daisy is likely to claim reinvestment relief to shelter £150,000 of her gain from immediate taxation. The gain deferred will become chargeable on the disposal of her shares or on the breach of the various EIS conditions within five years.

(ii) **The proposed listing**

EIS relief will be withdrawn if the company becomes listed within three years of the share issue.

Inheritance tax business property relief on the shareholdings is currently 100%. If the company were to become listed, this would fall to nil. Even Alex Bush would not have control, because his stake would fall to 910/2,100 = 43%.

Gary Hedge would lose retirement relief, because his stake would fall from 5% to 70/2,100 = 3%. However this will not be a relevant consideration if the listing occurs in 2003/04 or later as retirement relief will be phased out by then.

26 ALEX ZONG

> **Tutor's hints.** Take care with taper relief. It is deducted after current and brought forward capital losses.
>
> **Examiner's comments.** Poorly laid out answers and a failure to show workings (such as the private use adjustment) lead to a loss of marks.

(a) (i) **Schedule DI assessments**

The Schedule D Case I profits for each accounting period are:

		£
P/E 30.6.97	£28,000 – £3,300 (W) =	24,700
Y/E 30.6.98	£44,000 – £3,576 (W) =	40,424
Y/E 30.6.99	£53,000 – £3,898 (W) =	49,102
P/E 31.12.99	£29,000	29,000

Overlap profits on commencement were.

	£
1.10.96 to 5.4.97 (£24,700 × 6/9)	16,467
1.7.97 to 30.9.97 (£40,424 × 3/12)	10,106
	26,573

Alex's Schedule D Case I assessment for 1999/00 will be as follows.

	£
Y/E 30.6.99	49,102
P/E 31.12.99	29,000
	78,102
Relief for overlap profits	26,573
	51,529

Workings

1. **Capital allowances**

	Pool £	Private use £		Allowances £
Period ended 30.6.97				
Additions	15,200	4,000		
WDA (25% × 9/12)	2,850	750	× 60%	3,300
TWDV c/f	12,350	3,250		
Year ended 30.6.98				
WDA - 25%	3,088	813	× 60%	£3,576
WDV c/f	9,262	2,437		
Year ended 30.6.99				
Disposal		2,800		
Balancing charge		363	× 60%	(218)
Addition		13,500		
WDA 25%/(restricted)	2,316	3,000	× 60%	4,116
TWDV c/f	6,946	10,500		3,898

Note 1

Alex should elect to transfer plant to Lexon Ltd at its written-down value. This avoids the balancing charges that would otherwise arise in the final period. The market values of the lorry and plant (£4,300 + £8,200 = £12,500) and the motor car (£11,500) both exceed their respective written-down values.

(ii) **Capital gains tax**

The assets will be deemed to be disposed of at their market values:

	£	£
Goodwill		
Proceeds		40,000
Cost		nil
Capital gain		40,000
Freehold premises		
Proceeds		75,000
Cost	32,000	
Enhancement expenditure	6,700	
		38,700
		36,300
Indexation allowance to April 1998		
£32,000 × $\frac{162.6 - 153.8}{153.8}$ = 0.057	1,824	
£6,700 × $\frac{162.6 - 160.0}{160.0}$ = 0.016	107	
		1,931
		34,369

Total gains (before taper relief) total £74,369 (40,000 + 34,369).

Alex qualifies for incorporation relief since the business is transferred as a going concern, and all of the business assets are being transferred. However since Alex is receiving some shares and some cash (loan account) not all of the gain can be rolled over in this way. Alex will have a chargeable gain before taper relief of £4,648 (£74,369 × 10,000/160,000) which will be completely extinguished by the capital losses made in the year.

However, to avoid wasting taper relief and the annual exemption. Alex should consider increasing the amount of the loan account to £44,864:

	Answer bank £
£74,369 × 44,864/160,000 =	20,853
Less capital loss	(12,500)
Net gain for year	8,353

	£
Gain remaining after taper relief (£8,353 × 85%)	7,100
Less: Annual exemption	(7,100)
	nil

(iii) **Value added tax**

The incorporation of a business is outside the scope of VAT. This means there will be no VAT charged on any assets transferred to Lexon Ltd.

Lexon Ltd will be able to take over Alex's VAT registration number if it wishes. However, if this is done then the company assumes Alexs' VAT liabilities.

(b) (i) **Bad debt**

Bad debts relief is given six months after the time that payment was due, provided that the debt has been written off. Since an invoice was not raised until 15 June 1999, bad debt relief can not be claimed in the VAT return for the quarter ended 30 November 1999. The amount of the relief to be claimed in the following VAT return will be £1,050.

(ii) **Refund of VAT**

A claim must be made for the repayment of the VAT underclaimed. The amount due cannot just be put through on the next VAT return, since the error exceeds £2,000. Claims for the refund of VAT are subject to a three year time limit, and so the claim will cover the period 1 December 1996 to 30 November 1999. The repayment will be for £2,547 (£475 × 36 × 17.5/117.5).

(iii) **Discount**

Where a discount is offered for prompt payment, VAT is due on the net amount even if the discount is not taken. The output VAT due is therefore £565 (£3,400 × 95% × 17.5%).

27 CHOW TONG

Tutor's hints. There is no indexation allowance on assets acquired after 6 April 1998.

Examiner comment's. Many candidates wasted time by calculating the taxpayer's total liability for the year, when only the tax liability (which was at 40%) on the property activities was required.

(a) (i) **Treated as trading**

If Chow is treated as trading she will be liable to tax on the profit made under Schedule D Case I. The holiday apartment retained by her will be included at its market value of £75,000 (*Sharkey v Wernher 1956*). Chow's income tax liability arising on the property activities will be as follows.

	£	£
Sale proceeds (6 × £75,000)		450,000
Cost of property	132,000	
Cost of conversion	63,000	
Loan interest (£90,000 × 8% × 7/12)	4,200	
Legal fees (5 × £750)	3,750	
Advertising	1,200	
		204,150
Taxable profit		245,850
Income tax at 40%		98,340

Treated as not trading

If Chow is treated as not trading, she will be subject to capital gains tax on the profit made and such profit will be calculated using the normal CGT rules. The holiday apartment retained by her will not be charged to tax. Chow's CGT liability will be as follows.

	£	£
Proceeds (5 × £75,000)		375,000
Incidental costs of disposal (£3,750 + £1,200)		4,950
		370,050
Cost of property (£132,000 × 5/6)	110,000	
Cost of conversion (£63,000 × 5/6)	52,500	
		162,500
		207,550
Annual exemption		7,100
		200,450
Capital gains tax at 40%		80,180

(ii) There is no single test as to what constitutes trading, but certain tests, the **badges of trade**, will be used to determine whether or not the purchase and resale of property is a trading transaction. The tests are as follows.

(1) **The subject matter of the transaction**. Property which does not yield an income nor gives personal enjoyment to its owner is likely to form the subject matter of a trading transaction. Chow has not received any income from the property, and there is no indication that she purchased the property with a view to residing in it. This is a strong indication of trading.

(2) **The length of ownership**. The sale of property within a short time of its acquisition is an indication of trading. Chow immediately put the holiday apartments up for sale following the completion of the conversion.

(3) **Frequency of similar transactions**. Repeated transactions in the same subject matter will be an indication of trading. Although Chow's sale of the holiday apartments is an isolated transaction, this does not prevent the property activities being treated as an adventure in the nature of a trade.

(4) **Work done on the property**. Carrying out work on the property in order to make it more marketable, or taking steps to find purchasers, will indicate a trading motive. The conversion of the property into six separate holiday apartments at a cost of £63,000 is a clear indication of trading.

(5) **Circumstances responsible for the realisation**. A forced sale to raise cash for an emergency will by presumption indicate that the transaction

is not an adventure in the nature of a trade. There is no indication that Chow's sale of the holiday apartments was a forced sale.

(6) **Motive.** If a transaction is undertaken with the motive of realising a profit, this will be a strong indication of trading. There is no clear indication of Chow's motive, although such factors as obtaining planning permission lead to the conclusion that she undertook the property transaction with a view to a profit. However, the absence of a profit motive does not prevent a person from being treated as trading.

There is no requirement to pass each 'test'. Rather the Inland Revenue will look at each test to decide where the weight of evidence falls, ie trade or not.

Other factors

The property was acquired deliberately, rather than unintentionally such as by gift or inheritance, with the purchase being financed by a loan of £90,000. Both factors are an indication of trading.

Conclusion

Despite being an isolated transaction, Chow's sale of the holiday apartments is likely to be treated as an adventure in the nature of a trade.

(b) (i) **Tax relief**

Under the enterprise investment scheme (EIS), Chow will be entitled to tax relief of up to £30,000 (£150,000 at 20%) in 1999/00. She will be entitled to tax relief of £10,000 (£50,000 at 20%) for 2000/01 if £50,000 of the investment is delayed until that year. There will be no CGT on the disposal of the shares provided they are held for five years.

If Chow's property activities are taxed as a capital gain, then she will be entitled to EIS re-investment relief of the gains. This would reduce her CGT liability to £180 (200,450 – £200,000) @ 40% by deferring the capital gain. EIS re-investment relief will be available provided the investment is made before November 2002.

(ii) **Withdrawal of relief**

Tax relief given under the EIS will not be withdrawn as a result of Chow becoming a director of Knife-Edge Ltd, or as a result of the company obtaining a listing on the AIM. Tax relief will be withdrawn if Knife-Edge Ltd obtains a listing on the Stock Exchange before 15 March 2003 (three years from the date of subscription), or Chow sells shares before 15 March 2005 (five years from the date of subscription). Where shares are sold, the relief withdrawn will be limited to that given on those shares. The capital gain deferred will become chargeable when the shares are sold, or if Knife-Edge Ltd obtains a listing on the Stock Exchange before 15 March 2003.

(iii) **Loss on disposal**

If a loss is made on the disposal of shares, then relief will be available against either capital gains or income. The calculation of the loss will be based on the cost of the shares less any EIS relief obtained and not withdrawn.

28 MING KHAN AND NINA LEE

Tutor's hint. Chargeable gains are taxed at 20% if they fall below the higher rate threshold. They are, however, taxed at 40% to the extent that, when added to taxable income, they are at or above the threshold.

Examiner's comment. A common mistake in part(a) was not to restrict the loss relief for the second year of assessment to the balance remaining.

(a) **Period to 31.7.99**

Capital allowances	Pool
	£
Recording equipment	70,300
Electrical system	19,400
Sound insulation	13,200
Heating system	5,100
	108,000
WDA (25% × 15/12)	33,750
TWDV carried forward	74,250

The building is not an industrial building hence no IBAs are due on its cost.

The Schedule D Case I loss is therefore £105,000 (71,250 + 33,750): This is allocated as to Ming, £63,000 (60%) and Nina, £42,000, (40%) as follows.

The losses for the tax years are:

	Ming (60%)	Nina (40%)
1998/99 (1.5.98 to 5.4.99)	£	£
£63,000/£42,000 × 11/15	46,200	30,800
1999/00 (Balance of loss)	16,800	11,200
	63,000	42,000

The assessments for 1998/99 and 1999/00 will be nil.

The trading loss can be relieved in the following ways.

(i) **Carrying it forward under s 385 ICTA 1988 to set against future trading profits.**

(ii) **Claiming relief against total income under s 380 ICTA 1988.** The loss for 1998/99 can be set against total income for 1998/99 and/or 1997/98. The loss for 1999/00 can be set against total income for 1999/00 and/or 1998/99. Provided, in any particular year, that a s 380 claim is made first, a claim could also be made under s 72 FA 1991 to extend the set off to chargeable gains of the same year.

(iii) **Claiming relief under s 381 ICTA 1988 against total income of the three years preceding the year of the loss, earliest year first.** Thus the 1998/99 loss can be carried back to; 1995/96, 1996/97 and 1997/98 and the 1999/00 loss can be carried back to 1996/97, 1997/98 and 1998/99.

(b) **Ming Khan**

Ming should claim under s 380 ICTA 1988 to set the loss of £46,200 for 1998/99 against her total income for 1997/98.

	£	£
Schedule E - Salary (£42,000 × 11/12)		38,500
Compensation	60,000	
Exemption	30,000	
	30,000	
		68,500
Less: Loss relief (S 380)		46,200
		22,300
Personal allowance		4,335
		17,965

This will result in a tax repayment of:

£		£
10,035 (£28,000 – £17,965) × 23%		2,308
36,165 × 40%		14,466
46,200		16,774

Ming does not have any income for 1998/99 or 1999/00, and so a claim under s 380 ICTA 1988 in respect of her loss for 1999/00 is not available. She should therefore make a claim under s 381 ICTA 1988 against her total income for 1996/97.

	£
Schedule E - Salary	42,000
Loss claim (s 381)	16,800
	25,200
Personal allowance	4,335
	20,865

This will result in a tax repayment of:

£		£
7,135 × 23%		1,641
9,665 × 40%		3,866
16,800		5,507

Nina Lee

Nina's taxable income for 1995/96 and 1996/97 is £1,915 (£6,250 – £4,335). A claim under s 381 ICTA 1988 is not beneficial as it would waste personal allowances in these years and only save a small amount of tax.

Nina should utilise her loss of £30,800 for 1998/99 by claiming under s 380 ICTA 1988 against her total income for 1997/98. Although this does waste personal allowances it allows Nina to also set the loss against her chargeable gain and obtain an immediate repayment of CGT:

	£
Schedule A rental income	6,250
Less: Loss relief (S 380)	6,250
	nil
Tax refund: £1,500 at 10% + £415 at 23%	£245

	£
Chargeable gain	39,200
Less: Loss relief (£30,800 – £6,250)	24,550
	14,650
Annual exemption	7,100
	7,550

Capital gains tax due:	£
£7,550 × 20%	1,510
Previously paid on £32,100 (£39,200 – £7,100):	
£26,085 (£28,000 – £1,915) @ 20%	5,217
£6,015 @ 40%	2,406
Repayment due	6,113

Nina's loss of £11,200 for 1999/00 should be carried forward under s 385 ICTA 1998 against her Schedule DI trading profits for 2000/01 (year ended 31 July 2000).

(c) (i) **Bad debts**

For income tax purposes, relief will be given in the period of account when the bad debt is either written off or provided for by specific provision. No relief is available for a general provision. The relief will be for £20,000 (£23,500 × 100/117.5) less any amount that is recoverable.

For VAT purposes, relief will be given on the appropriate VAT return when the debt is over six months old, and has been written off. The six month time limit starts on the date the debt should have been paid (not the invoice/supply date). The relief will be for £3,500 (£23,500 × 17.5/117.5). However, if the partnership operates the cash accounting scheme, then relief is automatic, since output VAT would not have been accounted for to Customs in respect of the original invoice.

(ii) **Computer equipment - hire-purchase**

The partnership will be able to claim capital allowances on the cost of the computer equipment of £52,000 (£61,100 × 100/117.5). Since the computer equipment is to be replaced in three years time, it will be beneficial to make a claim for treatment as a short-life asset. Capital allowances of £52,000 will then be given over three years. If the computer is purchased before 2 July 2000 a first year allowance will be available.

The finance charge of £20,000 (36 × £2,000 = £72,000 − £52,000) will be a deductible expense for the partnership, and will be allocated to periods of account using normal accounting principles.

The input VAT of £9,100 will be reclaimed on the VAT return for the period in which the computer equipment is purchased.

Computer equipment - leasing

The lease rental payments of £24,000 pa (£28,200 × 100/117.5) will be a deductible expense for the partnership, and will be allocated to periods of account in accordance with the accruals concept.

The input VAT of £4,200 (£28,200 × 17.5/117.5) included in each lease rental payment will be reclaimed on the tax return for the period during which the appropriate tax point occurs.

No capital allowances can be claimed by the partnership.

Marking guide		Marks
(a)	Capital allowances	2
	Allocation of loss	2
	Section 385 ICTA 1988	1
	Section 380 ICTA 1988/Section 72	2
	Section 381 ICTA 1988	1
	Available	8
	Maximum	7
(b)	*Ming Khan*	
	Loss relief claims	2
	Refund 1997/98	3
	Refund 1996/97	2
	Nina Lee	
	Loss relief claims	2
	Refund 1997/98	3
	Available	12
	Maximum	11
(c)	*Bad debts*	
	Income tax	1
	VAT	2
	Computer equipment – Hire-purchase	
	Capital allowances	1
	Short-life asset	1
	Finance charge	1
	VAT	1
	Computer equipment – Leasing	
	Lease rental payments	1
	VAT	1
	Available	9
	Maximum	7
	Maximum	25

29 SMART AND SHARP

> **Tutor's hint.** Always start a partnership question by dividing partnership income between the partners before allocating the income to tax years.
>
> **Examiner's comment.** The NIC implications in part (b) caused problems for some candidates, and there is little excuse for not knowing the correct NIC calculations when the rates are given on the examination paper.

(a) The profits of each period of account must first be divided between the partners.

Period	Total £	Bob £	Nick £	Justin
Six months to 31.12.97				
Salaries (6/12)	130,000	90,000	40,000	
Balance	150,000	75,000	75,000	
	280,000	165,000	115,000	
Year to 31.12.98	£	£	£	
Salaries	260,000	180,000	80,000	
Balance	450,000	225,000	225,000	
	710,000	405,000	305,000	
Year to 31.12.99	£	£	£	
Salaries	260,000	180,000	80,000	
Balance	380,000	190,000	190,000	
	640,000	370,000	270,000	

	£	£	£	£
Year to 31.12.00 (1:1:1)	750,000	250,000	250,000	250,000
Year to 31.12.01 (1:1:1)	750,000	250,000	250,000	250,000
Year to 31.12.02 (1:1:1)	750,000	250,000	250,000	250,000

Next the amount of each partner's Schedule D Case II income in each tax year can be calculated.

Bob

Year	Basis period	£	£
1997/98	1.7.97-5.4.98 (£165,000 + $3/12 \times$ £405,000)		266,250
1998/99	Year to 31.12.98		405,000
1999/00	Year to 31.12.99		370,000
2000/01	Year to 31.12.00		250,000
2001/02	Year to 31.12.01		250,000
2002/03	Year to 31.12.02	250,000	
	Less: overlap relief	(101,250)	
			148,750

Nick

Year	Basis period	£	£
1997/98	1.7.97-5.4.98 (£115,000 + $3/12 \times$ £305,000)		191,250
1998/99	Year to 31.12.98		305,000
1999/00	Year to 31.12.99		270,000
2000/01	Year to 31.12.00		250,000
2001/02	Year to 31.12.01		250,000
2002/03	Year to 31.12.02	250,000	
	Less: overlap relief	(76,250)	
			173,750

Justin

Year	Basis period	£	£
1999/00	1.1.00-5.4.00 ($3/12 \times$ £250,000)		62,500
2000/01	Year to 31.12.00		250,000
2001/02	Year to 31.12.01		250,000
2002/03	Year to 31.12.02	250,000	
	Less: overlap relief	(62,500)	
			187,500

As the partnership is incorporated on 31 December 2002, 2002/03 is the year of cessation for all partners and overlap relief is available for the overlap profits that arose on commencement.

(b) **Partnership not incorporated**

If the partnership is not incorporated the partners will each have schedule D Case I income of £250,000. Their additional income tax and NIC liabilities will be:

	£
Income tax (£250,000 × 40%)	100,000
Class 2 (£6.55 × 52)	341
Class 4 (£26,000 – £7,530) × 6%	1,108
	101,449

The total NIC and income tax liabilities of the three partners will be:

3 × £101,449 = £304,347

Partnership incorporated

The annual tax liability of Smash Ltd will be:

	£
Trading profit	750,000
Less: director's remuneration (3 × £200,000)	(600,000)
Employer's Class 1 NIC (£200,000 – 4,335) × 3 × 12.2%	(71,613)
PCTCT	78,387

	£
Corporation tax at 20%	15,677
Employer's Class 1 NIC	71,613
	87,290

Tax liability of directors

The annual tax liability of each director will be as follows.

	£
Taxable income - Schedule E	200,000
Income tax at 40%	80,000
Employees Class 1 NIC	
(£26,000 – £3,432) × 10%	2,257
	82,257

The total annual tax liability of Smash Ltd and the three directors will be £334,061 (£87,290 + (£82,257 × 3)). This is an increase of £29,714 (£334,061 – £304,347) compared to the total annual tax liability of the three partners.

Conclusion

Since incorporating the partnership's business will result in an increase in the overall annual tax liability, incorporation does not appear to be beneficial.

(c) **Each partner will be entitled to overlap relief for his overlap profits when he ceases to be a member of the partnership.** This could be on incorporation of the business or on some other event when the partner leaves the partnership business. Relief is given by **deducting overlap profits in the final tax year the business is carried on.**

Relief for overlap profits may also be available if the partnership changes its accounting date. If a change of accounting date results in more than twelve months worth of profits being taxed in a tax year, **overlap relief is given to reduce the number of months worth of profit taxed in that year to twelve.**

(d) **CGT implications**

The incorporation of the partnership's business will be a disposal for CGT purposes. Provided that the disposal is in return for shares in Smash Ltd, any gains arising from the disposal of chargeable business assets can be held over against the base cost of the shares received. For this relief to apply the partnership's business must be transferred as a going concern, and all the assets of the partnership's business (excluding cash) must be transferred.

IHT implications

There are not normally any IHT implications of an incorporation itself as there is not normally a transfer of wealth. At present, were they to die, the existing partners would be entitled to BPR at the rate of 100% in respect of their partnership share. The new partner will not be entitled to BPR until he has been a partner for two years.

Following the incorporation of the partnership's business, BPR will only be available at 100% if the company remains unquoted and continues to carry on a qualifying trade. Again, Justin will not be entitled to any BPR until he has held the shares for two years.

30 SALLY AND TREVOR ACRE

Tutor's hints. In part (b) it was important to provide adequate justification for your choice of loss relief.

Examiner's comments. Candidates are advised to read the question carefully since a significant number confused the ages of the two partners.

(a) **Partnership assets**

	£
Market value	230,000
Less: cost	(170,000)
Unindexed gain	60,000
Less: indexation to April 1998	(9,690)
Gain on property	50,310
Gain on goodwill	100,000
Gains on partnership assets before taper relief	150,310

These gains are split between Trevor and Sally in their profit sharing ratio:

Trevor (30%) = £45,093

Sally (70%) = £105,217

Trevor is not old enough to qualify for retirement relief so his chargeable gain after taper relief is £38,329 (£45,093 × 85%).

Sally qualifies for retirement relief on her gain of £105,217 and on the gain made on the disposal of the leasehold premises as the disposal is an associated disposal:

Leasehold property

	£
Proceeds	90,000
Less: cost	
£85,000 × $\dfrac{78.055 + (79.622 - 78.055) \times 3/12}{81.100}$	(82,219)
Gain before taper relief	7,781

Sally's gains eligible for retirement relief:

	£
Partnership assets	105,217
Leasehold property	7,781
	112,998

The partnership business was carried on for three years and six months so the lower and upper limits for retirement relief are multiplied by 3½/10.

	£
Gains eligible for retirement relief	112,998
Less: retirement relief	
£70,000 + 50% (112,998 – 70,000)	(91,499)
	21,499
Sally's chargeable gain after taper relief (85%)	£18,274

(b) Each partner can claim for their share of the loss.

(i) Under s380 ICTA 1998 a partner can set their loss against their statutory total income in the year of the loss (1999/00) and/or in the preceding year

(1998/99). A s380 ICTA claim in any tax year can be extended to set any remaining loss against net chargeable gains of that year.

(ii) Under s388 ICTA 1988 the loss could be carried back to set against Schedule D Case II income of the three preceding years, latest year first.

(iii) Under s381 ICTA 1988 the loss could be set against the statutory total income of the three preceding years, earliest year first.

Sally's share of the loss is £47,600.

S388 ICTA 1988 relief would be:

	1997/98 £	1998/99 £
Schedule D Case II	51,800	36,400
Less: s388 ICTA 1988 relief	(11,200)	(36,400)
	40,600	-

Schedule A profits remain in 1998/99 to use the personal allowance and 10% rate band, so the tax relief is at 23% and 40%. Relief in 1997/98 is at 40%. This means all of the loss is saving tax at the marginal rates of 23% or 40%.

Under s380 ICTA 1988 in 1998/99, £36,400 of the loss would be relieved as above. In addition £5,835 of the loss would be relieved against Schedule A income wasting the benefit of the personal allowance and 10% rate band, so this claim cannot be as beneficial as the above claim.

Similarly in 1999/00 a s380 claim would waste the personal allowance and lower rate band. If Sally made a claim in order to then set her loss against her chargeable gains she would save some capital gains tax at 20% but this claim is less beneficial than the s388 ICTA 1988 claim, discussed above.

Relief under s381 ICTA 1988 will be:

	1996/97 £	1997/98 £
Schedule D Case II	26,250	51,800
Schedule A	5,835	5,835
	32,085	57,635
S 381 relief	(32,085)	(15,515)
	-	42,120

In 1996/97 relief wastes the personal allowance and the lower rate band. £26,250 is relieved at 23%. In 1997/98 relief is at 40%. This relief is not as beneficial as the s388 ICTA 1988 claim where all the loss saves tax at 23% or 40%.

The most beneficial claim for Sally is the s388 ICTA 1988 claim. Her taxable income each year if this claim is made is:

	1996/97 £	1997/98 £	1988/99 £	1999/00 £
Schedule D Case II	26,250	51,800	36,400	-
Less: s388 relief	-	(11,200)	(36,400)	
Schedule A	5,835	5,835	5,835	5,835
	32,085	46,435	5,835	5,835
Less: personal allowance	(4,335)	(4,335)	(4,335)	(4,335)
Taxable income	27,750	42,100	1,500	1,500

Sally's chargeable gain in 1999/00 is:

	£
Gain after taper relief (part a)	18,274
Less: annual exemption	(7,100)
	11,174

Trevor

Trevor's share of the loss is £20,400.

S388 ICTA 1988 relief would be:

	1997/98 £	1998/99 £
Schedule D Case II	22,200	15,600
Less: s388 ICTA 1988	(4,800)	(15,600)
	17,400	-
Schedule A	2,000	2,000
	19,400	2,000
Personal allowance	(4,335)	(2,000)
Taxable income	15,065	-

In 1998/99 £2,335 of the personal allowance and the £1,500 lower rate band, are wasted. The rest of the loss, £16,565, saves tax at 23% in either 1997/98 or 1998/99.

A s 380 claim in 1998/99 would relive £15,600 as above but it would also waste £2,000 of the personal allowance. This means this relief is not as beneficial as the s 388 claim discussed above.

A s 380 claim in 1999/00 would also waste £2,000 of personal allowances but it would also allow Trevor to set the remaining loss of £18,400 against chargeable gains 1999/00. Trevor would choose to set the £18,400 against gains on his non-business assets as these do not qualify for taper relief:

	£
Gains on non business assets	38,000
Less: loss relief	(18,400)
	19,600
Gains on partnership assets (part (a))	38,329
	57,929
Less: annual exemption	(7,100)
Chargeable gains	50,829

The £18,400 has saved CGT at 40% - £7,360.

This claim is clearly more beneficial than a s388 ICTA 1988 claim.

S381 ICTA 1988 relief would be:

	1996/97 £	1997/98 £
Schedule D Case II	11,250	22,200
Schedule A	2,000	2,000
	13,250	24,200
Less: loss relief	(13,250)	(7,150)
Taxable income	-	17,050

The personal allowance and the lower rate band are wasted in 1996/97. The rest of the loss, £14,565, saves tax at 23% in either 1996/97 or 1997/98.

The most beneficial claim for Trevor is the s380 and s72 claim in 1999/00. His resulting income is:

	1996/97 £	1997/98 £	1988/99 £	1999/00 £
Schedule D Case II	11,250	22,200	15,600	-
Schedule A	2,000	2,000	2,000	2,000
	13,250	24,200	17,600	2,000
Less: s380				(2,000)
Less: PA	(4,335)	(4,335)	(4,335)	
Taxable income	8,915	19,865	13,265	-

Trevor's chargeable gains in 1999/00 are, as calculated above, £50,829.

Marking guide			
			Marks
(a)	*Capital gains*		
	Goodwill		1
	Freehold property		1
	Leasehold property		2
	Trevor Acre		
	Share of chargeable gains		1
	Retirement relief not available		1
	Sally Acre		
	Share of chargeable gains		1
	Calculation of retirement relief		4
	Gain after taper relief		1
		Available	12
		Maximum	9
(b)	S 380 ICTA 1988 (against STI)		1
	S 72 FA 1991 (against gains)		1
	S 388 ICTA 1988 (terminal loss relief)		1
	S381 ICTA 1988 (relief for early year loss)		1
	Division of loss between partners		1
	Sally Acre		
	Alternative claim under s 380 ICTA 1988		1
	Claim under s 388 ICTA 1988		2
	Claim under s 381 ICTA 1988		1
	Taxable income and chargeable gains		2
	Trevor Acre		
	Claim under s 388 ICTA 1988		1
	Claim under s 380 ICTA 1988		1
	Claim under s 72 FA 1991		2
	Claim under s 381 ICTA 1988		1
	Taxable income and chargeable gains		2
		Available	18
		Maximum	16
		Maximum	25

31 TUTORIAL QUESTION: CHOOSING ASSETS TO SELL

(a) **Site A**

The gain would be based on the value at 31 March 1982 as follows.

	£
Proceeds	1,600,000
Less value on 31 March 1982	720,000
	880,000
Less indexation allowance: $\frac{171.0 - 79.4}{79.4} = 1.154 \times £720,000$	830,880
Chargeable gain	49,120
Corporation tax at 30%	£14,736

The gain using cost less the rolled over gain ie (base cost = £700,000 − £600,000) = £100,000) would clearly have been higher.

Site B

Since the asset was not held on 31 March 1982 but the old land was sold before 6 April 1988, the base cost less the rolled over gain must be reduced by one half of the gain originally rolled over. This compensates for the non-availability of rebasing to 31 March 1982 on either the old or the new asset.

		£
Proceeds of 1982 sale		900,000
Less cost		150,000
		750,000
Less indexation allowance: $\dfrac{81.9 - 79.4}{79.4} = 0.031 * £150,000$		4,650
Gain rolled over		745,350

	£	£
Proceeds		1,600,000
Less cost	900,000	
Less half of rolled over gain (£745,350 × 50%)	372,675	
	527,325	
		1,072,675
Less indexation allowance: $\dfrac{171.0 - 81.9}{81.9} = 1.088 \times £527,325$		573,730
		498,945
Corporation tax at 30%		£149,684

Selling site A would lead to a much lower corporation tax liability.

(b) To: A Director
    From: A N Accountant
    Date: 20 February 2000
    Subject: Retirement relief on the proposed disposal of your shareholding

The following conditions, which appear to be met in your case, apply to retirement relief on a disposal of shares and securities.

(i) The vendor must be aged at least 50, or retiring through ill health.

(ii) The company must be the vendor's personal company. This is so if the vendor holds at least 5% of the voting rights.

(iii) At least 5% of the voting rights must have been held for a qualifying period of at least one year during which the vendor was a full-time working officer or employee.

The maximum relief is all gains up to the lower limit, plus 50% of gains above the lower limit up to the upper limit. The limits in 1999/00 are £200,000 and £800,000 when the qualifying period is at least ten years, and are scaled down when it is shorter than this. In your case the limits will therefore be 9/10 of these figures, that is £180,000 and £720,000. The limits will decrease after 1999/00 as retirement relief is to be gradually phased out by 2003/04.

The gain eligible for relief is the total gain, multiplied by the ratio of the market value of the company's chargeable business assets to the market value of its chargeable assets. The latter excludes assets on which no chargeable gain would arise on disposal, such as debtors and stock; the former also excludes assets not used in the business, such as investments.

Any gain remaining chargeable after deducting retirement relief is eligible for taper relief. The shares are a business asset so in 1999/00 only 85% of the gain will remain chargeable after taper relief. If you actually retire after 31 March 2000, the amount of taper relief will increase but, from a tax planning point of view this has to be weighed against the reduction in the retirement relief limits.

32 VELO LTD

> **Tutor's hints.** There were a number of tricky technical points in this question but even if you did not know how to deal with these you should have still been able to achieve a pass mark in the question by applying your basic knowledge.
>
> **Examiner's comments.** This was the least popular question on the paper and produced very few good answers.

(a) (i) *Sale of factory*

This will result in the following capital gain:

	£
Proceeds	920,000
Less: cost	(326,000)
Unindexed gain	594,000
Less: Indexation allowance	
$£326,000 \times \dfrac{171.5 - 114.3}{114.3}$ $(= 0.500)$	(163,000)
Indexed gain	431,000

Rollover relief is available to defer the above gain to the extent that the proceeds are re-invested in the following replacement property:

		Proceeds reinvested
		£
(1)	Freehold factory	725,000
(2)	Leasehold office	80,000
(3)	Fixed plant and machinery (overhead crane)	53,000
		858,000

The balance of the proceeds not reinvested of £(920,000 – 858,000) = £62,000 is chargeable in the year ended 31 March 2000.

Rollover relief defers the gain reinvested of £(431,000 – 62,000) = £369,000. The leasehold office building and the overhead crane are both depreciating assets, and so any proportion of the gain rolled over against them will only be held over until the earlier of their disposal or ten years from the date of acquisition. However, in this situation the legislation would appear to allow the claim to be effectively made wholly against the value of the freehold factory. The base cost of the freehold factory will be £356,000 (725,000 – 369,000).

There would also be a balancing charge under the IBA regime as follows:

	£
Original cost (not land or offices (exceeds 25% of cost))	160,000
Less: IBAs given (y/e 31.3.90 – 31.3.99)	
$10 \times 4\% \times £160,000$	(64,000)
Residue before sale	96,000
Less: proceeds (limited to cost)	(160,000)
Balancing charge	64,000

(ii) *Purchase of new factory and crane*

Velo Ltd can claim IBAs on the new factory. The eligible expenditure is the lower of the purchase price and the original cost incurred by the person incurring the construction expenditure ie the original cost of £(478,000 + 30,000) = £508,000. The cost of the drawing office is eligible expenditure.

The unexpired tax life of the building remaining on 1 March 2000 is 16 years 4 months. This means Velo Ltd is entitled to IBAs of $\dfrac{£508,000}{16\,^{4}/_{12}} = £31,102$ per annum commencing in the year to 31.3.00 until the expenditure is written off.

Although the crane is a long-life asset, because Velo Ltd has not exceeded the £100,000 annual limit, it will be treated as plant and machinery. It will therefore qualify for a 40% FYA (£53,000 @ 40% = £21,200) in the y/e 31.3.00 as Velo Ltd is a medium-sized company. Thereafter a WDA of 25% can be claimed on the reducing balance.

(iii) *Leasehold factory and computer equipment*

A Schedule D Case I deduction can be claimed in respect of the leasehold office as follows:

	£
Premium paid	80,000
Less: £80,000 × (15 – 1) × 2%	(22,400)
Total deductible	57,600

£57,600/12 = £3,840 deductible per annum

Amount deductible for y/e 31.3.00	£
1/12 × £3,840	320
Add: rent paid $\left(\dfrac{16,200}{12}\right)$	1,350
Total deduction	1,670

Normally the amortisation (depreciation) of the lease will be deducted in the accounts and must be added back as an appropriation.

The computer equipment is a short life asset and a claim should be made to 'de-pool' the expenditure. This must be made by 31.3.02. If the equipment is disposed of before 31.3.04, a balancing charge or allowance will be made. Otherwise, its tax written down value is added to the general pool at that time. It should be noted that the election is not advantageous if the equipment is not sold before 31.3.04 at less than tax written down value.

For the y/e 31.3.00, the allowance will be a first year allowance of 40% × £14,000 = £5,600.

(b) (i) *Heating and ventilation systems*

A joint election can be made by Velo Ltd and the purchaser of the building to identify the disposal price of the systems and the corresponding amount on which the purchaser can claim allowances. The time limit for the election is two years after the purchaser acquires the interest (ie 25 March 2002). The amount cannot exceed the original cost of the plant (£54,000) and it must not be less than the tax written down value of £28,000.

It would be beneficial for Velo Ltd, if the price was not to exceed £38,000 (the pool WDV). The most beneficial figure would be £28,000, giving a WDA on the rest of the pool for y/e 31.3.00 of £(38,000 – 28,000) = £10,000 @ 25% = £2,500.

(ii) *Overhead crane*

The overhead crane is a long-life asset. As it was acquired in y/e 31.3.00 and Velo Ltd intends to acquire another crane on 1 March 2000 costing £53,000 the £100,000 limit regarding long-life assets will be exceeded.

If both cranes are purchased in y/e 31.3.00, the first crane will not affect the long-life pool calculation as it is bought and sold in the same year. However, there will be no first year allowance on the second crane and the WDA will be

6% instead of 25%. It would therefore be better for the new crane to be acquired after 31.3.2000.

(iii) *Effect on rollover relief*

If the heating and ventilation system and the crane are separately identified, the sale proceeds of the factory will be reduced to:

£(575,000 − 28,000 − 64,000) = £483,000.

This means the full proceeds are reinvested in qualifying assets and so the whole gain can be deferred.

Marking guide

		Marks
(a)	*Sale of factory*	
	Gain	1
	Rollover relief/Amount reinvested	1
	Immediate gain	1
	Depreciating assets	1
	Allocation of gain	1
	Balancing charge	2
	New factory	
	Expenditure qualifying for IBAs	2
	25 year life/Balance remaining	2
	IBAs commencing year to 31.3.00	2
	New crane	
	Limit - £100,000	1
	FYA	1
	Subsequent WDA	1
	Leasehold offices	
	Premium paid/Amortisation	2
	Rent paid (deduction)	1
	Computer equipment	
	Short life asset	1
	Balancing allowance	1
	FYA	1
	Available	22
	Maximum	17
(b)	*Heating and ventilation systems*	
	Joint election	1
	Lower and upper limits	1
	Balancing charge	1
	WDA	1
	Overhead crane	
	Limit of £100,000	1
	Tax planning	1
	WDA if two cranes purchased	1
	Rollover relief	
	Reduction in gain immediately chargeable	1
	Available/maximum	8
	Maximum	25

33 SALLY JONES

> **Tutor's hint.** You might reasonably have been uncertain about the treatment of the ex gratia payment. The £30,000 exemption is only available if the payment is not treated as a lump sum payment under an unapproved retirement benefit scheme. How a payment is treated will depend on all the circumstances, particularly the age of the recipient and whether or not the recipient goes on to other employment.
>
> **Examiner's comment.** In part (b), many candidates had difficulty with the retirement relief calculation.

(a) **If a company buys its own shares for more than the amount originally subscribed, general tax rules state that there is a distribution of the excess.**

However, a capital gains tax disposal occurs rather than a distribution, when an unquoted trading company (or the unquoted parent of a trading group) other than a company whose trade consists of dealing in shares, securities, land or futures, **buys back its own shares in order to benefit its trade. No relief is given if a main objective is tax avoidance.** On the other hand, **if the conditions for the relief are satisfied the relief is compulsory.**

The conditions to be satisfied by the vendor shareholder are as follows.

(i) The vendor must be **resident and ordinarily resident in the UK** when the purchase is made.

(ii) **The shares must have been owned by the vendor or her spouse throughout the five years preceding the purchase.** (Sally has owned her shares for six years.) This is reduced to three years if the vendor is the personal representative or the heir of a deceased member, and previous ownership by the deceased will count towards the qualifying period.

(iii) **The vendor and her associates must as a result of the purchase have their interest in the company's share capital reduced to 75% or less of their interest before the disposal.** Associates include spouses, minor children, controlled companies, trustees and beneficiaries. Sally's holding falls from 51.67% to 11/40 = 27.5%, a 47% reduction.

(iv) **The vendor must not after the transaction be connected with the company or any company in the same 51% group.** A person is connected with a company if he can control more than 30% of the ordinary share capital, the issued share capital and loan capital or the voting rights in the company. Sally's shareholding will fall to 27.5%.

The conditions appear to be met in Sally's case. **The relief is also available where a company purchases shares to enable the vendor to pay any inheritance tax arising on a death.** The 'benefit to the trade' test and the conditions in (i) - (iv) above do not then apply.

(b) (i) INCOME TAX

	Non-savings £
Schedule E income	
Salary £24,000 × 9/12	18,000
Pension £950 × 3	2,850
Bonus	5,700
Ex gratia payment (first instalment)	40,000
STI	66,550
Less personal allowance	4,335
Taxable income	62,215

	Answer bank

	£	£
Income tax on non-savings income		
£1,500 * 10%		150
£26,500 * 23%		6,095
£34,215 * 40%		13,686
		19,931
Less tax reductions		
Additional personal allowance £1,970 * 10%	197	
Widow's bereavement allowance £1,970 * 10%	197	
		394
Tax liability		19,537

Notes

(1) Bonuses are taxed in the year of receipt. However, for directors the definition of 'receipt' is very wide. An amount not actually received is treated as received as soon as the company's period of account ends (if the amount has already been determined by then), or when the amount is determined (if that is after the end of the period of account). The first of these alternatives applies here, making the bonus to be received on 30 April 2000 taxable in 1999/00.

(2) Ex gratia payments may qualify for a £30,000 exemption. However, that exemption is denied when a payment is regarded as a lump sum payment under an unapproved pension scheme. The payment to Sally is almost certain to be so regarded, because she has reached an age at which she might reasonably retire and there is no indication that she will be taking up any other employment.

Ex gratia payments on the termination of employment are taxed in the year they are received.

(ii) CAPITAL GAINS TAX

Zen Ltd is Sally's personal trading company, and retirement relief is available, based on a six year qualifying period.

	£	£
Gain		170,000
Less retirement relief		
Full relief £200,000 * 60%	120,000	
Partial relief £(170,000 – 120,000) * 50%	25,000	
		145,000
Chargeable gain		25,000

Taper relief is available as the shares are a business asset that has been owned for two years.

Gain after taper relief (85% × £25,000)	£21,250
CGT: £(21,250 – 7,100) * 40%	£5,660

(c) Zen Ltd will be able to deduct the following amounts in computing its taxable profits.

(i) Sally's monthly salary, plus employer's National Insurance contributions of 12.2% of the amount by which the salary exceeds the lower limit of £4,335. This is deductible in the period of account in which the salary is charged in the accounts (since none will be paid more than nine months later than the end of that period).

(ii) Sally's bonus, deductible in the period of account in which the bonus is treated as received by Sally. Thus the bonus determined before 31 March 2000 will be deductible in the year ended 31 March 2000. (Note that if Sally had been treated as receiving the bonus at any time up to nine months after the end of that year, it would still have been deductible in that year.) Employer's National Insurance contributions of 12.2% of the full amount will also be due and deductible.

(iii) The ex gratia payment paid on 31 March 2000 is deductible in the year ended 31 March 2000 because it was all paid in that year or within the subsequent nine months. This deduction is, however, subject to its being shown that the payment was made wholly and exclusively for the purposes of the company's trade (a test which applies to all the payments, but which may be harder to satisfy in the case of the ex gratia payment). Employer's National Insurance contributions are not due on genuinely ex gratia payments.

34 TUTORIAL QUESTION: REGISTRATION AND ACCOUNTING

Tutor's hint. Any discussion of partial exemption or of overseas trade was clearly ruled out by the question, and would have earned no marks.

ABC Certified Accountants
6 Somewhere Road, London, EC4Y 1SX

The Managing Director
XYZ Ltd
1 Anywhere Street
London, WC2 5SJ

Date: 23 October 1999
Our ref: Misc 1
Your ref: 123

Dear Sir,

Thank you for your recent letter.

We set out below the main points which you need to be aware of in respect of VAT.

Registration

If the company makes taxable supplies of goods or services, it must register with HM Customs & Excise if its taxable turnover in any period of up to 12 months to the end of a calendar month has exceeded the registration limit, or if you anticipate that it will exceed the registration limit in the 30 day period starting on any day.

The registration limit is currently £51,000.

Accounts

You should **record all income and expenditure exclusive of any VAT. The VAT should be recorded in a separate account showing the balance due to or from HM Customs & Excise.**

The only exception (when expenditure should be recorded inclusive of VAT) is expenditure, the VAT on which is irrecoverable. The main categories are cars with some non-business use and business entertaining.

Accounting for VAT

VAT is normally accounted for on a **quarterly basis**, the months which end the quarters depending on the type of business. A business may, however, arrange for its VAT quarters to coincide with its own accounting quarters. If VAT repayment claims normally arise (because input VAT normally exceeds output VAT), **a business can apply for monthly accounting in order to improve its own cash flow**. All VAT returns and payments must be made within one month of the end of the relevant period, and you should note that substantial penalties can be imposed on any business which is persistently late in paying VAT.

The normal accounting system for VAT ignores the time when cash is received from debtors and paid to suppliers. Small businesses, in particular, can suffer cash flow problems from the need to account for VAT before receiving payment from customers. Consequently, **taxable persons with an annual taxable turnover of up to £350,000 are entitled to use the cash accounting scheme. Users of the scheme account for VAT on the basis of cash receipts and payments**. This ensures that automatic bad debt relief is given and that VAT never has to be accounted on a supply before a customer has paid for it. Once in the cash accounting scheme a business will only have to leave if it's turnover in a particular year exceeds the built-in tolerance limit of £437,500 and also exceeds £350,000 in the following twelve months.

An entirely **separate scheme, available when annual taxable turnover does not exceed £300,000, is the annual accounting scheme. This is designed to reduce the compliance burden on small businesses by requiring only one VAT return each year. However, throughout the year they make payments on account of the ultimate liability under direct debits**. If annual turnover is £100,000 or more, the business must pay 90% of the previous year's net VAT liability during the year by means of nine monthly payments starting at the end of the fourth month of the year. If taxable turnover in the previous year was up to £100,000, four quarterly payments are required, each of 20% of the previous year's net VAT liability, starting at the end of the fourth month of the year. However, if the net VAT liability for the previous year is below £2,000, the trader need not make any interim payments.

At the end of the year the trader completes an annual VAT return which must be submitted to HM Customs and Excise along with any payment due by two months after the end of the year.

Records

You will have to **keep VAT records for up to six years** including:

(a) details of all input and output VAT together with invoices (copies of invoices issued);

(b) details of all credits given or received together with credit notes (copies of credit notes issued);

(c) details of errors or corrections;

(d) details of any self-supplies;

(e) a detailed VAT ledger account.

(f) all other documentation relating to purchases and sales, such as day books.

Finally, we enclose copies of the relevant VAT booklets which you will need. We hope that you have found the information in this letter helpful but if you have any queries, please let us know.

Yours faithfully

ABC Certified Accountants

35 SCHOONER LTD

Tutor's hints. Take care with written questions to answer all parts of the question.

Examiner's comments. Many candidates failed to score high marks in part (b) because they did not deal with each aspect of the question separately.

(a) The deemed time of supply of goods is known as the tax point. The **basic tax point is the date on which the goods are removed or made available to the customer.** If a VAT invoice **is issued or payment is received** before the basic tax point, the earlier of these dates automatically becomes the tax point. If the earlier date rule does not apply and if the **VAT invoice is issued within 14 days after the basic tax point, the invoice date becomes the tax point** (although the trader can elect to use the basic point for all his supplies if he wishes).

Schooner will account for output tax on the deposit of £50,000 and on the payment on account of £100,000 on the quarterly return for the period during which the payments are received. The total output tax to be accounted for on this return will be £22,340 (17.5/117.5 × £150,000). Output VAT on the balance of the payment £38,910 (£350,000 × 17.5% – £22,340) will be accounted for on the following quarterly return.

(b) (i) **The equipment bought outright and the equipment bought on hire purchase will attract first year allowances** of £180,000 (40% (£250,000 + £200,000)). These first year allowances will be deducted in computing the Schedule D Case I profits for the year ended 31 December 2000.

The annual charge of £145,000 incurred in respect of the leased equipment will be deducible in computing schedule D Case I profits for the year to 31 December 2000. **In addition, the total financing charge** of £76,000 (£276,000 – £200,000) **incurred over the life of the hire purchase contract will be deductible in computing schedule D Case I profits.** The amount to be deducted in the year to 31 December 2000 will be the same as the amount that is deducted in computing the profits for accounts purposes on normal accounting principles.

(ii) **VAT of £28,000 (£17.5% × £160,000) will have to be accounted for as output VAT in respect of the equipment which is acquired from other EU countries. However, this VAT may also be treated as input VAT on the same VAT return so there is no overall cash flow effect. VAT** of £15,750 (£90,000 × 17.5%) **will have to be accounted for in respect of the equipment imported from outside the EU at the point of entry into the UK. This amount can then be deducted as input VAT on the next VAT return.**

Deductible input VAT of £35,000 (£200,000 × 17.5%) will be incurred in respect of the hire purchase equipment. In addition, deductible input VAT of £25,375 (£145,000 × 17.5%) per annum will be incurred on the lease rental payments.

(c) (i) As the loan from Alex Barnacle will be interest free, it will have no effect on Schooner Ltd's schedule D Case I profits.

As the debenture will be issued for trading purposes, interest of £30,000 (£300,000 × 10%) will be deductible in computing schedule D Case I profits in the year to 31 December 2000. In addition, the 5% discount of £15,000 and the professional fees of £8,000 will be deductible for Schedule D Case I purposes over the life of the debenture. Using the accruals basis this means that £4,600 (£23,000/5) will be deductible in the year to 31 December 2000.

Schooner Ltd will not be able to obtain a Schedule D Case I deduction in respect of any costs associated with the share issue.

(ii) As Schooner Ltd is a close company Alex will be able to obtain tax relief for the interest paid on the loan as a charge on income. This means that the interest will be deductible in computing Alex's statutory total income.

It is assumed that, as Schooner Ltd is an unquoted trading company, the shares will be issued under the Enterprise Investment Scheme (EIS). This means that Chloe Dhow will be entitled to tax relief on the first £150,000 of her investment. The relief will be given as a tax reducer equal to the lower of £30,000 and Chloe's income tax liability for 1999/00. There will be no tax reduction in respect of the additional £30,000 invested.

If the EIS shares are held for five years there will in addition be relief from capital gains tax as any gain arising is exempt.

Marking guide

			Marks
(a)	*Tax point*		
	Goods removed or made available		1
	Invoice issued or payment received		1
	Issue of invoice within 14 days		1
	Output VAT		
	Payments on account		1
	Balance of output tax		1
		Maximum/available	5
(b)	*Effect on Schedule D Case I profits*		
	First year allowances		2
	Lease rental payment		1
	Finance charge		2
	VAT		
	EU acquisition		2
	Non EU importation		2
	VAT – leasing		1
	VAT – hire purchase		1
		Available	11
		Maximum	9
(c)	*Schedule D Case I profits*		
	Personal loan		1
	Debenture interest		1
	Discount/incidental costs		2
	Shares and incidental costs		2
	Tax relief		
	Charge on income		2
	Relief under the EIS		5
		Available	13
		Maximum	11
		Maximum	25

36 HIGHRISE LTD

> **Tutor's hint.** Your first step should have been to work out the profits that would be included in each set of accounts. Only then should you consider the corporation tax accounting periods.
>
> *Other points.* Schedule A losses for companies are relieved in the same way as management expenses:
>
> - first they are set off against non-Schedule A income and gains of the company for the current period; and any excess
> - is carried forward for set off against future income (of all descriptions); or
> - is available for surrender as group relief
>
> **Examiner's comments.** Many candidates gave away easy marks by not mentioning the due dates of the different mainstream corporation tax liabilities.

(a) **One set of accounts for the eighteen months to 31 December 1999**

If one set of accounts is prepared, the tax adjusted Schedule D Case I profits before capital allowances arising in the eighteen months to 31 December 1999 will be £432,000 (£141,000 + £126,000 + £165,000).

For corporation tax purposes **there will be two accounting periods, one covering the first twelve months and the other covering the balancing period of six months.** As a result corporation tax will be payable as follows:

	Year to 30 June 1999 £	Six months to 31 December 1999 £
Schedule D profits before capital allowances (12:6)	288,000	144,000
Capital allowances (W1)	(35,000)	(7,500)
	253,000	136,500
Schedule A (W2)	22,000	0
Chargeable gain (£42,000 – £38,000)	4,000	0
PCTCT	279,000	136,500

Corporation tax

	£	£
£279,000 × 21% × 9/12	43,943	
£279,000 × 20% × 3/12	13,950	
£136,500 × 20%	-	27,300
	57,893	27,300

£57,893 will be due and payable by 1 April 2000 and £27,300 will be due and payable by 1 October 2000.

Two sets of accounts

Tax adjusted trading profits included in accounts prepared for the six months to 31 December 1998 will be £141,000 and the tax adjusted profits included in the accounts for the twelve months to 31 December 1999 will be £291,000 (£126,000 + £165,000).

The corporation tax computations resulting from each set of accounts will be

	Six months to 31 December 1998 £	Year to 31 December 1999 £
Schedule D profits before capital allowances	141,000	291,000
Capital allowances (W1)	(2,500)	(34,375)
	138,500	256,625
Schedule A (W2)	30,000	0
Chargeable gain (W3)	42,000	0
	210,500	256,625
Less: Schedule A loss	–	(8,000)
	210,500	248,625

Corporation tax

	£	£
£210,500 × 31% (W4)	65,255	0
Less: (£750,000 – £210,500) × 1/40	(13,488)	0
£248,625 × 21% × 3/12	0	13,053
£248,625 × 20% × 9/12	0	37,294
Mainstream corporation tax	51,767	50,347

£51,767 will be due and payable by 1 October 1999 and £50,347 will be due and payable by 1 October 2000.

The company should be advised to prepare one set of accounts as the total tax liability is £16,921 (£51,767 + £50,347 – £57,893 – £27,300) smaller.

Workings

1   **Capital allowances**

   Separate capital allowance computations are required for each corporation tax accounting period.

   One set of accounts

   Year to 30 June 1999

	£	£	Allowances £
TWDV b/f		20,000	
WDA @ 25%		(5,000)	5,000
		15,000	
Addition qualifying for FYA	75,000		
FYA @ 40%	(30,000)		30,000
		45,000	
		60,000	35,000

   Six months to 31 December 1999

WDA at 25% × 6/12		(7,500)	7,500
		52,500	

   Two sets of accounts

   Six months 31 December 1998

	£	
TWDV b/f	20,000	
WDA at 25% × 6/12	(2,500)	£2,500
	17,500	

   Year to 31 December 1999

	£	£	£
WDA at 25%		(4,375)	4,375
Addition qualifying for FYA	75,000		
FYA @ 40%	(30,000)		30,000
		45,000	
		58,125	34,375

2   **Schedule A**

   The company's Schedule A profits are computed on an accruals basis. Profits and losses on all properties are pooled.

   One set of accounts

   12 months to 30.6.99

	£
Bodford (£48,000 × 6/12)	24,000
Ampton (£1,000 × 10)	10,000
Redecoration	(12,000)
Schedule A	22,000

There is no Schedule A income in the six months to 31.12.99 as both buildings have been sold.

Two sets of accounts

Six months to 31.12.98

The building at Ampton will be let until 31 December 1998 so the schedule A income accruing in the six months to 31 December 1998 will be £48,000 × 6/12 = £24,000 and there was no income accruing after this.

The building at Bodford will be let for £1,000 a month, so the rental income accruing in the six months to 31.12.98 is £1,000 × 6 = £6,000.

	£
Ampton	24,000
Bodford	6,000
Schedule A	30,000

Year ended 31.12.99

	£
Ampton (sold)	-
Bodford	
Rent accruing (£1,000 × 4)	4,000
Redecoration	(12,000)
Schedule A loss	(8,000)

A company's Schedule A loss can be set against its non-Schedule A income and gains arising in the same period.

3 **Allowable loss**

Capital losses can be set against gains in the same or future accounting periods only. They can not be carried back.

4 **Rate of tax**

Six months to 31 December 1998

Upper limit is £1,500,000 × 6/12 = £750,000.
Lower limit is £300,000 × 6/12 = £150,000
PCTCT = £210,500
'Profits' = £210,500

As profits are between the lower and upper limits, marginal relief applies.

(b) Highrise Ltd's acquisition of Shortie Ltd will mean that it will be possible for Shortie Ltd to group relieve some of the loss forecast for the year to 31 March 2000. The maximum loss available for group relief will be the lower of:

(i) £38,750 (£155,000 × 3/12)

(ii) 3/12 of Highrise Ltd's PCTCT for the year to 31 December 2000.

If within three years of the acquisition of Shortie Ltd there is a major change in the nature or conduct of Shortie Ltd's trade it will not be possible for Shortie Ltd to carry forward any schedule D Case I losses that arose before the change in ownership.

Shortie Ltd's capital loss of £37,000 is a pre-entry loss. It will also be necessary to ascertain the amount of the unrealised pre-entry loss attributable to the investment in Minute Ltd. This can either be done on a time basis when the shareholding is disposed of, or based on the market value of the shareholding as at 1 January 2000. It will not be possible for Highrise Ltd to utilise the pre-entry capital losses against any gain arising on the disposal of its 5% shareholding in Tiny Ltd, by transferring the shareholding to Shortie Ltd (no gain no loss) prior to disposal outside of the group.

37 BARGAINS LTD

> **Tutor's hint.** The rules treating benefits to participators in close companies as distributions only apply when the normal Schedule E rules taxing benefits do not apply.
>
> **Examiner's comment.** Many candidates ignored the fact that the cars were only provided for nine months.

(a) (i) The company's first accounting period will run from the start of trade on 1 April 1999 to its accounting date, 31 December 1999. **Any deductible pre-trading expenditure will be treated as incurred on the first day of trading,** and will therefore be deductible in this accounting period.

(ii) The **pre-trading expenditure on advertising will be deductible** for corporation tax purposes. The **expenditure on refurbishment will also be deductible except to the extent that it is capital expenditure.** Expenditure needed to make the premises fit for use will be capital expenditure (*Law Shipping Co Ltd v CIR 1923*). Expenditure leading to significant improvements, such as the installation of a heating system where there was none before, will also be capital expenditure. Expenditure on routine repairs and redecoration, on the other hand, will be revenue expenditure.

The VAT incurred on both the advertising expenditure and the refurbishment expenditure will be recoverable, because it is VAT on services supplied not more than six months before registration.

(b) Rodney and Reggie will be taxed under Schedule E as follows.

Rodney: £10,575 * 25% * 9/12 = £1,983 (annual business mileage 2,100 * 12/9 = 2,800)

Reggie: £10,575 * 15% * 9/12 = £1,190 (annual business mileage 14,400 × 12/9 = 19,200)

There will be no Schedule E charge on Del, but the provision of a car to him will be treated as a distribution of £10,575 * 35% * 9/12 = £2,776 net. Del will be taxed as if he had received a dividend of this amount, giving him gross income of £2,776 * 100/90 = £3,084, a tax credit of £308 and no further tax liability unless he is a higher rate taxpayer. The actual cost of providing the car will be a disallowable expense for the company. The company will be treated as though it had paid a dividend of £3,084. Any motor expenses incurred by the company in respect of Del's car will be disallowable.

The VAT on the cars will not be recoverable because of the private use. Capital allowances will be available on the full cost (including VAT) of the cars provided for Rodney and Reggie, but not on the cost of the car provided for Del because its provision is treated as a distribution. The annual writing down allowances will be 25% on a reducing balance basis. Because the first accounting period is only 9 months long, the allowance in that period will be 2 × £10,575 * 25% * 9/12 = £3,966. Any motor expenses incurred by the company in respect of servicing, insurance and general running of both Rodney and Reggie's cars will be tax deductible for the company.

(c) On making the loan to Del, the company will become liable to account for an amount of tax of £42,000 * 25% = £10,500. This is, in general, due nine months after the end of the accounting period, so it is due by 1 October 2000. However, if the company becomes a large company the tax will be subject to the quarterly payments on account regime. This tax is recovered when the loan is repaid.

Del will only be taxed on the loan as income to the extent that it is written off. He will then be treated as receiving a net dividend equal to the amount written off.

Del will, however, be treated as receiving (and the company will be treated as paying) a dividend equal to the Schedule E benefit for interest-free loans. This will be the interest which Del would have had to pay at the official rate. The tax consequences will be the same as for the deemed distribution in respect of Del's car.

(d) The company will use the VAT secondhand scheme. The input VAT on an item bought for resale will not be recovered, but the output VAT on its sale will be (gross selling price - gross purchase price) * 7/47. There is no output VAT when an item is sold at a loss.

38 TARGET LTD

> **Tutor's hint.** In parts (a) and (b) it was important to spot that Target Ltd would become a consortium company.
>
> **Prizewinner's point.** Note that under FRS 4 *Capital instruments* the debenture interest, discount and incidental costs should have been written off so as to achieve a constant rate on the outstanding balance in each period. However, the calculations below were those expected from candidates.
>
> **Examiner's comments.** The loan relationship aspects were generally not well answered. This was disappointing since this topic was dealt with in the Finance Act article published in the Students' Newsletter written specifically for this paper.

(a) **One third of Target Ltd's ordinary share capital acquired**

Target Ltd	£
Schedule D Case I	nil
Capital gain	51,300
Less s 393A Loss relief (W1)	51,300
PCTCT	-

Expansion Ltd	£
Schedule D Case I	214,000
Schedule D Case III (£120,000 × 8% × 8/12)	6,400
	220,400
Less: consortium relief (W)	(14,400)
PCTCT	206,000

Corporation tax	£
£206,000 at 21% × 3/12	10,815
£206,000 × 20% × 9/12	30,900
Less: Income tax suffered (£6,400 × 20%)	1,280
MCT	40,435

Capital loss c/f £9,600

Working

If Expansion Ltd acquires one third of Target it will become a consortium member on 1 July 1999 since Target Ltd is a consortium company. Target Ltd is able to surrender one third of its trading loss to Expansion Ltd. Target Ltd must take into account its own current year profits when calculating the surrender. Only the current year loss can be surrendered, and this is restricted to the corresponding period of 1 July 1999 to 31 December 1999.

	£
Target Ltd's loss	137,700
Utilised itself under S 393A	(51,300)
	86,400
Available to consortium members (one third per member)	28,800

Time apportion £28,800 × 6/12 in order to calculate share of loss for Expansion Ltd in the year to 31.12.99.

Brought forward trading losses can not be surrendered or set against chargeable gains. Trading losses of £9,200 will remain to be carried forward.

(b) **Two thirds of Target Ltd's ordinary share capital acquired**

Target Ltd will become an associated company of Expansion Ltd and the lower and upper limits for corporation tax purposes are therefore £150,000 and £750,000 respectively.

Target Ltd

Target Ltd's mainstream corporation tax position will be the same as in part (a) above.

Expansion Ltd	£
Schedule D Case I profit	214,000
Schedule D Case III	6,400
	220,400
Less: Consortium relief (£28,800 × 2 × 6/12)	28,800
PCTCT	191,600
FY98	
Corporation tax £191,600 × 31% × 3/12	14,849
Less: marginal relief: 1/40 (750,000 – 191,600) × 3/12	(3,490)
FY99	
Corporation tax at £191,600 × 30% × 9/12	43,110
Less: marginal relief: 1/40 (750,000 – 191,600) × 9/12	(10,470)
	43,999
Less: income tax suffered	1,280
MCT	42,719
Capital loss c/f	£9,600

(c) **All of Target Ltd's ordinary share capital acquired**

Target Ltd and Expansion Ltd will be members of the same group relief group and also of the same capital gains group.

Target Ltd

Target Ltd's mainstream corporation tax position will be the same as in part (a) above.

Expansion Ltd	£
Schedule D Case I (W2)	199,225
Schedule D Case III	6,400
Capital gain (W1)	3,225
	208,850
Less group relief (£137,700 × 6/12)	68,850
PCTCT	140,000

Corporation tax	£
£140,000 at 21% × 3/12	7,350
£140,000 × 20% × 9/12	21,000
Less: Income tax suffered	1,280
MCT	27,070

1 **Chargeable gains**

Target Ltd should transfer the office building to Expansion Ltd. This transfer will be on a no gain/no loss basis and the gain of £51,300 will be realised by Expansion Ltd on disposal of the office outside the group. £38,475 (£51,300 × ¾) of this gain can be rolled over into the base cost of the new factory to be acquired in January 2000.

	£
Capital gain	51,300
Less rolled over (75% business use)	38,475
	12,825
Capital losses b/f	9,600
Gain remaining chargeable	3,225

Tutorial note. There is full reinvestment of the sale proceeds relating to the business part of the office £105,000 (£140,000 × ¾), so all of the gain on this part of the building is rolled over.

2 **Schedule D Case I**

The loan relationship legislation does not define 'trading purposes'. If the debenture issue is for trading purposes, then the debenture interest, the 3% discount and the incidental costs of obtaining the finance will be deductible Schedule DI expenses. Expansion Ltd's Schedule D Case I profit for the year ended 31 December 1999 will be:

	£
Previous Schedule DI profit	214,000
Debenture interest (£250,000 at 10% × 6/12)	(12,500)
Discount (£250,000 × 3% = £7,500) × 6/60	(750)
Incidental costs (£15,250 × 6/60)	(1,525)
Revised Schedule DI profit	199,225

Tutorial note. If the issue of debentures is not for trading purposes, then there will be a net loss on loan relationships of £8,375 (£6,400 − £12,500 − £750 − £1,525). Expansion Ltd's PCTCT would (as above) be:

	£
Schedule DI profit	214,000
Capital gain	3,225
	217,225
Less loss on loan relationships	8,375
	208,850
Less group relief (£137,700 × 6/12)	68,850
PCTCT	140,000

Either of these approaches would be acceptable. The former is followed in this answer.

Marking guide	Marks
One third of ordinary share capital acquired	
Target Ltd	1
Schedule DI/Schedule DII	2
Consortium relief	3
Corporation tax	1
Income tax	1
Two thirds of ordinary share capital acquired	
Schedule DI/Schedule DIII	1
Consortium relief	1
Corporation tax	2
Income tax	1
All of ordinary share capital acquired	
Transfer of office building	1
Rollover relief	2
Calculation of gain	2
Issue of debentures	3
Schedule DI profit	2
Group relief	1
Corporation tax	1
Available/Maximum	25

39 HYDRA LTD

Tutor's hint. Presentation is important in a question like this. Look carefully at how we have set out part (a).

Examiner's comment. The trading loss brought forward and the capital loss caused problems for a number of candidates with both being subject to group relief claims.

(a) MAINSTREAM CORPORATION TAX LIABILITIES

	Hydra Ltd £	Boa Ltd £	Cobra Ltd £	Mamba Ltd £
Schedule DI profit	0	120,000	85,000	0
Capital gain (W1)	70,000	0	0	8,000
	70,000	120,000	85,000	8,000
Trade charge	(20,000)	0	0	0
	50,000	120,000	85,000	8,000
Group relief				
Hydra Ltd (W2)		(45,000)		
Mamba Ltd (W2)			(10,000)	
PCTCT	50,000	75,000	75,000	8,000
	£	£	£	£
MCT at 20%	10,000	15,000	15,000	1,600
Trading loss c/f	£15,000			
Capital loss c/f			£15,000	

Workings

1. Roll-over relief has been claimed in respect of Hydra Ltd's capital gain, based on the replacement asset purchased by Boa Ltd. Since the proceeds from the disposal of Hydra Ltd's factory were £350,000, and the new office building purchased by Boa Ltd only cost £280,000, £70,000 of Hydra Ltd's capital gain is immediately chargeable.

2. There are four associated companies in the group, so the small companies' limit is £75,000 (£300,000/4)

Mamba Ltd is a 75% subsidiary of Cobra Ltd, but is not a 75% subsidiary of Hydra Ltd (80% × 80% = 64%). Mamba Ltd's trading loss can therefore only be surrendered to Cobra Ltd

Hydra Ltd's trading loss of £45,000 has been surrendered to Boa Ltd in order to obtain relief at the marginal rate and bring its profits down to the lower limit of £75,000.

(b) Currently, Mamba Ltd is only a 64% (80% × 80%) subsidiary of Hydra Ltd which means that the two companies do not form a group relief group and Mamba Ltd can only surrender its losses to Cobra Ltd. The result of transferring the shareholding in Mamba Ltd to Hydra Ltd is that all four companies would then be in the same group for group relief purposes. This would give Mamba Ltd the flexibility of being able to transfer trading losses to (or from) any of the other group companies.

No chargeable gain or allowable loss would arise on the transfer. The companies would remain within the same capital gains group so any intra-group transfers of assets would still take place on a no gain/no loss basis. It would, therefore, probably be beneficial to make the transfer.

(c) **The formation of a VAT group**

Two or more companies under common control can be treated as members of a VAT group provided that each of them either is resident in the UK or has an established place of business in the UK, and:

(i) one of them controls each of the others;

(ii) one person (which could be an individual or a holding company) controls all of them; or

(iii) two or more persons carrying on a business in partnership control all of them.

The consequences of group registration are as follows.

(i) The group must appoint a **representative member which must account for the group's output VAT and input VAT**. However, all members of the group are jointly and severally liable for any VAT due from the representative member.

(ii) **Any supply of goods or services by a member of the group to another member of the group is normally disregarded for VAT purposes.** A supply is not disregarded unless the companies concerned stay in the same VAT group until after the goods are removed or made available, or the services are performed.

(iii) Any other supply of goods or services by or to a group member is normally treated as a supply by or to the representative member.

(iv) Any VAT payable on the import of goods by a group member is payable by the representative member.

Desirability of including Mamba Ltd in the VAT group

As Mamba Ltd makes zero-rated supplies, then VAT repayment claims would normally arise. In such circumstances it can apply for monthly accounting in order to improve its cash flow position.

If Mamba Ltd is included in the group registration, no such benefit will be available as it is likely that the group as a whole will be in a net VAT paying position each period. Whilst this may reduce the administration burden on Mamba Ltd, it will not get the same cash flow benefit.

40 ONGOING LTD

> **Tutor's hint.** A loss can normally be carried back to set against profits of the previous twelve months. However, a loss and any trade charges arising in the twelve months prior to the cessation of trade can be carried back to set against the profits of the previous 36 months.
>
> **Examiner's comment.** In part (a) too many candidates did not know how to deal with the loss relief claim under s 393A ICTA 1988 where there were two trading losses.

(a) (i)

	Year to 30.6.96 £	Year to 30.6.97 £	6 mths to 31.12.97 £	Year to 31.12.98 £	Year to 31.12.99 £	Year to 31.12.00 £
Schedule D Case I	88,500	59,000	62,500	47,000	0	0
Schedule A	6,000	0	1,500	0	0	0
Capital gain (W1)	0	0	0	0	0	58,800
	94,500	59,000	64,000	47,000	0	58,800
Less: s 393 A current (W2)	0	0	0	0	0	(58,800)
Less: trade charges	(12,000)	(12,000)	(6,000)	(12,000)	0	0
	82,500	47,000	58,000	35,000	0	0
Less: s 393A carryback (W3)	0	(29,500)	(58,000)	(35,000)	0	0
	82,500	17,500	0	0	0	0
Less: non-trade charges	0	0	0	0	0	0
PCTCT	82,500	17,500	0	0	0	0
MCT @ 24.75%	£20,419					
MCT @ 23.25%		£4,069				

(ii) The following corporation tax refunds will be due resulting from the s 393A loss relief claims.

Original MCT before loss relief

	Period ended 30.6.97 £	Period ended 31.12.97 £	Period ended 31.12.98 £
Schedule D Case I	59,000	62,500	47,000
Schedule A	-	1,500	-
Trade charges	(12,000)	(6,000)	(12,000)
Non-trade charges	-	(1,000)	(1,000)
PCTCT	47,000	57,000	34,000
MCT 24%	8,460		
MCT 21%	2,468	11,970	7,140
Original MCT	10,928	11,970	7,140
MCT after s 393A relief	(4,069)	-	-
Tax refund due	6,859	11,970	7,140

(iii) **Ongoing Ltd - year ended 31 March 2001**

	£
Schedule D Case I (£93,000 – £12,000)	81,000
Less: s 393(1) relief	(14,500)
	66,500
Schedule D Case III	3,500
	70,000
Less: Group relief (W4)	(52,500)
PCTCT	17,500
CT @ 20%	£3,500

(b) (i) For accounting periods ending after 30 June 1999 **companies that are subject to the full rate of corporation tax will have to pay their corporation**

tax liability in quarterly instalments. For the first accounting period to which this applies, 60% of the corporation tax liability is due by instalments with the remaining 40% being due nine months after the end of the period. The position for Hazell Ltd is as follows.

Year ended 30 June 2000

CT liability	
£2,000,000 × 30% (FY99)	£600,000
Due instalments (£600,000 × 60%)	£360,000

The instalments will be £360,000 × ¼ = £90,000 and were due for payment on:
14 January 2000
14 April 2000
14 July 2000
14 October 2000

The balance of £240,000 is due on 1 April 2001.

(ii) As a notice requiring a return was received in good time, Hazell Ltd will, under self assessment, be required to submit its return and accounts to the Revenue within twelve months of the end of the accounting period, ie by 30 June 2001. Assuming that the return is filed on time, the Revenue will have until 30 June 2002 to give written notice that they are going to enquire into it.

Workings

1   **Chargeable gains**

	y/e 31.12.98	y/e 31.12.00
	£	£
Gain	10,800	72,000
Less: loss b/f	(10,800)	(13,200)
Chargeable gain	nil	58,800

2   **Loss relief y/e 31.12.99**

	£
Loss	68,000
S 393A relief y/e 31.12.99	-
y/e 31.12.98	(35,000)
Unrelieved on cessation of trade	33,000

All charges paid in the year to 31.12.99 are also unrelieved on the cessation of trade.

3   **Loss relief - y/e 31.12.00**

	£
Loss	140,000
Less: S 393A relief y/e 31.12.00	(58,800)
Add: unrelieved charges of final period	11,250
	92,450
Less: s 393A carryback y/e 31.12.99	0
y/e 31.12.98	0
6 m/e 31.12.97	(58,000)
6/12 of y/e 30.6.97	(29,500)
Unrelieved	4,950

In addition, the non-trade charges paid in the final year remain unrelieved on cessation.

Tutorial note. As the trade has ceased trade charges paid in this period are added to the loss carried back.

4 Group relief

Ongoing Ltd can claim to reduce profits in the year ended 31 March 2001 by any of Goodbye Ltd's losses that arose in the 'corresponding period'. The 'corresponding period' in respect of Goodbye Ltd's loss for the year to 31 December 2000 is 1.4.00 to 31.12.00. Therefore, the maximum group relief claim is the lower of:

(i) Available profits £70,000 × 9/12 = £52,500

(ii) Available losses £140,000 × 9/12 = £105,000

Marking guide		Marks	
(a)	(i) Schedule A/Chargeable gains	1	
	Use of y/e 31.12.99 loss	1	
	y/e 31.12.99 trade charges not used	1	
	y/e 31.12.00: current period relief	1	
	Add final period charges to loss	1	
	6 m/e 31.12.97 relief	1	
	y/e 30.6.97 (50% relief)	2	
	CT liabilities	2	
	Available/Maximum		10
	(ii) PCTCT for each year	1	
	Refunds: y/e 30.6.97	1	
	6 m/e 31.12.97	1	
	y/e 31.12.98	1	
	Available/Maximum		4
	(iii) Schedule D I	½	
	S 393(1) relief	½	
	Schedule D III	½	
	Group relief	1½	
	Corporation tax	1	
	Available/Maximum		4
(b)	Estimated CT liability	1	
	Large companies pay by instalments for periods ending after 30.6.99	1	
	60% due by instalments	1	
	Due dates for instalments	1	
	Due date for balance	1	
	Filing date	1	
	Enquiries	1	
	Available/Maximum		7
			25

41 OCEAN PLC

Tutor's hint. When a question specifies a structure for your answer, you should use it. The structure will make your task a lot easier.

Examiner's comment. Several candidates did not appreciate the difference between selling a subsidiary and selling its assets.

(a) **Tax implications for Ocean plc**

(i) **Capital gains**

Ocean plc will have chargeable gains on its disposals of shares in Tarn Ltd and Loch Ltd. It is not selling its shares in Pool Ltd, so will not have a chargeable gain there.

(ii) **Group status**

Tarn Ltd will cease to be a subsidiary for all purposes from the date of disposal. Group relief should be available to Ocean plc for Tarn Ltd's losses up to the date of disposal, unless there were arrangements to sell Tarn Ltd before that date. The losses up to the date of disposal will be computed on a time-apportioned basis unless the result would be unfair or unreasonable.

Loch Ltd's position in relation to the Ocean plc group will be the same except that it will become a consortium-owned company, giving Ocean plc access to 60% of Loch Ltd's post-disposal losses.

Tarn Ltd and Pool Ltd (dormant) will cease to count as associated companies from the end of the accounting period of disposal.

(iii) **VAT**

Loch Ltd will be able to remain in any Ocean plc VAT group. Tarn Ltd will have to leave any such VAT group.

(b) **Tax implications for Tarn Ltd, Loch Ltd and Pool Ltd**

(i) **Capital gains**

Tarn Ltd will have chargeable gains on shops transferred to it from Ocean plc within the six years before the sale of shares. The gains will be computed as if it had sold the shops at the times of transfer for their then market values. The gains will, however, be included in Tarn Ltd's chargeable profits for the accounting period of the sale of shares.

Pool Ltd will have chargeable gains or allowable losses in respect of the sale of its assets. Rollover relief against acquisitions by other members of the Ocean plc group may be available. Alternatively, if other companies in that group have allowable losses, assets standing at a gain could be routed through those other companies to use their losses.

(ii) **VAT**

Pool Ltd, being dormant, will have to de-register. If it transfers it business as a going concern and Sea plc is registered for VAT, that transfer will be outside the scope of VAT.

(iii) **Trading losses**

Tarn Ltd and Loch Ltd will be able to carry forward their losses against future profits from the same trade. However, in the case of Tarn Ltd (the control of which is changing) the carry-forward of losses will be denied if, within three years before or after the transfer, there is a major change in the nature or conduct of its trade.

Pool Ltd will lose the benefit of any losses which it cannot use against profits of the current period or earlier periods.

(iv) **Capital allowances**

Pool Ltd will have balancing adjustment (allowances or charges) on the assets it sells where it has had capital allowances on those assets.

(c) **Tax implications for Sea plc**

(i) **Capital gains**

Sea plc will have base costs for the shares and assets equal to the price its pays.

(ii) **Group status**

Tarn Ltd will become a subsidiary for all tax purposes. Sea plc will be able to claim group relief for Tarn Ltd's losses from the date of purchase. Tarn Ltd will also count as an associated company from the start of the accounting period.

Loch Ltd will become a consortium-owned company, allowing Sea plc to claim relief for 40% of Loch Ltd's loss.

(iii) **VAT**

Tarn Ltd will be able to join any Sea plc VAT group.

(iv) **Capital allowances**

Sea plc will be able to claim capital allowances on the qualifying assets which it buys from Pool Ltd.

42 STAR LTD

Tutor's hints. This is a very common type of question. Ensure that you can answer it well.

Examiner's comments. This was a popular question and most candidates had few problems with parts (a) and (b).

(a)

	Star Ltd £	Zodiac Ltd £	Exotic Ltd £
Schedule D Case I	-	650,000	130,000
Capital gain	130,000	-	-
Charges on income	(10,000)		
	120,000	650,000	130,000
Less: S393A relief	(20,000)		
Less: group relief (W)		(60,000)	(45,000)
Profits chargeable to corporation tax	100,000	590,000	85,000
Dividends plus tax credit (FII)			15,000
'Profits'	100,000	590,000	100,000
CT @ 20%	20,000		17,000
CT @ 30%		177,000	

Star Ltd's brought forward trading losses of £7,500 and Zodiac Ltd's capital loss of £8,000 remain to be carried forward.

Working

1. There are three associated companies so the lower and upper limits are £100,000 and £500,000 respectively. Star Ltd's loss should initially be set against its own profits to relieve the £20,000 that would otherwise be taxed at the marginal rate of 32.5%. Next £45,000 should be surrendered to Exotic Ltd, to bring profits down to the lower limit. The balance of the loss should be surrendered to Zodiac Ltd where it will save tax at the full rate.

(b) (i) **As the proceeds of the sale of the warehouse will be reinvested within 36 months of sale rollover relief will potentially be available.** Part of the gain equal to the proceeds not reinvested, £90,000, will be immediately chargeable if the freehold office is acquired. The remaining gain of £40,000 could be rolled over by deducting it from the base cost of the office.

None of the gain will be immediately chargeable if the leasehold office is acquired as all of the proceeds will be reinvested. However, as the leasehold is a depreciating asset the gain will not be deducted from the base cost of the new asset. Instead, it will be deferred or held over until the earlier of:

(1) 10 years after acquisition of the leasehold
(2) the date the leasehold ceases to be used in the trade
(3) the date of sale of the leasehold.

Zodiac Ltd and Star Ltd are members of the same capital gains group so rollover relief will be available if Zodiac Ltd purchases a freehold warehouse. As all of the sale proceeds would be reinvested, no gain would be immediately chargeable but the base cost of Zodiac Ltd's warehouse will be reduced by £130,000.

(ii) Whichever of the claims are made, Star Ltd's profits will fall below the small companies' limit. This means that Star Ltd should not relieve any of its loss under s393A ICTA 1988 but that it should increase the amount of the loss surrendered to Zodiac Ltd by £20,000 where 30% relief will be obtained.

If none of the gain is immediately chargeable, Star Ltd will also have unrelieved trade charges of £10,000. These will be carried forward for relief against future Schedule D Case I profits.

(c) **The inclusion of Exotic Ltd in the group VAT registration results in the group being partially exempt, thus restricting the recovery of input tax on the overhead expenditure of £450,000.**

$$\frac{\text{Taxable supplies}}{\text{Total supplies}} = \frac{1,900,000 + 1,800,000}{1,900,000 + 1,800,000 + 950,000} = 79.57\% = 80\% \text{ (round up to nearest whole number)}.$$

The irrecoverable input is therefore £15,750 (£450,000 × 17.5% = £78,750 × 20% (100 − 80)).

If Exotic Ltd is excluded from the group VAT registration, Star Ltd will have to charge output tax on its management fee of £50,000. Exotic Ltd cannot register for VAT (it does not make any taxable supplies), and so will be unable to recover this as input tax. The additional VAT cost is £8,750 (£50,000 × 17.5%).

The exclusion of Exotic Ltd from the VAT group throughout the year ended 31 March 2000 would therefore have reduced the group's overall VAT liability by £7,000 (£15,750 − £8,750).

		Marks
Marking guide		
(a) Schedule DI profit		1
Capital gain/Charge on income		1
Lower and upper limits		1
Loss relief- S 393A		1
Group relief		2
FII/profit		1
Corporation tax		1
Losses carried forward		<u>1</u>
	Available/Maximum	9
(b) Reinvestment within three years		1
Freehold office building		
Immediate gain		1
Base cost		1
Leasehold office building		
Whole gain rolled over		1
Depreciating asset		1
Date of sale/Ten years/ceasing to be used		1
Freehold warehouse		
Same capital gains group		1
Rollover/deduct from base cost		1
Loss relief		
Profits less than £100,000		1
Additional surrender		1
Charge on income		<u>1</u>
	Available	11
	Maximum	10
(c) Partially exempt group		1
Calculation of irrecoverable VAT		2
VAT on £50,000 fee		1
VAT on management fee irrecoverable		1
Conclusion		<u>1</u>
	Maximum	<u>6</u>
	Maximum	<u>25</u>

43 TUTORIAL QUESTION: DOUBLE TAXATION RELIEF FOR INDIVIDUALS

(a) MR POIROT: UK INCOME TAX LIABILITY

Mr Poirot is UK resident and ordinarily resident for 1999/00 but he is not UK domiciled. His 1999/00 income tax liability is as follows.

	Non-savings	Savings (excl dividend)
	£	£
Schedule E	45,000	
Bank deposit interest £800 × 100/80		1,000
	45,000	1,000
Less personal allowance	4,335	
Taxable income	40,665	1,000

Income tax on non savings income £
£1,500 * 10% 150
£26,500 * 23% 6,095
£12,665 * 40% 5,066
Income tax on savings (excl dividend) income
£1,000 × 40% 400
11,711
Less tax reduction
 Married couple's allowance £1,970 * 10% 197
Tax liability 11,514

(b) MR WAIN: UK INCOME TAX LIABILITY

	Non-savings £	Savings (excl dividend) £	Dividend £	Total £
Schedule E	31,644			
Schedule D Case III		1,490		
Schedule D Case V £2,400 * 100/60			4,000	
STI	31,644	1,490	4,000	37,134
Less personal allowance	4,335			
Taxable income	27,309	1,490	4,000	32,799

Income tax on non-savings income £
£1,500 * 10% 150
£25,809 * 23% 5,936
Income tax on savings (excl dividend) income
£691 × 20% 138
£799 * 40% 320
Income tax on dividend income
£4,000 × 32.5% 1,300
7,844
Less double taxation relief (W) 1,300
Tax liability 6,544

Working: double taxation relief
Overseas tax suffered on dividends £4,000 * 40% £1,600

UK tax on £4,000 of dividends £4,000 × 32.5% £1,300

Double taxation relief is therefore restricted to £1,300.

44 TUTORIAL QUESTION: DOUBLE TAX RELIEF FOR COMPANIES

Calculation of mainstream corporation tax liability

Stripe Ltd y/e 31.3.00

	£
Schedule DI - UK	800,000
overseas	600,000
Schedule DV (W1)	244,622
Capital gains	95,000
Less: Charges paid	(85,000)
PCTCT	1,654,622

	£
Corporation tax @ 30%	496,387
Less: DTR (W2) (£180,000 + 59,822)	(239,822)
MCT	256,565

Workings

1   **Schedule DV - Stripe Ltd**

	£
Dividend income (withholding tax @ 12% = £25,200)	210,000
Underlying tax £305,000 × $\frac{210,000}{1,850,000}$	34,622
	244,622

Total foreign tax suffered: £25,200 + £34,622 = £59,822

2   **Double tax relief - Stripe**

		UK profits £	*DI - overseas* £	*DV* £
PCTCT		810,000	600,000	244,622
CT @ 30%		243,000	180,000	73,387
Less: DTR				
(i)	DI overseas lower of UK CT - £180,000 overseas tax - £222,000 £600,000 × 37%		(180,000)	
(ii)	DV lower of UK CT - £73,387 overseas tax - £59,822 (W1)			(59,822)
		243,000	-	13,565

45 BARNEY HALL

> **Tutor's hint.** This question has been amended to reflect changes in the syllabus.
>
> **Examiner's comments.** In part (b) it was often not apparent which aspect of the question was being answered. When answering a question of this nature it is essential that each section is clearly labelled with a heading.

(a) *Residence in the UK during a tax year*

A person will be resident in a given tax year if, in that year he either:

(i) **is present in the UK for 183 days or more** (excluding days of arrival and departure); or

(ii) **he makes substantial visits to the UK.** Visits averaging 91 days or more a year for each of four or more consecutive years will make the person resident for each of these tax years (for someone emigrating from the UK, the four years are reduced to three).

If days are spent in the UK because of exceptional circumstances beyond the control of the individual's control (eg illness), those days are ignored for the purposes of the 91 day rule (but not the 183 day rule).

A person who is **leaving the UK permanently after being resident** in the UK who can produce evidence to that effect (eg sale of UK house, setting up permanent home abroad), **will be treated as being non-UK resident from the date of departure.** In other cases, the decision will be postponed for three years and then retrospective adjustments will be made.

If a person goes abroad for full-time service under a contract of employment such that:

(i) his absence from the UK is for a period which includes a complete tax year; and

(ii) interim visits to the UK do not amount to six months or more in any one tax year or three months or more per tax year on average;

he is normally regarded as **being not resident and not ordinarily resident for the whole of the period of the contract**.

A person **coming to the UK to take up permanent residence or with the intention of staying for at least three years is treated as resident in the UK from the date of arrival. A person who comes to the UK to work for a period of at least two years is treated as resident for the whole period from arrival to departure**.

Someone who comes to the UK for 'temporary' purposes (such as for a brief spell of employment) **is not UK resident unless he spends 183 days or more in the UK in that year.**

(b) (i) *Working overseas for a period of fifteen months*

Barney will be resident and ordinarily resident in the UK for 1999/00 and 2000/01, as he will not be abroad for a complete tax year. He will therefore be assessable in 1999/00 on his world-wide income which will consist of the following:

	Non-savings Income £	Savings (excl dividend) Income £	Total £
Schedule E Case I	33,600		
Benefits: travel for self	2,400		
Subsistence £850 × 5	4,250		
Travel for spouse	700		
	40,950		
Less: allowable deduction (benefits – see note)	(7,350)		
	33,600		
Schedule A	2,600		
Schedule D Case V (£5,460 × 100/30)		7,800	
Statutory total income	36,200	7,800	44,000

Barney will be able to claim a deduction for the following amounts paid or reimbursed by his employer from his Schedule E benefits:

(i) Cost of travel from any place in the UK to take up the overseas employment, and travel back to any place in the UK on its termination.

(ii) Board and lodging outside the UK provided for the purpose of enabling him to perform the duties of the overseas employment.

(iii) The cost of up to two return journeys for his spouse and children under the age of 18, provided that he is absent from the UK for a continuous period of at least 60 days, as is the case here.

Barney will be able to claim double taxation relief of the lower of the tax in the UK on the bank interest (ie £7,800 × 40% (savings income is top slice) = £3,120) and the tax in Yalam (ie £7,800 × 30% = £2,340), that is £2,340.

Barney is liable to CGT on the disposal of assets situated anywhere in the world because he is UK resident. His gain on the land is:

	£
Proceeds $180,000/8	22,500
Less: Cost $84,000/6	(14,000)
Unindexed gain	8,500
Less: Indexation allowance to April 1998	

$$\frac{162.6 - 154.4}{154.4} (= 0.053) \times £14,000 \qquad (742)$$

Indexed gain	7,758

No taper relief yet available.
This gain will be taxable in 1999/00.

His gain on the gift of the shares is estimated to be:

	£
Deemed proceeds (MV) $\frac{218-210}{4}$ = 2 + 210 = 212p × 8,000	16,960
Less: Cost	(9,450)
Unindexed gain	7,510
Less: Indexation allowance to April 1998	

$$\frac{162.6 - 154.4}{154.4} \times £9,450 \qquad (502)$$

Indexed gain	7,008

Gift relief is not available on small holdings of quoted shares.

Gain after taper relief (95% × £7,008)	£6,658

This gain will be taxable in 2000/01

(ii) *Working overseas for a period of eighteen months*

Barney will be working abroad for a period which includes the whole tax year of 2000/01. He should therefore be treated as not resident or ordinarily resident in the UK for the whole of the period between 1 November 1999 to 30 April 2001, provided that he does not make interim visits as described in (a) above.

For income tax he will only be taxable on UK source income during his absence. He will also be liable to tax on his world-wide income up to his departure. His 1999/00 statutory total income will therefore be:

	Non-savings Income £	Savings (excl dividend) Income £	Total £
Schedule E Case I (£33,600 × 7/12)	19,600		
Schedule A	2,600		
Schedule D Case V £5,460 × 100/30 × 7/12		4,550	
Statutory total income	22,200	4,550	26,750

In this case, double taxation relief will be restricted to the UK tax payable on the interest, as the UK tax rate (20%) is less than the Yalamese tax rate. The DTR will therefore be £4,550 × 20% = £910.

For capital gains tax purposes, it is not possible for Barney to treat 1999/00 as a split year as he has previously always been resident in the UK. Therefore the gain made in 1999/00 will still be taxable in that year.

The gain on the gift of shares to his daughter is made during a period when Barney is treated as not resident and not ordinarily resident. It is therefore not taxable in the year 2000/01. **However, since there are less than five tax years between the year of Barney's departure (1999/00) and his rearrival in the UK (2001/02), the gain will be caught by the temporary non-residence provisions.** This means that the gain will be taxable in 2001/02, as a gain of that year.

(c) *Inheritance tax on gift to daughter*

This gift to Barney's daughter will be a potentially exempt transfer:

		£
Value of shares (as in (b))		16,960
Less:	AE 2000/01	(3,000)
	AE 1999/00 b/fwd	(3,000)
Potentially exempt transfer		10,960

No lifetime tax is payable. If Barney dies within seven years of the transfer, there will be no tax to pay on the PET as it is within the nil rate band. However, it will use up £10,960 of the nil rate band available on later transfers and the death estate.

It does not matter if Barney gives shares situated in Yalam to his daughter, instead of the UK shares. This is because Barney will remained domiciled in the UK and, as such is subject to IHT on assets situated anywhere in the world.

Marking guide

			Marks
(a)	*Residence in the UK*		
	183 day rule		1
	91 day rule		1
	Exceptional circumstances		1
	Leaving the UK permanently		2
	Coming to the UK permanently/three years		1
	Coming to the UK for 2 years/temporary purposes		2
		Available	8
		Maximum	6
(b)	*Working overseas for 15 months*		
	Assessed on world-wide income		1
	Calculation of STI		2
	Benefits/Deduction of expenses		2
	DTR		1
	Plot of land gain		1
	Shares gain		1
	Taxation of gains in year of disposal		1
	Working overseas for 18 months		
	Not resident or ordinarily resident		1
	Liability to UK income tax		1
	STI/DTR		1
	Capital gains tax on land		1
	Capital gains tax on shares		2
		Available/maximum	15
(c)	*Inheritance tax on gift*		
	Value of transfer		1
	Treatment of PET		1
	UK Domicile – liability to IHT on worldwide assets		2
		Available/maximum	4
		Maximum	25

46 EYETAKI INC

Tutors hint. To score well you needed to be able to answer all parts of this question.

Examiner's comments. This was the least popular question on the paper and was generally answered quite badly.

(a) (i) Eyetaki Inc **will be liable to UK corporation tax if it is trading through a branch or agency in the UK (trading within the UK). The company will not be liable to UK corporation tax if it is merely trading with the UK.**

From 1 January 2000 to 28 February 2000, Eyetaki Inc employed a UK agent, and maintained a stock of cameras in the UK. **Provided that contracts for the sale of cameras were concluded in Eyeland, Eyetaki Inc will probably not be liable to UK corporation tax on** profits made during this period.

On 1 March 2000, Eyetaki Inc appears to have opened a **permanent establishment** in the UK by renting an office and showroom, and it is likely that the sales managers will be empowered to **conclude contracts in the UK**. Eyetaki Inc will therefore be liable to UK tax on the profits made in the UK from 1 March 2000 to the date that the trade is transferred to Uktaki Ltd (presumably 31 July 2000).

Corporation tax will be at the full rate regardless of the level of profits made in the UK, or by Eyetaki Inc, since there is no double taxation treaty between the UK and Eyeland.

(ii) **Uktaki Ltd's accounting periods**

Uktaki Ltd's first chargeable accounting period starts when the company commences trading on 1 August 2000 and ends 12 months later on 31 July 2001. The next period runs from 1 August 2001 to the end of Uktaki Ltd's period of account, 31 December 2001.

(b) Each part of the building must be considered separately.

(i) The part to be used to assemble cameras from components imported from Eyeland will qualify for industrial buildings allowance (IBA) since it is to be used in a **trade consisting of a subjection of goods to a process.**

(ii) The part used to **store goods which are to be subjected to a process, and to store manufactured goods not yet delivered** will also qualify for IBAs. Whether the cameras are sold wholesale or retail should not affect the building's classification as an industrial building.

(iii) The **showroom and general offices will only qualify for allowances if they represent 25% or less of the total cost of the building.** Otherwise, the industrial buildings allowance will be restricted to the other qualifying proportion of the building.

Allowances

A writing-down allowance at the rate of 4% on a straight-line basis will be given, commencing with the accounting period that the building is brought into use.

Enterprise zone

If the building is in an enterprise zone, the full cost of the building (excluding the land) will qualify for industrial buildings allowance, regardless of the proportion of the cost represented by the showroom and general offices.

Allowances

If the building is in an enterprise zone, a 100% initial allowance is available. If the initial allowance is not taken in full, a writing-down allowance at the rate of 25% of cost on a straight-line basis is given.

(c) **Eyeland is not a member of the European Union (EU)**

Uktaki Ltd will have to account for VAT on the value of goods imported from outside the EU at the time of their importation. The value of the goods will include carriage costs, and all taxes, dues and other charges levied on importation. An input VAT deduction will be given on the company's next VAT return.

If Uktaki Ltd arranges for a guarantee to be given, the VAT due on importation can be accounted for on a monthly basis rather than on importation.

Eyeland becomes a member of the European Union

No VAT will have to be paid on importation if goods are purchased from a supplier in another EU state to whom Utaki Ltd has supplied its VAT registration number. Instead, output VAT will be accounted for in the period which includes the date of acquisition of the goods. The date of acquisition is the earlier of the date of issue of a VAT invoice or the 15th of the month following the removal of the goods. **This VAT payable (output tax) is also input VAT which can be deducted in the normal way on that same VAT return.**

(d) As goods are purchased at an over valuation from an overseas holding company, the UK transfer pricing legislation will apply. This means **Utaki Ltd will have to substitute a market price for the transfer price when calculating its profit chargeable to UK corporation tax. The market price will be an 'arm's length' one that would be charged if the parties to the transaction were independent of each other.**

(e) The director is to come to the UK in order to take up employment for a period in excess of two years, and so will be treated as UK resident for the entire period. The director will only be treated as ordinarily resident in the UK if there is the intention to stay in the UK for three years or more, or if he actually remains for three years.

   (i) **Emoluments for UK duties**

   The director will be subject to UK tax on emoluments for duties performed in the UK regardless of his residence status.

   (ii) **Emoluments for duties performed in Eyeland**

   The director will be subject to UK tax on emoluments for duties performed in Eyeland if he is both resident and ordinarily resident in the UK. If the director is resident, but not ordinarily resident in the UK, only such emoluments remitted to the UK will be taxable in the UK.

   (iii) **Investment income arising in Eyeland**

   The director is domiciled in Eyeland, and so will only be subject to UK tax on investment income arising in Eyeland if it is remitted to the UK.

Marking guide		Marks
(a) Liability to corporation tax		
Trading within the UK/Trading with the UK		1
1 January 2000 to 28 February 2000		2
1 March 2000 to 31 July 2000		2
Rate of corporation tax		1
Accounting periods		2
	Available	8
	Maximum	7
(b) Qualification as an industrial building		
Camera assembly		1
Storage of goods		2
Showroom and general offices		1
Writing-down allowance		1
Designated enterprise zone		1
	Available/Maximum	6
(c) Not a member of the European Union		2
Member of European Union		2
	Available/Maximum	4
(d) Substitution of market price in calculating PCTCT		2
Market price = arms length price		1
	Maximum/Available	3
(e) Resident status of director		2
Emoluments for duties performed in the UK		1
Emoluments for duties performed in Eyeland		1
Investment income arising in Eyeland		1
	Available/Maximum	5
	Maximum	25

47 MAGEE PLC

Tutor's hint. Your answer to part (b) should have quantified the tax saving obtained by making a distribution.

(a) (i) **A company incorporated in the UK is UK resident**. Gavin Ltd should therefore not be incorporated in the UK.

(ii) **UK residence would depend on whether central management and control is exercised in the UK**. Superficially it would appear likely since the board will meet in the UK. However, the place of exercise of central management and control is a matter of fact and if the directors (or others) actually exercised control outside the UK, Gavin Ltd would not be UK resident.

(iii) Gavin Ltd would not be UK resident for corporation tax purposes as it would be neither incorporated in the UK nor controlled from the UK. Thus the final option would meet Magee plc's requirements.

(b) (i) **A controlled foreign company (CFC) is one which is controlled by UK resident persons, and which is resident in a country with a lower level of tax. A lower level of tax is defined as less than three quarters of the amount which would have been payable had the company been resident in the UK**. Legislation includes a list of countries which are not regarded as low tax countries.

For the rules to apply, a UK company together with connected or associated persons **must have at least a 25% stake** in the overseas company.

A CFC's profits may be apportioned among the persons having an interest in it, and corporation tax charges may then be levied on UK corporate shareholders. However, no tax charge arises if the CFC distributes 90% of its profits.

(ii) (1) If no dividend is paid, the effect on Magee plc's corporation tax liability will be as follows.

	£
Tax on apportioned profits £420,000 * 30%	126,000
Less foreign corporation tax £450,000 * 8%	36,000
Increase in corporation tax liability	90,000

(2) If a dividend of 90% of Gavin Ltd's profits is paid (the minimum to avoid an apportionment), the position will be as follows.

	£
Gavin Ltd's tax adjusted profits	420,000
Less tax thereon £450,000 * 8%	36,000
Gavin Ltd's distributable profits	384,000

	£
Dividend received by Magee plc £384,000 * 90%	345,600
Underlying tax £345,600 * 36,000/364,000	34,180
Schedule D Case V income	379,780
Corporation tax £379,780 * 30%	113,934
Less underlying tax relief	34,180
Increase in corporation tax liability	79,754

The distribution would save corporation tax of £(90,000 − 79,754) = £10,246, so it should be made.

(c) If Alex only stays abroad for 14 months, he will leave the UK in 2000/01 (in December 2000) and return in 2001/02 (in February 2002). There is therefore no possibility of his becoming non-UK resident, and so his earnings will be taxable in full.

If the period abroad is 18 months, it will include a complete tax year (2001/02), and Alex will be treated as not UK resident for the whole of the period abroad. This will ensure that his earnings are not within the scope of Schedule E, so they will escape UK income tax. However, non-resident status will be lost if visits to the UK amount to six months or more in any one tax year or three months or more a year on average. Alex should take care that his visits to the UK do not break the three months rule.

(d) The reimbursements will be taxable emoluments. **If Tony Smith's duties of employment are performed wholly abroad, he may claim a Schedule E deduction equal to the reimbursement by Magee plc of his own travelling expenses** from the UK to Ruritania at the start of his employment abroad, and back to the UK at its end. If Tony Smith's duties of employment are performed partly abroad, the same deduction is available provided that the duties performed abroad can only be performed abroad and the journey is made wholly and exclusively to perform them or to return to the UK after performing them.

Provided that Tony Smith is **absent from the UK for a continuous period of at least 60 days the same deduction will also be available in respect of the reimbursed cost of up to two return trips per tax year to visit him by his wife and his 15 year old child. However, this deduction will not be available in respect of visits by his 20 year old child, as the age limit is 18.**

48 PADDINGTON LTD

> **Tutor's hints.** The examiner has said that you can expect questions to require knowledge of open end investment companies.
>
> **Examiner's comments.** In part (a) the inclusion of information for the UK resident subsidiary confused many candidates.

(a) **Mainstream corporation tax liability**

	Total £	UK £	Overseas £
Schedule D Case I	79,000	79,000	
Trading loss brought forward	7,000	7,000	
	72,000	72,000	
Capital gain	6,000	6,000	
Schedule D Case V (W1)	246,400		246,400
	324,400	78,000	246,400
Charge on income	12,000	12,000	
PCTCT	312,400	66,000	246,400
Corporation tax (W2)	89,030	18,809	70,221
Double taxation relief (W3)	70,221	-	70,221
Mainstream corporation tax liability	18,809	18,809	Nil

Workings

1 **Dividend from Waterloo Ltd**

Paddington Ltd owns 10% or more of Waterloo Ltd, so relief for the underlying tax paid in Westoria is available.

	£
Dividend received £213,400 × 80%	170,720
Withholding tax at 3%	5,280
	176,000
Underlying tax $176{,}000 \times \dfrac{117{,}600}{294{,}000}$	70,400
Schedule D Case V income	246,400

2 **Corporation tax**

The upper limit of £1,500,000 is divided by three, since both Victoria Ltd and Waterloo Ltd are associated companies.

	£
£312,400 at 30%	93,720
Marginal relief 1/40 × (500,000 – 312,400)	4,690
	89,030
UK income £89,030 × 66,000/312,400	18,809
Overseas income £89,030 × 246,400/312,400	70,221

3 **Double taxation relief**

Double taxation relief is restricted to the lower of:

		£
(i)	Overseas tax (£5,280 + £70,400)	75,680
(ii)	UK corporation tax on overseas income	70,221

(b) As a result of its reduction in corporation tax rates from 30% to 10%, Westoria will become a 'low tax country', since its rate of tax will be **less than three quarters of that payable on the equivalent profits in the UK.** Waterloo Ltd will therefore be classified as a controlled foreign company unless it meets one of the following exclusion tests.

(i) It is **quoted on a recognised Stock Exchange**.

(ii) Its **profits are less than £50,000.**

(iii) It has an **acceptable distribution policy** (90% of taxable profits must be distributed.)

(iv) The **exempt activities test**. This test is unlikely to be satisfied because Waterloo Ltd appears to be engaged in the non-qualifying business, of dealing in goods for delivery from a connected person (Paddington Ltd).

(v) **The motive test.** (Waterloo Ltd must not exist for the main purpose of avoiding UK tax. The fact that Waterloo Ltd was set up prior to the reduction in the rate of Westoria's corporation tax, supports this argument.)

If Waterloo Ltd is classified as a controlled foreign company, then Paddington Ltd will be assessed to UK corporation tax on its share (80%) of the profits of Waterloo Ltd, rather than on the dividends remitted to the UK. Relief would be given for tax paid in Westoria.

(c) Unit trusts and OEICs are similar in nature but, as the name suggests, OEICs are incorporated companies rather than trusts. OEICS are easier to market overseas. Dividends from OEICs are treated in exactly the same way as any other company dividend.

(d) ISAs are available to anyone who is resident and ordinarily resident in the UK and aged 18 or over.

No income tax arises on ISAs. Tax credits are paid on dividends from shares held in the account between 6 April 1999 and 5 April 2004 and no CGT arises on disposals. Withdrawals may be made at any time without penalty.

There is an annual subscription limit of £5,000 (although in 1999/2000 this is £7,000) of which a maximum of £1,000 can be in cash (this limit is raised to £3,000 for 1999/2000 only) and £1,000 in life insurance. A husband and wife will each have their own limits.

49 LUCY LEE

> **Tutor's hint.** This question has been amended to take changes in the syllabus into account.
>
> **Examiner's comment.** The mistake made by some candidates was to waste time writing at length about tax avoidance and the related decided cases, despite there only being two marks available.

(a) **Tax avoidance**

Tax avoidance is the reduction of tax by legal, although possibly artificial means. Thus tax avoidance is using the existing law to reduce your tax bill.

Artificial arrangements may be limited by the courts and statutory provisions exist to counteract specific forms of tax avoidance.

Tax evasion

Tax evasion is the attempted reduction of tax liabilities by misrepresenting the facts or by concealing information and it is illegal. Thus tax evasion means you have deliberately not paid the tax due.

(b) (i) **Employment of husband**

If Lucy employs her husband, paying him £28,000 pa, her income tax liability will be reduced as follows.

	£
Salary	28,000
Employers' NIC (£28,000 – 4,335) × 12.2%	2,887
	30,887
Income tax saved at 40%	12,355

Her NIC will not be affected as her profits will not be reduced to below the upper limit of £26,000.

As a result of the salary, additional income tax and NIC will be payable by Lucy's husband and also the business:

	£
Schedule E	28,000
Less: personal allowances	(4,335)
Taxable income	23,665

	£
Income tax on non-savings income	
£1,500 at 10%	150
£22,165 at 23%	5,098
	5,248
Employees' NIC	
(£26,000 – £3,432) × 10%	2,257
Payable by husband	7,505
Employer's NIC (payable by business)	2,887
	10,392

This results in an overall tax saving of £1,963 (£12,355 – £10,392).

The salary paid to Lucy's husband is only deductible if it is wholly and exclusively for business purposes. As the previous personal assistant was paid less, it is unlikely that the additional salary will be deductible unless it can be justified.

(ii) **New business venture**

(1) The **partnership is a separate taxable person from Lucy's own business for VAT purposes** and as its taxable supplies are below the registration threshold it is not liable to register for VAT.

However, **disaggregation rules exist whereby if the partnership is effectively an extension of Lucy's own business, then the two will be classed as one taxable person**, and the partnership will then have to account for VAT. As both businesses are engaged in similar activities, and the partnership uses Lucy's office premises, equipment and employees, the disaggregation rules are likely to apply.

(2) **Accounting for output VAT**

The tax point is normally the date the service is completed.

However **if an invoice is issued or payment is received earlier than the above date, then this earlier date becomes the tax point.**

If an invoice is issued in the 14 days after the date the service is completed, then the 'normal' tax point is replaced by the invoice date.

Deposit of £500

The VAT point is the date the deposit is received

Output VAT of £74.47 (500 × 7/47) must be accounted for in the return period in which the deposit is received. VAT is payable to Customs one month after the end of the return period.

Balance of contract price

The VAT point is the date the contract is completed (as an invoice is not issued within the next 14 days).

Output VAT of £74.47 must be accounted for in the return period in which this occurs.

VAT is due one month after the end of the return period.

(iii) **Wedding gift to daughter**

The gift by Lucy to her daughter will be a PET, but exemptions are available as follows.

		£
Gift		12,500
Marriage exemption		(5,000)
Annual exemption	2000/01	(3,000)
	1999/00	(3,000)
PET		1,500

The £1,500 will be fully exempt if Lucy survives seven years from the date of the gift.

Lucy's gift of £12,500 to her husband will be exempt as it is a transfer to a spouse.

The same exemptions will be available to Lucy's husband when he makes a gift of £12,500 to his daughter.

If Lucy's gift to her husband is conditional upon him giving it to their daughter, her gift may be caught under the associated operations rule. The associated operations rule is a piece of anti-avoidance legislation used by the Inland Revenue to attack schemes set up to avoid inheritance tax by using several transactions instead of just one transaction.

(c) (i) If the company continues trading the loss could be:

(1) carried forward to set against future schedule D Case I profits arising from the same trade.

(2) set against other profits (before the deduction of charges) incurred in the nine months to 31.12.00. Any trade charges that become unrelieved as a result of this set off can be carried forward to set against future Schedule D profits.

(3) Once the set off described in (2) above has been made any remaining loss could be carried back to set against total profits (after the deduction of trade charges) incurred in the previous twelve months.

(ii) If the company ceases trading the loss could be set against other profits (before the deduction of charges) incurred in the same period.

Any remaining loss could then be carried back to set against total profits (after the deduction of trade charges) incurred in the previous 36 months. Any unrelieved trade charges arising in the final 12 months of trading may be added to the loss carried back.

50 LI AND KEN WONG

> **Tutor's hint.** This was a fairly wide-ranging question, covering several taxes. When faced with such a question, it is worth spending a little time thinking creatively before planning your answer in detail.
>
> **Examiner's comment.** In part (a), many candidates did not appreciate that voluntary registration in the current position would not be beneficial.

(a) If Li accepts the contract, she will have to register for VAT. She will have to absorb the VAT on her work for the public, because of the competitive nature of the market. She is already a higher rate taxpayer in any case (profits £40,000 – £2,600 × 1.175 – £1,800 = £35,145).

The net effect of the contract would be as follows.

	£	£
Additional revenue		15,000
Less additional costs		
VAT absorbed £40,000 × 7/47	5,957	
Secretary – Salary	9,000	
– NICs (£9,000 – £4,335) × 12.2%	569	
		(15,526)
		(526)
Add VAT recoverable on expenses £2,600 × 17.5%		455
Decrease in profit		(71)
Decrease in spending money £71 × 60%		£43

The contract is marginally loss-making in the short term.

(b) The cost of two part-time secretaries at £4,650 each would be 2 × (£4,650 – 4,335) × 12.2%) (NICs) = £9,379. This is £190 cheaper than one full-time secretary, a post-tax saving of £190 × 60% = £114.

A self-employed secretary would, at £9,200, be even cheaper, but the Revenue could well query a full-time secretary's self-employed status and require Li to account for employer's NICs.

(c) There will be no special income tax effects for Li other than the drop in her income. The basis period rules for opening years will apply to Li's son, but Li's own basis periods will continue undisturbed.

Li will be treated as disposing of a share in the goodwill to her son. If goodwill is not revalued in the accounts, this will be at cost plus indexation (to April 1998), giving Li no gain and no loss. If it has been revalued, the disposal will be at balance sheet value plus indexation to April 1998, giving a gain on which taper relief would be available. The Revenue could argue for market value to be used based on the family connection between Li and her son, but not (unless the admission is not a bona fide commercial arrangement) based on the partnership connection.

Giving Li's son a share in the business will constitute a potentially exempt transfer by Li, but 100% business property relief should be available if it becomes chargeable.

(d) Capital allowances will be as follows.

	31 March £	30 April £
First period		
Acquisition	6,000	6,000
WDA 25%/25% × 13/12	(1,500)	(1,625)
	4,500	4,375
Second period		
WDA 25%	(1,125)	(1,094)
	3,375	3,281
Third period		
WDA 25%	(844)	(820)
	2,531	2,461

Note: FYAs are not available on cars.

Profits will be as follows.

	31 March £	30 April £
First period		
12 × £1,600 – £1,500	17,700	
12 × £1,600 + £2,000 – £1,625		19,575
Second period		
12 × £2,000 – £1,125	22,875	
11 × £2,000 + £2,500 – £1,094		23,406
Third period		
12 × £2,500 – £844	29,156	
12 × £2,500 – £820		29,180

Taxable profits will be as follows.

Year	Basis period	Working	31 March £	30 April £
1999/00	6.4.99 - 5.4.00		17,700	
	6.4.99 - 5.4.00	£19,575 × 12/13		18,069
2000/01	1.4.00 - 31.3.01		22,875	
	1.5.99 - 30.4.00	£19,575 × 12/13		18,069
2001/02	1.4.01 - 31.3.02		29,156	
	1.5.00 - 30.4.01			23,406

The date of 30 April is better in these early years, because it delays the impact on taxable profits of the rise in accounting profits (as profits are being taxed 11 months later). Over the whole life of the business, the taxable profits will be the same regardless of the accounting date: any difference on commencement will be compensated for by a difference on relief for overlap profits on cessation or on a change of accounting date.

(e) There is no need to make a charge for services, and a charge will not be imputed (unlike the position for goods).

Any charge will be income for Li, taxable at 40%. No charge should be made, because Ken would get no tax relief for the charge in relation to the short lease, and relief at only 23% for the charge in relation to the compensation claim.

Marking guide		Marks
(a)	Register for VAT	1
	Absorb VAT	1
	Decrease in profits	<u>3</u>
		5
(b)	Part-time secretaries	2
	Self-employed	<u>1</u>
		3
(c)	Basis periods	1
	CGT	3
	IHT	<u>2</u>
		6
(d)	Capital allowances	3
	Profits	2
	Taxable profits	3
	Conclusion	<u>1</u>
	Available	9
	Maximum	7
(e)	No need to charge	2
	Not beneficial	2
		<u>4</u>
		<u>25</u>

51 WHITE STALLION LTD

Tutor's hint. In part (c), you might have thought that delays in some transactions could have led to the application of the Ramsay principle. However, although the limits of application of that principal are uncertain, they are not *that* uncertain.

Examiner's comment. In part (a), many candidates mistakenly included the expensive cars in a car pool.

(a) THE TAX IMPLICATIONS OF THE RESTRUCTURING

   (i) **Gains and losses on the branch premises**

   (1) Apton

	£
Proceeds	145,000
Less cost	75,000
	70,000
Less indexation allowance	
$\dfrac{167.5 - 101.9}{101.9} = 0.644 \times £75,000$	48,300
Chargeable gain	<u>21,700</u>

   (2) Bindle

   The lease factors required are as follows.

   40 years: 95.457

   31 years 3 months: 88.371 + 3/12 (89.354 − 88.371) = 88.617

	£
Proceeds	100,000
Less cost £90,000 × 88.617/95.457	83,551
	16,449
Less indexation allowance	
$\dfrac{167.5 - 130.3}{130.3} = 0.285 \times £83,551 = £23,812$	16,449
No gain and no loss	<u>0</u>

(3) Cotter

	£	£
Proceeds		85,000
Less cost	88,000	
Less cost used in part disposal		
£88,000 × 27/(27 + 70)	24,495	
	63,505	
		21,495
Less indexation allowance		
$\frac{167.5 - 133.5}{133.5} = 0.255 \times £63,505$		16,194
Chargeable gain		5,301

The chargeable gains, which will be included in the company's profits chargeable to corporation tax, total £(21,700 + 0 + 5,301) = £27,001.

(ii) **The redundancy payments**

These payments will be deductible expenses for corporation tax purposes. Because the trade is not ceasing, the limit of statutory amount + 3 × statutory amount will not apply. Thus the loss will be increased by £45,800.

(iii) **The sale of the motor cars**

Balancing adjustments will arise as follows.

	Car pool £	Each expensive car £
Y/e 31.7.98		
Addition		14,000
WDA		(3,000)
Balance c/f	11,500	11,000
Y/e 31.7.99		
Disposals	(24,000)	(9,000)
Balancing (charge)/allowance	(12,500)	2,000

The reduction in the trading loss will be £12,500 − 4 × £2,000 = £4,500.

(iv) **The transfer of the head office**

The sale of the old head office will give rise to a chargeable gain as follows.

	£
Proceeds	285,000
Less cost	140,000
	145,000
Less indexation allowance	
$\frac{167.5 - 101.9}{101.9} = 0.644 \times £140,000$	90,160
Chargeable gain	54,840

This gain will be included in profits chargeable to corporation tax. No rollover claim will be possible, because the proceeds not reinvested, £(285,000 − 140,000) = £145,000, exceed the gain.

The new head office, being in an enterprise zone, will qualify for a 100% initial allowance. This will increase the trading loss by £(140,000 − 40,000) = £100,000. The company may choose not to take the whole allowance immediately. The amount not taken as initial allowance will be allowed at £100,000/4 = £25,000 a year, starting in the year of purchase.

In addition, £16,700 of the gain on the Apton branch can be rolled over against the new head office, leaving a chargeable gain of £(145,000 − 140,000) = £5,000, the proceeds not reinvested.

(v) The review of debtors

If a specific provision for doubtful debts is raised, or specific debts are written off, the debit entry will be deductible, increasing the trading loss.

If the debts over six months old are written off, a VAT refund of £32,000 × 7/47 = £4,766 may be claimed. The VAT on newer but bad debts will be recoverable when they are six months old.

The increase in the allowable loss is therefore likely to be £(56,500 × 40/47) = £48,085 assuming all debtors are inclusive of 17½% VAT.

(b) LOSS RELIEF CLAIMS

(i) The possible claims

Loss relief could be claimed as follows.

(1) The loss could be carried forward against future profits of the same trade. Relief by this method would be slow.

(2) The loss could be set against total profits of the year ended 31 July 1999. These consist of the capital gains of £21,700 + £5,301 + £54,840 − £16,700 (rollover claim) = £65,141. The rate of relief would be 20.667% (8/12 × 21% + 4/12 × 20%).

(3) So long as claim (2) is made, the balance of the loss could be set against total profits of the preceding twelve months, later years first. Relief in the year ended 31 July 1998 would be at 21%

(ii) The best claim

Claims (2) and then (3) should be made, so as to obtain relief as quickly as possible.

(iii) Aspects of restructuring to defer

The loss to be carried back should be maximised, so as to maximise the relief. Aspects of the restructuring which either reduce the loss or increase the other profits of the year ended 31 July 1999 should therefore be deferred until after 31 July 1999. These are as follows.

(1) The sale of the Apton and Cotter branches.

(2) The sale of the six cheap cars in the car pool.

(3) The sale of the four expensive cars, because the writing down allowances (£2,750 per car) would exceed the balancing allowances.

(4) The sale of the head office.

All other aspects should be carried out by 31 July 1999, and the full 100% initial allowance on the new head office should be claimed.

(c) **Tax avoidance is the attempted reduction of tax liabilities by legal, although possibly artificial, means. Tax evasion is the attempted reduction of tax liabilities by misrepresenting the facts or by concealing information, and it is illegal.**

Tax avoidance schemes can in general succeed, but very artificial schemes may be struck down under the Ramsay principle. There are also statutory provisions to counteract specific forms of avoidance. Tax evasion will, if discovered, always fail, and may lead to criminal and civil penalties.

If White Stallion Ltd were to defer aspects of its restructuring until after 31 July 1999, that would not amount to an artificial transaction of the type covered by the Ramsay principle, and would not be avoidance. However, any pretended deferral (such as lying about the date of sale of an asset) would be evasion.

52 FRED BARLEY

Tutor's hint. Question like this are very common. This means you must ensure that you are fully aware of all the tax aspects arising on the transfer of a business.

Examiner's comments. Candidates who confuse the different reliefs available such as retirement relief and BPR cannot expect to pass this paper.

(a) **Income tax implications of sale of business**

The sale of the business to Simon will result in a cessation for Fred and a corresponding commencement for Simon. In the absence of any election, plant and machinery will be transferred to Simon for capital allowance purposes at its market value on 31 May 2000 resulting in the following allowances and balancing charge.

	£
Seven months to 31.12.96	
Addition	34,000
WDA at 25% × 7/12	(4,958)
	29,042
Year to 31.12.97	
WDA at 25%	(7,261)
	21,781
Year to 31.12.98	
WDA at 25%	(5,445)
	16,336
Year to 31.12.99	
WDA at 25%	(4,084)
	12,252
Five months to 31.5.00	
Less: disposal (limited to cost)	(34,000)
Balancing charge	21,748

However, since Simon and Fred are connected persons, the balancing charge can be avoided by electing for the plant and machinery to be transferred to Simon at its tax written down value of £12,252. Such an election must be made jointly by 31 May 2002.

Assuming this election is made Fred's Schedule D Case I profits/(loss) will be:

	£
Seven months to 31.12.96 (£70,000 – £4,958)	65,042
Year to 31.12.97 (£122,000 – £7,261)	114,739
Year to 31.12.98 (£81,000 – £5,445)	75,555
Year to 31.12.99 (£34,000 – £4,084)	29,916
Five months to 31.5.00	(36,000)

The taxable profits in each year will be:

	£
1996/97 (1.6.96 – 5.4.97) (£65,042 + 3/12 × £114,739)	93,727
1997/98 (y/e 31.12.97)	114,739
1998/99 (y/e 31.12.98)	75,555
1999/00 (y/e 31.12.99)	29,916
2000/01 (five months to 31.5.00)	-

A claim could be made under s 380 ICTA 1988 for the loss to be set against Fred's total income of £29,916 in 1999/00. As Fred has no income in 2000/01, a s 380 ICTA 1998 claim will not be possible in 2000/01. The loss available for relief under s 380 ICTA 1988 is:

	£
Schedule D Case I	36,000
Overlap relief	28,685
	64,685

Alternatively, a claim could be made to relieve the loss of the last twelve months of trading under s 388 ICTA 1988. The loss of the last twelve months is:

	£	£
1.6.99 - 5.4.00		
$7/12 \times £29,916$	17,451	
$3/5 \times (£36,000)$	(21,600)	
		(4,149)
6.4.00 - 31.5.00		
$2/5 \times (£36,000)$	(14,400)	
Overlap relief	(28,685)	
		(43,085)
		47,234

This would be relieved against Schedule D Case I income of £29,916 in 1999/00 and against £17,318 of income in 1998/99.

Clearly a S 388 ICTA 1988 claim will be worthwhile, resulting in a tax refund of £12,616 (£5,689 + £6,927).

Simon will take over the plant and machinery at its tax written down value of £12,252 on 1 June 2000. His capital allowances for the year to 31 May 2001 will be £3,063 and his Schedule D Case I loss will be £15,063 (£12,000 + £3,063). The loss available for relief under s 381 in each of the opening years will be:

2000/01 (1.6.00 – 5.4.01)	
(£15,063 × 10/12)	£12,553
2001/02 (y/e 31.5.01)	
£15,063 – £12,553 (already relieved in previous year)	£2,510

The loss could be carried forward for relief under s 385 ICTA 1988 but as this would not result in relief until at least 2002/03 a claim under s 381 ICTA 1988 would be better. A s 381 claim would result in £12,553 being set against income of 1997/98 and £2,510 being set against income of 1998/99.

These claims should result in immediate tax refunds totalling £6,025 ((£12,553 + £2,510) × 40%)

A s 381 claim must be made by the 31 January which is nearly two years after the end of the year in which the relevant loss was made.

(b) **Capital gains implications - Fred**

Since Fred and Simon are connected persons, the market value of the assets transferred will be used, rather than the sale proceeds.

Farm land and farm buildings

As Fred is 50 years old, he qualifies for retirement relief. As he ran the business for four years the upper and lower limits are multiplied by 4/10. Provided that Fred and Simon jointly elect, gift relief will also be available.

	£	£
Deemed proceeds		600,000
Cost		115,000
Unindexed gain		485,000
Indexation to April 1998 £115,000 × $\frac{162.6-153.0}{153.0}$ (0.063)		7,245
		477,755
Retirement relief		
(4/10 × £200,000) × 100%	80,000	
(£320,000 (*Note 2*) − £80,000) × 50%	120,000	
		200,000
		277,755
Gain held over (*Note 3*)		217,755
Chargeable gain		60,000

The farmland and buildings are business assets that have been owned for three years since 6.4.98 (including the bonus year) so the gain chargeable after taper relief is:

£60,000 × 77.5% = £46,500

Note 2. The retirement relief upper limit is £320,000 (£800,000 × 4/10). We are using the upper and lower limits for 1999/00 as instructed by the question. As retirement relief is being phased out, the limits are actually lower in 2000/01.

Note 3. The consideration paid by Simon exceeds the cost of the land and buildings and the retirement relief available by £60,000 (£375,000 − £115,000 − £200,000). Therefore only £217,755 (£277,765 − £60,000) of the gain qualifies to be held over as a gift of business assets.

Investments	£
Deemed proceeds	250,000
Cost	35,000
	215,000
Indexation to April 1998 £35,000 × $\frac{162.6-157.5}{157.5}$	1,133
	213,867

The chargeable gain after taper relief is £203,174 (95% × £213,867).

Fred's chargeable gain	£
Chargeable gains £46,500 + £203,174	249,674
Annual exemption	7,100
	242,574

CGT liability	£
£28,000 × 20%	5,600
£214,574 × 40%	85,830
242,574	91,430

The CGT of £91,430 will be due on 31 January 2002. It would be beneficial if at least £60,000 of the consideration paid by Simon was allocated to other assets. The hold over of the gain on the farm land and farm buildings would then not be restricted.

Capital gains tax - Simon

Simon will take over the farm land and farm buildings at a base cost of £382,245 (£600,000 − £217,755), and the investments at a base cost of £250,000.

(c) **Inheritance tax**

The transfer of value to Simon on 31 May 2000 will be a PET that will only become chargeable to IHT if Fred dies within seven years of the transfer. If Fred dies within three years of the transfer the IHT payable will be:

	£
Value transferred (£1,000,000 − £375,000)	625,000
Less: Business property relief (*Note 4*) (£625,000 − £250,000)	(375,000)
	250,000
Less: Annual exemptions	
2000/01	(3,000)
1999/00	(3,000)
	244,000

	£
IHT	NIL
£231,000 × 0%	5,200
£13,000 × 40%	5,200

The IHT of £5,200 will be reduced by taper relief if Fred survives for at least three years after making the transfer of value. Simon will have to pay any IHT due within six months of the end of the month of Fred's death.

Note 4. BPR is only available to set against the value of business assets transferred. It will not be available if Simon has sold the business or the business has ceased to qualify at the date of Fred's death. APR is not available because Simon purchased the farmland and farm buildings at their agricultural value.

It would be beneficial if Simon purchased the investments, plus other assets worth £125,000 at full value, and the farm land and buildings were gifted. That way APR/BPR would be available @ 100% on the full gift.

Tax Planning
BPP Mock Exam: June 2000

Question Paper:	
Time allowed	3 hours
FOUR questions ONLY to be answered	

Disclaimer of liability

Please note that we have based our predictions of the content of the 2000 exams on our long experience of the ACCA exams. We do not claim to have any endorsement of the predictions from either the examiner or the ACCA and we do not guarantee that either the specific questions, or the general areas, that are forecast will necessarily be included in the exams, in part or in whole.

We do not accept any liability or responsibility to any person who takes, or does not take, any action based (either in whole or in part and either directly or indirectly) upon any statement or omission made in this book. We encourage students to study all topics in the ACCA syllabus and the mock exam in this book is intended as an aid to revision only.

paper 11

DO NOT OPEN THIS PAPER UNTIL YOU ARE READY TO START
UNDER EXAMINATION CONDITIONS

Mock exam: questions

FOUR questions ONLY to be attempted.

1   Moon Ltd is the holding company for a group of companies. The group structure is as follows.

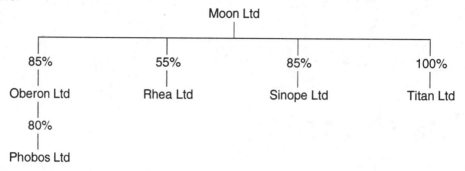

Each percentage holding represents a holding of ordinary share capital. The shareholdings were all held throughout the year ended 31 March 2000 except for Moon Ltd's 100% shareholding in Titan Ltd that was acquired on 1 October 1999. All of the companies have an accounting date of 31 March. The results of each company (except Titan Ltd) for the year ended 31 March 2000 are as follows:

	Tax adjusted Schedule D Case I profit £
Moon Ltd	278,000
Oberon Ltd	47,000
Rhea Ltd	124,000
Sinope Ltd	72,000
Phobos Ltd	4,000

Sinope Ltd's tax adjusted profit of £72,000 is entirely in respect of an overseas branch. Overseas taxation of £25,920 has been paid on the branch profits.

Titan Ltd previously had an accounting date of 30 September, but has produced accounts for the six month period to 31 March 2000 to make its accounting date coterminous with the other group companies. Due to a reorganisation following its takeover by Moon Ltd, Titan Ltd made a tax adjusted Schedule D Case I loss of £95,000 for the six month period to 31 March 2000. On 31 December 1999 the company received bank interest of £1,500, and on 15 February 2000 it paid a patent royalty of £4,000 (gross). For the year ended 30 September 1999, Titan Ltd has profits chargeable to corporation tax of £18,000. It did not pay any charges in this year.

(a) **Required:**

 (i) Explain the possible ways that Titan Ltd can relieve its Schedule D Case I trading loss for the six month period to 31 March 2000.

(5 marks)

 (ii) State, giving appropriate reasons, the companies to which Titan Ltd can surrender its Schedule D Case I trading loss. (3 marks)

 (iii) Advise the Moon Ltd group as to which loss relief claims as specified in (a) and (b) above would be the most beneficial. Your answer should be supported by appropriate calculations. (7 marks)

You are not expected to calculate the mainstream corporation tax liabilities for any of the companies.

(b) Moon Ltd, Rhea Ltd and Oberon Ltd are registered as a group for VAT purposes but, the inclusion of Rhea Ltd in the group is now being reconsidered. The forecast sales and purchases of the companies for the year to 31 March 20001 are:

Mock exam: questions

	Moon Ltd £	Oberon Ltd £	Rhea Ltd £
Sales			
Standard rated	400,000		
Zero rated		50,000	
Exempt			150,000
Purchases	(50,000)	(10,000)	(30,000)
Overheads	(80,000)		
Management fee	20,000	(10,000)	(10,000)

The purchases, overhead expenditure and management fees are all standard rated. Each of the company's purchases relate to its own sales. The overhead expenditure cannot be attributed to any of the three companies sales. All of the above figures are exclusive of VAT.

Required

(i) **State what the consequences of VAT group registration are** (4 marks)

(ii) **Advise whether it would be beneficial for Rhea Ltd to leave the VAT group.** (6 marks)

(25 marks)

2   Albert Bone, a widower aged 64, died on 31 March 2000. The main beneficiary under the terms of Albert's will is his son Harold, aged 37. At the date of his death Albert owned the following assets.

(a) 76,000 £1 ordinary shares in Hercules plc. On 31 March 2000 the shares were quoted at 139-147, with bargains on that day of 137, 141 and 143.

(b) Building society deposits of £115,900.

(c) A life assurance policy on his own life. Immediately prior to the date of Albert's death, the policy had an open market value of £42,000. Proceeds of £55,000 were received following his death.

Albert was a beneficiary of two trusts.

(a) Under the terms of the first trust, Albert was entitled to receive all of the trust income. The trust owned 50,000 units in the Eureka unit trust, which was quoted at 90-94 on 31 March 2000. Accrued distributable income at 31 March 2000 was £800 (net).

(b) Under the terms of the second trust, Albert was entitled to receive the income at the discretion of the trustees. The trust's assets were valued at £95,000 on 31 March 2000.

Until 15 March 1991, Albert owned his main residence. On that date, he had made a gift of the property to Harold. Albert continued to live in the house with Harold, rent free, until the date of his death. On 15 March 1991 the property was valued at £65,000, and on 31 March 2000 it was valued at £180,000.

Albert has also made the following gifts during his lifetime.

(a) On 3 December 1992, he made a gift of £92,000 into a discretionary trust.

(b) On 18 October 1995, he made a gift of £39,500 to a granddaughter as a wedding gift.

(c) On 20 April 1996, he made a gift of ordinary shares (a 52% holding) in a quoted trading company, into a discretionary trust. The shareholding was valued at £302,000, and had been owned for 10 years. The trust still owned the shares at 31 March 2000.

Any inheritance tax arising from the above gifts was paid by Albert.

At the date of his death, Albert owed £900 in respect of credit card debts, and he had also verbally promised to pay the £750 hospital bill of a neighbour. Albert's funeral expenses came to £1,200.

Under the terms of his will, Albert left specific gifts to his grandchildren totalling £40,000. The residue of his estate was left to Harold.

Required:

(a) **Calculate the IHT that will be payable as a result of Albert's death. Your answer should show who is liable to pay the tax, and by what date. You should also include an explanation as to your treatment of Albert's main residence, and a calculation of the amount of the inheritance that Harold will receive.**

You should ignore Albert's income tax liability for 1999/00, and should assume that the tax rates and allowances for 1999/00 apply throughout. (17 marks)

(b) **Harold is to make a gift of some of his inheritance to his son, aged 8, so as to utilise his son's personal allowance. Advise Harold of whether or not such a gift would be effective for income tax purposes. Your answer should include any tax planning advice that you consider to be appropriate.** (4 marks)

(c) **Harold plans to invest the balance of his inheritance so as to achieve capital growth, since he already has sufficient income. He will require the capital in five years time when he is to purchase a new house. Briefly advise Harold of investments that would be appropriate for such an investment strategy.** (4 marks)

(25 marks)

3 (a) Ukul Ltd is a UK resident company involved in management consultancy. The company has a branch in the country of Ulandi, which is controlled from that country and which does not deal with UK persons or with connected or associated persons. This branch has experienced substantial growth in recent years, and now accounts for 75% of Ukul Ltd's business. Ukul Ltd's results for the year ended 31 March 2000, split between the UK and Ulandi, are as follows.

	Total £	UK £	Ulandi £
Profit per accounts (before taxation)	116,000	29,000	87,000
Tax-adjusted profits			
Under UK legislation	120,000	30,000	90,000
Under Ulandian legislation	n/a	n/a	87,000

The branch in Ulandi is subject to Ulandian corporation tax at the rate of 18%. The Ulandian branch remits 50% of its profits after tax to the UK. Ulandi does not impose any type of withholding tax on remittances out of the country. There is no double taxation treaty between the UK and Ulandi, and Ulandi is not a member of the European Community. All of the above figures are in pounds sterling.

Required

Calculate Ukul Ltd's mainstream corporation tax liability for the year ended 31 March 2000. (3 marks)

(b) Ukul Ltd is planning to incorporate its branch in Ulandi. It will achieve this by transferring the branch's trade to a newly formed 100% subsidiary that will be resident in Ulandi. As far as the Ulandian tax system is concerned, the subsidiary would be taxed in exactly the same way as the branch. The subsidiary would remit 50% of its distributable profits (ie accounting profits after tax) as dividends to the UK.

Ukul Ltd is planning to replace its computer systems in the near future. A substantial proportion of this expenditure will be in respect of computers that are to be used in Ulandi. The Ulandian tax system does not give any relief for capital expenditure.

Required

Advise Ukul Ltd of the tax implications arising from the incorporation of its branch in Ulandi. You answer should include a calculation of what Ukul Ltd's mainstream corporation tax liability for the year ended 31 March 2000 would have been, if the branch had been incorporated as a 100% subsidiary at the beginning of that year. (9 marks)

(c) Sasha Khan, who is employed by Ukul Ltd's Ulandian branch in Ulandi, is to be assigned to the UK for a period of 15 months. During this period, she will be employed and paid by Ukul Ltd in the UK. For the 15 month period, Sasha will stay in rented accommodation, and will rent out her main residence situated in Ulandi. Sasha is resident and domiciled in Ulandi.

Required

Advise Sasha of the UK tax implications arising from her 15 month period of employment in the UK. You are not expected to discuss personal allowances, expense claims or double taxation relief claims. (4 marks)

(d) **Briefly describe the self assessment rules that apply for companies for accounting periods ending after 30 June 1999. In particular, mention how the profits of controlled foreign companies, the pricing of goods sold to non-resident group companies and interest on overdue/overpaid corporation tax are dealt with under self assessment.** (9 marks)

(25 marks)

4 Benny Fitt is the managing director of Usine Ltd, an unquoted trading company. Benny, aged 39, is paid a salary of £45,000 per annum. You should assume that today's date is 20 December 1999. Benny has asked for your advice on the following matters.

(a) On 1 October 1999 Usine Ltd provided Benny with a new 2,600 cc petrol powered motor car with a list price of £28,400. The motor car was subsequently fitted with a sun-roof costing £700. Benny made a capital contribution of £2,500 towards the cost of the motor car. During 1999/00 Benny will drive 1,100 business miles. He has a business meeting planned for 8 April 2000, which is a round trip of 220 miles from his home. The round trip from work to the meeting would be 190 miles, and Benny drives a total of 45 miles each day to work and back. It may be possible to bring this meeting forward to 4 April 2000. Benny has the use of a company credit card. During 1999/00 this will be used to pay for motor repairs of £460, business accommodation of £380, entertaining of customers £720 and petrol of £425. Included in the figure for petrol is £180 in respect of private mileage which is not reimbursed to Usine Ltd.

Required

Advise both Benny and Usine Ltd of the tax implications arising from the provision of the company motor car and the company credit card. Your answer should include an explanation of why it would be beneficial if Benny:

(i) **brought his business meeting forward to 4 April 2000; and**

(ii) **paid Usine Ltd £180 for his private petrol.**

You should ignore VAT, and confine your answer to the implications for 1999/00.
(11 marks)

(b) On 10 December 1999 Usine Ltd dismissed their sales director, and paid him a lump sum redundancy payment of £45,000. This consisted of the following.

	£
Statutory redundancy pay	2,100
Payment in lieu of notice	3,100
Holiday pay	2,800
Ex gratia compensation for loss of office	34,000
Agreement not to work for a rival company	3,000
	45,000

A new sales director is to commence employment on 1 January 2000. She is to be paid a lump sum payment of £10,000 upon the commencement of employment. The new director currently lives 120 miles from Usine Ltd's head office, so the company has offered her two alternative arrangements.

(i) Usine Ltd will pay £9,500 towards the cost of the director's relocation, and will also provide an interest free loan of £50,000 in order for the director to purchase a property.

(ii) Usine Ltd will provide accommodation for the director. The company owns a house which it purchased in 1989 for £86,000, and improved at a cost of £8,000 during 1998. The house has a rateable value of £4,400, is currently valued at £105,000, and has recently been furnished at a cost of £10,400. Usine Ltd will pay for the annual running costs of £3,200.

Required:

Explain the income tax implications of the lump sum payments of £45,000 and £10,000, and the two alternative arrangements offered to the new sales director.

You are not expected to consider the tax implications of Usine Ltd, and you should confine your answer to the implications for 1999/00. (9 marks)

(c) Usine Ltd runs an occupational pension scheme for its employees. Employees contribute 4% of their salary, and the company contributes a further 8%. The benefits on retirement are based upon final salary. At present the scheme is not approved by the Inland Revenue, but Usine Ltd is planning to amend the conditions of the scheme so that Inland Revenue approval can be obtained.

Required

Advise Usine Ltd of the tax advantages for both itself and for its employees if Inland Revenue approval is obtained for the occupational pension scheme. (5 marks)

(25 marks)

5 Yaz Pica commenced trading as a self-employed printer on 1 January 2000. He is to make up his accounts to 31 December 2000, and has produced the following quarterly profit forecast:

Mock exam: questions

	Quarter ending 31.3.00 £	Quarter ending 30.6.00 £	Quarter ending 30.9.00 £	Quarter ending 31.12.00 £	Total for year £
Sales					
Standard rated	19,400	28,600	40,200	51,200	139,400
Zero rated	5,100	7,500	9,700	12,500	34,800
	24,500	36,100	49,900	63,700	174,200
Purchases	(14,900)	(16,700)	(18,400)	(20,600)	(70,600)
Opening stock	(3,600)	(3,800)	(4,400)	(5,700)	(3,600)
Closing stock	3,800	4,400	5,700	7,200	7,200
Subcontractor costs	-	(3,100)	(8,800)	(12,400)	(24,300)
Expenses					
Standard rated	(9,900)	(5,200)	(5,600)	(6,100)	(26,800)
Exempt	(1,100)	(1,300)	(1,600)	(1,800)	(5,800)
Profit/(Loss)	(1,200)	10,400	16,800	24,300	50,300

Yaz registered for VAT on 1 January 2000, even though the VAT registration turnover limit was not exceeded until May 2000. All of Yaz's sales are to members of the general public. The purchases are all standard rated. Because of the pressure of work, Yaz was late submitting his first VAT return due on 30 April 2000.

The opening stock of £3,600 represents purchases made during December 1999. On 10 December 1999 Yaz purchased printing equipment for £18,000, and spent £1,400 on an advertising campaign that ran throughout December. All the expenses included in the profit forecast are allowable for tax purposes, but do not include capital allowances or the cost of the advertising campaign.

The above figures are all net of VAT.

On 1 May 2000 Yaz started sub-contracting some of his work to another printer, Albert Elite. As a result of the continued expansion of the business it is likely that as from 1 October 2000 Albert will work for Yaz on a full-time basis. Yaz considers Albert to be self-employed because he issues invoices for the work done. Albert is not registered for VAT.

Until 30 November 1999 Yaz was employed on a salary of £42,000 pa, and PAYE of £6,927 has been deducted during 1999/00. He is single and has no other income or outgoings.

Required

(a) (i) **Calculate the amount of income tax that Yaz will have to pay on 31 January 2001 if he makes up his accounts for the year ended 31 December 2000.** (6 marks)

(ii) **Advise Yaz of whether it will be beneficial to make up his accounts for the three month period to 31 March 2000, rather than for the year ended 31 December 2000.** (4 marks)

You are only expected to calculate Yaz's income tax liability for 1999/00. NIC should be ignored.

(b) (i) **With hindsight, it is evident that Yaz should not have registered for VAT until 1 July 2000. Explain why this is the case, and calculate the additional profit that Yaz would have made if he had registered for VAT as from 1 July 2000 rather than from 1 January 2000.** (5 marks)

(ii) **State the implications of Yaz being late in submitting any further VAT returns during 2000.** (2 marks)

(iii) **Advise Yaz of the advantages of using the annual accounting scheme, and explain when he will be permitted to join.** (3 marks)

(c) **Briefly explain the criteria that will be used in deciding whether Albert should be treated as employed or self-employed. State the implications for Yaz if Albert is incorrectly treated as self-employed rather than employed.**

(5 marks)

(25 marks)

6   ABC Ltd is an unquoted trading company that is under the control of three sisters, Agnes, Betty and Chloe, and is a close company. The share capital of ABC Ltd consists of 100,000 £1 ordinary shares, of which Agnes owns 20,000, Betty 40,000 and Chloe 40,000. Agnes and Betty are full-time working directors of the company, but Chloe is neither a director nor an employee.

Agnes is 57 years old, and is to retire on 31 December 1999. She will sell her 20,000 shares in ABC Ltd to Betty and Chloe for £20 per share. ABC Ltd's shares are currently worth £30 each for a minority shareholding. Agnes acquired her shares at their par value on 1 July 1992, the date of ABC Ltd's incorporation. She became a full-time working director of ABC Ltd on 1 July 1993 having not previously worked for the company. The market value of ABC Ltd's assets at 31 December 1999 is forecast to be as follows.

	£
Goodwill	500,000
Freehold property - factory and warehouse	1,050,000
Plant and machinery (costing more than £6,000 per item)	400,000
Investments in quoted companies	700,000
Motor cars	100,000
Current assets	750,000
	3,500,000

Agnes personally owns a freehold office building that is used rent free by ABC Ltd. This cost £78,000 on 1 June 1993, and is to be sold to Betty and Chloe for its current market value of £200,000 on 31 December 1999.

ABC will make an interest free loan of £200,000 to Chloe in order to help her finance the acquisitions from Agnes. This loan will be repaid over the next four years. ABC Ltd has an accounting date of 30 September and is expected to have profits chargeable to corporation tax of £800,000 for the year ended 30 September 2000. No dividends will be paid during the year. This is similar to its level of profits in the prior year.

Agnes, Betty and Chloe are all 40% taxpayers. Agnes has not made any lifetime gifts of assets, and has an estate (excluding the above assets and the consideration to be paid by Betty and Chloe) valued at £400,000 which she has left to her children.

Required

(a) **Calculate Agnes' CGT liability for 1999/00. Your answer should include an explanation of the amount of retirement relief that will be available to Agnes. You should assume that holdover relief is *not claimed* in respect of the gift of business assets.** (11 marks)

(b) **Calculate the IHT liabilities that would arise if Agnes were to die on 30 June 2002. You should assume that the shareholding in ABC Ltd is still owned by Betty and Chloe at that date, and that the market values and tax rates for 1999/00 apply throughout.** (7 marks)

(c) **Briefly advise both ABC Ltd and Chloe of the tax implications arising from the provision of the interest free loan of £200,000.** (4 marks)

(d) **As an alternative to Agnes selling her shareholding in ABC Ltd to Betty and Chloe, it has been suggested that the shareholding should instead be purchased by ABC Ltd for £20 per share. The purchase will not qualify for the special** treatment applying to a company's purchase of its own shares, and will therefore be treated as a distribution.

Advise Agnes of the tax implications for her arising from the company making a distribution. (3 marks)

(25 marks)

MOCK EXAM: ANSWERS

**DO NOT TURN THIS PAGE UNTIL YOU
HAVE COMPLETED THE MOCK EXAM**

WARNING! APPLYING OUR MARKING SCHEME

If you decide to mark your paper using our marking scheme, you should bear in mind the following points.

1. The BPP solutions are not definitive: you will see that we have applied the marking scheme to our solutions to show how good answers should gain marks, but there may be more than one way to answer the question. You must try to judge fairly whether different points made in your answers are correct and relevant and therefore worth marks according to our marking scheme.

2. If you have a friend or colleague who is studying or has studied this paper, you might ask him or her to mark your paper for you, thus gaining a more objective assessment. Remember you and your friend are not trained or objective markers, so try to avoid complacency or pessimism if you appear to have done very well or very badly.

3. You should be aware that BPP's answers are longer than you would be expected to write. Sometimes, therefore, you would gain the same number of marks for making the basic point as we have shown as being available for a slightly more detailed or extensive solution.

It is most important that you analyse your solutions in detail and that you attempt to be as objective as possible.

Mock exam: answers

1

> **Tutor's hint.** As instructed by the question you should not have calculated the mainstream corporation tax liability for any of the companies.
>
> **Examiner's comments.** Most candidates had few problems with part (a), although some confused the income and corporation tax loss reliefs.

(a) *Loss relief*

   (i) The Schedule D Case I trading loss of Titan Ltd can be relieved in the following ways:

   - Under s 393(1) ICTA 1988, it can set off its trading loss against income from the same trade in future accounting periods. Relief is available against the first available profits.

     S 393(I): 1 mark

   - Under s 393A(1) ICTA 1988 the loss can be set against total profits (before deducting any charges) of the current accounting period ie the six months to 31 March 2000. The only other income is the bank interest of £1,500, so such a claim would not be beneficial as it would merely result in unrelieved patent royalties of £4,000. However, if the carryback claim discussed below is to be made, this claim must be made first. The unrelieved patent royalties can be added to the loss carried forward under s 393(1) ICTA 1988.

     S 393A: current: 1 mark

   - After a s 393A(1) ICTA 1988, described above has been made relief can be given for any remaining loss against total profits (after deducting trade charges but before deducting non-trade charges) of an accounting period falling wholly or partly within the 12 months of the start of the period in which the loss was incurred ie y/e 30.9.99.

     S 393A (I): carryback: 1 mark

     A claim for relief against current or prior period profits must be made within two years of the end of the accounting period in which the loss arose ie by 31.3.02.

     However, no relief is available against profits made in accounting periods on one side of (in this case before) a change of ownership of a company where the loss making period is on the other side of (in this case, after) the change in ownership and there has been a major change in the nature or conduct of the trade within three years before or after the change. On 1 October 1999, there was such a change in ownership of Titan Ltd, and therefore the carry back of loss relief may be restricted. It is possible that the reorganisation mentioned would be treated as a major change in the conduct of the business.

     Restriction: 1 mark

   - Group relief enables Titan Ltd to surrender trading losses and excess charges on income to other group companies. Since the accounting periods of Titan Ltd and the claimant company will not be the same, only relief for the period of overlap can be given ie 6/12 of the claimant company's profits chargeable to corporation tax in y/e 31.3.00 can be relieved.

     Group relief: 2 marks

   (ii) *Group relief*

   Group relief applies between UK companies within a 75% group. Members of a 75% group are the holding company and its 75% subsidiaries so in this case the 75% group will be:

   Group definition: 1 mark

Notes   *Mock exam: answers*

Group members:
1 mark

(1) Moon Ltd
(2) Titan Ltd (100% holding by Moon Ltd)
(3) Sinope Ltd (85% holding by Moon Ltd)
(4) Oberon Ltd (85% holding by Moon Ltd)

Excluded companies:
1 mark

Phobos Ltd is not in the group (80% × 85% = 68% holding only) nor is Rhea Ltd (55% holding only).

This means that Titan Ltd will be able to surrender its loss to Moon Ltd, Sinope Ltd and Oberon Ltd but not to Phobos Ltd or Rhea Ltd

(iii) *Choice of loss reliefs*

Rate s 393A relief: 1 mark

In making a choice between loss reliefs the most important factor is the rate at which relief will be obtained. If relief is claimed under s 393A(1) against the profits of the twelve months to 30 September 1999, the rate of relief will be 20.5% (6/12 @ 21% and 6/12 @ 20%). In addition additional trade charges will become unrelieved in the six months to 31.3.00 and will have to be carried forward

A group relief claim will be more beneficial. The amount that can be relieved is:

Amount:
1 mark

	£
Schedule D Case I loss	95,000
Excess trade charges £(4,000 – 1,500)	2,500
	97,500

Associates:
1 mark

Relief should, in general, be given first to companies whose profits fall within the marginal relief band. The associated companies here are Moon Ltd and all the subsidiaries (Oberon, Rhea, Sinope and Titan) and subsidiary (Phobos Ltd). The limits for small companies are therefore:

Limits:
1 mark

Lower: £300,000 ÷ 6 = £50,000
Upper: £1,500,000 ÷ 6 = £250,000

Sinope Ltd:
2 marks

Only Sinope Ltd is currently affected by marginal relief. However, it should also be taken into account that Sinope Ltd has paid overseas taxation at the rate of 36% (25,920/72,000 × 100) and so would lose DTR if group relief were surrendered to it. Therefore, the best use of the relief would be against Moon Ltd profits which are just above the upper limit. The maximum relief would be 6/12 × £278,000 = £139,000, so a full group relief claim can be made, as the actual loss to be surrendered is only £97,500. The first £(278,000 – 250,000) = £28,000 will be relieved at 30% and the remaining £(97,500 – 28,000) = £69,500 relieved at 32.5%.

Moon Ltd:
2 marks

(b) (i) **Companies under common control may apply for group registration.** The effects and advantages of group registration are as follows.

Consequences:
1 mark each

- Each VAT group must appoint a representative member which must **account for the group's output VAT and input VAT, thus simplifying VAT accounting** and allowing payments and repayments of VAT to be netted off. However, all members of the group are jointly and severally liable for any VAT due from the representative member.

- **Any supply of goods or services by a member of the group to another member of the group is, in general, disregarded for VAT purposes,** reducing the VAT accounting work. However, VAT does have to be accounted for on certain services supplied to a UK group company via an overseas group member.

- Any other supply of goods or services by or to a group member is in general treated as a supply by or to the representative member but any special status of the representative member (eg charitable status) is ignored unless the member by or to whom the supply was made also has that special status.

- Any VAT payable on the import of goods by a group member is payable by the representative member.

(ii) The inclusion of Rhea Ltd in the VAT group makes the group partially exempt. The following proportion of non-attributable input VAT on overhead expenditure will be recoverable:

Partial exemption: 1 mark

$$\frac{\text{Taxable supplies}}{\text{Total supplies}} = \frac{450{,}000}{600{,}000} = 75\%$$

Non-attributable VAT
£80,000 × 17.5% = £14,000

Irrecoverable amount
25% × £14,000 = £3,500

Irrecoverable VAT: 2 marks

However, as the irrecoverable input VAT is below the de minimis limit of £625 per month on average and is less than 50% of all input VAT incurred, it is in fact recoverable.

Deminimis: 1 mark

Thus group registration does not result in any irrecoverable VAT.

If Rhea Ltd is not included in the group registration VAT will have to be charged on the management fee of £10,000. As Rhea Ltd does not make taxable supplies it cannot register for VAT and it would not be able to recover this VAT. If Rhea Ltd is included in the group registration VAT does not have to be charged on the management fee. This means inclusion within the group is recommended.

Management fee: 1 marks

Conclusion: 1 mark

Notes *Mock exam: answers*

> **Marking guide**
>
> | | | | | Marks |
> | --- | ----- | -------------------------------------- | ------------------ | ----- |
> | (a) | (i) | *Loss relief* | | |
> | | | S 393(1) ICTA 1988 | | 1 |
> | | | S 393A(1) ICTA 1988 – current year | | 1 |
> | | | S 393A(1) ICTA 1988 – previous 12 months | | 1 |
> | | | Restriction on carry back | | 1 |
> | | | Group relief | | 2 |
> | | | | Available | 6 |
> | | | | Maximum | 5 |
> | | (ii) | *Group relief* | | |
> | | | Group definition | | 1 |
> | | | Companies qualifying | | 1 |
> | | | Companies not qualifying | | 1 |
> | | | | Available/Maximum | 3 |
> | | (iii) | *Loss relief claims* | | |
> | | | S 393A(1) claim | | 1 |
> | | | Group relief claim amount | | 1 |
> | | | Associates/limits | | 2 |
> | | | Sinope Ltd | | 2 |
> | | | Moon Ltd | | 2 |
> | | | | Available | 8 |
> | | | | Maximum | 7 |
> | (b) | (i) | *VAT* | | |
> | | | Consequences of group registration | | 4 |
> | | | Partial exemption group | | 1 |
> | | | Calculate irrecoverable VAT | | 2 |
> | | | De minimis limit | | 1 |
> | | | VAT on Management charge | | 1 |
> | | | Conclusion | | 1 |
> | | | | Available/Maximum | 10 |
> | | | | Maximum | 25 |

2

> **Tutor's hint**. The £nil band of £231,000 has been used throughout this question as that is what was required by the examiner.
>
> **Examiner's comment**. There was confusion as to the seven year cumulation period, with some candidates ignoring the chargeable lifetime transfer made more than seven years before death altogether, despite this having an impact on subsequent transfers.

(a) **Lifetime tax on lifetime gifts**

Gift with reservation: 1 mark

(i) Main residence - 15.3.91

This was a PET so no lifetime tax was due.

CLT: 1 mark

(ii) CLT - 3.12.92

	£
Gift	92,000
Less: Annual exemption (92/93)	(3,000)
Annual exemption (91/92)	(3,000)
	86,000

This falls within the £nil band so the lifetime tax is:

£86,000 × 0% = £nil

PET: 1 mark

(iii) PET - 18.10.95

No lifetime tax due on PET

(iv) CLT - 20.4.96

The gift was a CLT on which IHT would have been due:

	£
Gift	302,000
BPR @ 50%	(151,000)
Annual exemption (96/97)	(3,000)
	148,000

CLT: 2 marks

BPR at 50% is available for controlling interests in quoted shares.

In the previous seven years, £86,000 of the £nil band had been used, leaving £145,000:

	£
£145,000 × 0%	Nil
3,000 × ¼	750
	750

The gross value of this chargeable transfer is therefore £148,750 (£148,000 + £750).

Death tax

As a result of Albert's death IHT will, in addition, be due on gifts made after 31 March 1993 and on the value of his chargeable estate at death.

IHT on death: 2 marks

Gifts made after 31 March 1993

		£
PET 18.10.95		39,500
Marriage exemption		(2,500)
Less: Annual exemption	(95/96)	(3,000)
	(94/95)	(3,000)
		31,000

In the seven years before 18.10.95, £86,000 of the £nil band had been used leaving £145,000.

There is therefore no IHT due on the PET as it falls within the £nil band.

CLT 20.4.96 £148,750 (see above).

In the previous seven years, £117,000 (£86,000 + £31,000) of the £nil band had been used leaving £114,000:

£		£
114,000 × 0%		Nil
34,750 × 40%		13,900
148,750		13,900
Less: taper relief (20%)		(2,780)
		11,120
Less: lifetime tax paid		(250)
		10,870

£10,870 must be paid by the trustees of the discretionary trust by 30 September 2000. Alternatively, as the trust property consisted of a shareholding in a company that was controlled by Albert immediately prior to the transfer, the trustees could pay the IHT in ten equal annual instalments commencing on 30 September 2000.

Due date/ instalment option: 1 mark

Mock exam: answers

Chargeable estate on 31 March 2000

	£	£
Free estate		
76,000 shares in Hercules plc at lower of		
(i) $139 + \frac{1}{4}(147 - 139) = 141p$		
(ii) $\frac{137+143}{2} = 140p$		106,400
Building society deposit		115,900
Life assurance policy		55,000
Accrued trust income		800
Less: Funeral expenses		(1,200)
Credit card debts		(900)
Net free estate		276,000
Settled property (W2)		
Eureka unit trust (50,000 × 90p (W1))	45,000	
Less: accrued trust income (800 × $^{100}/_{80}$)	(1,000)	
		44,000
Gift with reservation		180,000
Chargeable estate		500,000

In the seven years before death £179,750 of the £nil band had been used leaving £51,250:

	£		£
51,250 × 0%			Nil
448,750 × 40%			179,500
500,000			179,500

IHT of £179,500 is payable in respect of the chargeable estate of £500,000. The estate rate is, therefore, 35.9%.

IHT of £15,796 (£44,000 × 35.9%) will be payable by the trustees of the interest in possession trust by 30 September 2000. Harold will have to pay IHT of £64,620 (£180,000 × 35.9%) in respect of the gift with reservation. This IHT is also payable by 30 September 2000 although Harold may elect to pay it in ten equal annual instalments commencing on 30 September 2000.

IHT of £99,084 (£276,000 × 35.9%) will be payable by the executor's of Albert's estate by the earlier of 30 September 2000 and the date of the delivery of the account.

Harold will receive an inheritance of £136,916 (£276,000 − £40,000 − £99,084).

Treatment of main residence

As Albert continued to live **rent free** in the main residence, the gift in March 1991 was a **gift with a reservation of benefit. The gift is treated in the same way as any other gift** (ie as a PET when made). In addition, **as the reservation still existed at the date of Albert's death, the residence is included in Albert's chargeable estate at its value on the date of his death.**

The IHT due on the main residence **as a result of Albert's death is the higher of:**

(i)   **any additional IHT due as a result of treating the gift as a PET;**
(ii)   **the IHT due as a result of including the residence in the death estate.**

As the PET was made more than seven years before Albert's death, there is no additional tax due under (i). This means the IHT due is the IHT that will be due as a result of including the main residence in Albert's death estate.

Notes (margin):
- Shares: 1 mark
- Rest of free estate: 2 marks
- Settled property: 1 mark
- Gift with reservation: 1 mark
- B/f total: 1 mark
- Liability: 1 mark
- Estate rate: 1 mark
- IHT due date: 1 mark
- Due date: 1 mark
- Harold: 1 mark
- Gift with reservation: 1 mark

Workings

1. Units in unit trust

    Units in a unit trust are always valued at the lower of the quoted prices.

2. An interest in a discretionary trust is never part of a chargeable estate at death.

(b) There is a legislation to prevent the parent of a minor child transferring income to the child in order to use the child's personal allowance. **Income which is derived from capital transferred by the parent remains income of the parent for tax purposes.** There is a **de-minimis limit where the income does not exceed £100** so it could be effective for Harold to transfer a very small amount of capital in order to generate income below this threshold.

Income: 2 marks

It would be better for a deed of variation to be used to vary the terms of Albert's will so that the capital passes directly to Harold's son and any income arising from the capital is treated as that of his son. There would be no effect on the IHT due on Albert's estate. A deed of variation must be signed by all of the beneficiaries under a will and must be entered into within two years of Albert's death.

Deed: 2 marks

(c) As Harold wishes to achieve capital growth rather than income he could consider investing in the following.

Each valid investment: 1 mark

(i) **Gold and antiques.**

(ii) **National saving certificates.** These must normally be held for five years but the return is tax free

(iii) **Zero coupon bonds.** These bonds have no income. Investor's get their return by buying the bond for less than its redemption value

(iv) **Certificates of deposit.** These work in a similar way to zero coupon bonds

(v) **Equity shares.** The potential for capital growth is unlimited, (depending on the share). However, shares may be a high risk investment as their value can fall as well as rise

(vi) **Unit trust and investment trusts.** These offer a number of options for growth

(vii) **Individual savings account (ISA).** In 2000/2001 £5,000 can be invested in an ISA. This investment can be made up of cash, life insurance and stocks and shares. A fund specifically aimed at capital growth can be chosen. No income tax or capital gains tax will arise on ISAs.

Notes **Mock exam: answers**

Marking guide		Marks
(a) *Lifetime transfers*		
Gift with reservation		1
Chargeable transfer 3.12.92		1
PET 18.10.95		1
Chargeable transfer 20.4.96		2
Additional IHT on death		2
Due date/instalment option		1
Estate at death		
Ordinary shares		1
Other assets/debts and funeral expenses		2
Settled property		1
Gift with reservation		1
Cumulative total		1
IHT liability		1
Rate of IHT on estate		1
IHT due by estate/due date		1
Other IHT liabilities/due dates		1
Harold		1
Gift with reservation		1
	Available	20
	Maximum	17
(b) Income tax treatment		2
Variation of terms of will		2
	Maximum/Available	4
(c) Each valid investment 1 mark per investment		4
	Available/Maximum	4
	Maximum	25

3

> **Tutor's hint.** An overseas branch of a UK company is simply a branch, its profits are automatically part of the UK company's profits and the rules on controlled foreign companies are irrelevant. All this changes once the branch is incorporated.
>
> Recent changes are often examined. Pay particular attention to part (d).

(a) UKUL LTD CORPORATION TAX COMPUTATION

Schedule D Case V: 1½ marks

	£
Schedule D Case I	30,000
Schedule D Case V	90,000
Profits chargeable to corporation tax	120,000

CT: ½ mark
DTR: 2 marks

	£
Corporation tax £120,000 × 20%	24,000
Less DTR: lower of £87,000 × 18% = £15,660	(15,660)
£90,000 × 20% = £18,000	
Mainstream corporation tax	8,340

Not CFC: 2 marks

(b) The Ulandian tax rate of 18% means that the subsidiary will escape being treated as a controlled foreign company (UK rate 20% × 75% = 15%). Even if this were not so, it would pass the exempt activities test.

The main implication of incorporation is that only profits remitted to the UK would be taxable in the UK. Thus if the branch had been a subsidiary in the year ended 31 March 2000, Ukul Ltd's tax computation for that year would have been as follows.

Mock exam: answers

	£
Schedule D Case I	30,000
Schedule D Case V (W1)	43,500
	73,500
Corporation tax £73,500 × 20%	14,700
Less DTR (W2)	7,830
Mainstream corporation tax	6,870

There are two other important implications of the incorporation of the branch. *Associate company: 1 mark*

(i) Ukul Ltd will have an associated company, halving the limits for small companies rate and marginal relief.

(ii) Capital allowances will not be available on equipment (such as the computers) bought by the subsidiary. They would have been available if bought by the branch. *Capital allowances: 1 mark*

There will be no immediate gains on the branch assets on incorporation, so long as all of those assets are transferred in exchange for shares. *No gains: 1½ marks*

Working 1: Schedule D Case V

Schedule D Case V: 2½ marks

	£
Dividend £87,000 × (100 – 18)% × 50%	35,670
Underlying tax £35,670 × 15,660/71,340	7,830
	43,500

Working 2: DTR *DTR: 2 marks*

DTR is the lower of:

(i) UK tax £43,500 × 20% = £8,700
(ii) Overseas tax £7,830 (W1) ie £7,830

(c) Sasha will be **resident in the UK for any tax year in which she spends at least 183 days in the UK.** This will apply to at least one tax year and possibly two, depending on her dates of arrival and departure. She will remain domiciled in Ulandia. *Residence: 2 marks*

Her earnings from UK employment will be taxable in the UK. Earnings from her Ulandian employment and rental income from Ulandia will also be taxable in the UK if they are remitted to the UK while Sasha is resident in the UK. *Taxation: 2 marks*

(d) Under self-assessment companies must work out their own corporation tax liability and must pay their CT liability by the due date. *Due date: 1 mark*

Any interest paid as a result of the late payment of this corporation tax is a deductible expense in calculating profits chargeable to corporation tax. Correspondingly, interest received on an overpayment is taxable. *Interest: 2 marks*

Within 12 months of the end of each period, companies are normally required to submit a corporation tax return that includes a self-assessment of the amount of corporation tax payable for that period. Records relating to the return must be kept for six years after the end of the accounting period and the Revenue may enquire into the return. Notice of the enquiry must normally be given within 12 months of the filing date. *Records: 1 mark* *Enquiries: 2 marks*

Companies have to include details of any apportionable profits of a controlled foreign company within their tax returns. *CFC: 2 marks*

If sales are made to a non resident group company at an undervalue, the company concerned will have to adjust the transfer price to a true market price on its self-assessment return. *Transfer pricing: 2 marks*

Notes **Mock exam: answers**

Marking guide	Marks	
(a) Schedule D Case V	1½	
DTR - UK tax	½	
- Overseas tax	½	
- Set off lower	1	
UK CT @ 20%	½	
Available	4	
Maximum		3
(b) Not CFC	2	
Dividend received	1	
Relief for underlying tax	½	
Calculation underlying tax	1	
DTR	2	
Associated company	1	
No gains on branch assets	1½	
Capital allowances	1	
Available	10	
Maximum		9
(c) Residence	2	
Taxation - UK income	1	
Remitted Ulandi income	1	
Available/Maximum		4
(d) Due date	1	
Interest	2	
Records	1	
Enquiries	2	
CFC	2	
Transfer pricing	2	
Available	10	
Maximum		9
		25

4

> **Tutor's hint.** It was important to answer all parts of this question.
>
> **Examiner's comments.** This was a popular question although answers were somewhat disappointing given that most of the material being examined was of a Paper 7 level.

(a) **Benny Fitt**

Benefits in kind assessable on Benny are:

Car benefit: 2 marks

	£
Car benefit (£28,400 + £700 − £2,500) × 35% × 6/12	4,655
Fuel benefit (£2,270 × 6/12)	1,135
Expense payments (£380 + £720)	1,100
	6,890

Other BIK: 1 mark

Expense claim: 1 mark

Tax: 1 mark

Benny will be able to claim a deduction under s 198 ICTA 1988 for the expense payments of £1,100. The tax due on these benefits for 1999/00 will be £2,316 (£6,890 − £1,100 = £5,790 at 40%). The tax on the car and fuel benefits will be collected under PAYE, with any remaining liability being due on 31 January 2001.

Mock exam: answers

Usine Ltd

Capital allowances are available on the cost of the motor car. The writing-down allowance on the car is initially restricted to £3,000 per annum.

Capital allowances: 2 marks

Credit card expenses of £1,265 (£460 + £380 + £425) are allowable for Schedule D Case I purposes. However, the cost of entertaining is not allowable.

Expenses: 1 mark

Class 1A NIC of £706 (£4,655 + £1,135 = £5,790 at 12.2%) will be due on 19 July 2000

Class 1A: 1 mark

Effect of earlier business meeting

Mileage: 2 marks

If the business meeting is brought forward to 4 April 2000 then it falls into 1999/00 rather than 2000/2001. For 1999/00 the 2,500 business mileage limit is £1,250 (£2,500 × 6/12). The business mileage for the meeting will be 220 miles, being the actual distance travelled from home to the meeting. If the meeting is brought forward to 4 April 2000, then Benny's business mileage for 1999/00 will be £1,320 (£1,100 + £220) and his income tax liability for 1999/00 will be reduced by £532 (£4,655 – £3,325) × 40%).

Tax saving: 1 mark

Usine Ltd's Class 1A NIC liability will be reduced by £162 (£1,330 at 12.2%).

Private petrol

If Benny pays £180 for his private petrol there would be no assessable fuel scale benefit. This would reduce his income tax liability by £454 (£1,135 at 40%). The net saving for Benny is £274 (£454 – £180).

Tax saving: 1 mark

Usine Ltd's Class 1A NIC liability will be reduced by £138 (£1,135 at 12.2%).

(b) **Leaving employee**

Redundancy payment

Any payment that the sales director was contractually obliged to receive is taxable income.

Normally wages in lieu of notice are an ex gratia payment (since generally there is no contractual entitlement to receive this). Statutory redundancy pay is exempt. The first £30,000 of ex gratia payments are exempt. However although exempt itself, the statutory redundancy payment reduces the exempt amount of £30,000. The redundancy payment of £45,000 is therefore taxable as follows.

Wages in lieu: 1 mark

	£	£
Holiday pay		2,800
Restrictive covenant		3,000
Ex-gratia payment (£34,000 + £3,100)	37,100	
Less: exempt amount (£30,000 – £2,100)	27,900	
		9,200
Taxable		15,000

Taxable amount: 2 marks

Lump sum payment on taking up employment

Lump sum: 1 mark

The lump sum payment of £10,000 to the new sales director will be taxable, unless the payment represents compensation for a right or asset given up on taking up employment with Usine Ltd.

Beneficial loan

In 1990/00 there will be a taxable benefit of £1,250 (£50,000 × 10% × 3/12). However, the director will be able to claim a tax reducer of £75 (£1,250 × 30,000/50,000 at 10%).

Loan: 1 mark

Relocation costs

There will be no taxable benefit in respect of eligible removal expenses up to £8,000. The exemption covers such items as legal and estate agents' fees, stamp duty, removal costs, and the cost of new domestic goods where existing goods are not suitable for the new residence.

Accommodation

The benefit in kind in respect of the accommodation in 1999/00 will be as follows.

	£
Rateable value (£4,400 × 3/12)	1,100
Additional benefit (£105,000 – £75,000) = 30,000 at 10% × 3/12	750
Furniture (£10,400 × 20% × 3/12)	520
Running costs (£3,200 × 3/12)	800
	3,170

(c) The following tax advantages will result from Usine Ltd's occupational pension scheme obtaining Inland Revenue approval.

(i) Contributions paid will be deductible in calculating the company's Schedule D profits.

(ii) Usine Ltd's contributions will not be taxable benefits for employees. There will be no NIC liability.

(iii) An employee's contributions will be deductible from his Schedule E income.

(iv) The pension fund will not be subject to tax on either income or capital gains (although the tax credit attached to dividends cannot be recovered).

(v) A tax-free lump sum may be taken by an employee upon retirement.

(vi) Provision can be made for a tax-free lump sum to be paid on an employee's death in service.

Mock exam: answers

	Marking guide	Marks	
(a)	**Benny**		
	Car benefit	2	
	Other benefits	1	
	Expense claim	1	
	Income tax liability	1	
	Usine Ltd		
	Capital allowances	2	
	Deductible expenses	1	
	Class 1A NIC	1	
	Business meeting		
	Business mileage	2	
	Tax saving	1	
	Private petrol		
	Tax saving	1	
	Available	13	
	Maximum		11
(b)	*Lump sum payments*		
	Wages in lieu of notice	1	
	Taxable amount	2	
	Lump sum on taking up employment	1	
	Beneficial loan	1	
	Relocation costs	2	
	Accommodation		
	Additional benefit	2	
	Furniture/running costs	1	
	Available	10	
	Maximum		9
(c)	Advantages of approval		
	1 mark per advantage		
	Available	6	
	Maximum		5
Maximum			25

5

> **Tutor's hint.** The VAT aspects of questions such as this are of increasing importance.
>
> **Examiner's comments.** The annual accounting scheme was often confused with the cash accounting scheme.

(a) (i) *Payments of income tax 31.1.2001*

This payment will be the full payment of income tax for 1999/00. No payments on account will have been made because the 1998/99 liability was met under PAYE. The first payment on account for 2000/01 will also have to be paid.

Notes Mock exam: answers

Income tax 1999/00

		Non-savings Income
	£	£
Schedule E (8/12 × £42,000)		28,000
Schedule D Case I		
Profits per accounts (y/e 31.12.00)	50,300	
Less: pre-trading expenditure	(1,400)	
First year allowance 40% × £18,000	(7,200)	
	41,700	
1999/00 taxable (41,700 × 3/12)		10,425
STI		38,425
Less: personal allowance		(4,335)
Taxable income		34,090

Sch E: 1 mark

Sch D: 3 marks

Tax: 1 mark

Tax on non-savings income   £
£1,500 × 10%   150
£26,500 × 23%   6,095
£6,090 × 40%   2,436
     8,681
Less: PAYE   (6,927)
Tax for 1999/00   1,754
Add: payment on account 2000/01 – 50%   877
Total tax due 31.1.01   2,631

PAYE: 1 mark

Payments: 1 mark

(ii) If accounts are made up to 31 March 2000, there will be a trading loss as follows:

	£
Loss per accounts	1,200
Pre trading expenditure	1,400
First year allowance	7,200
Loss for 1999/00	9,800

Loss: 1 mark

There will be a *nil* Schedule D Case I assessable amount for 1999/00. Under s 381 ICTA 1988 the loss can be set against the total income of the preceding three years on a first in, first out basis ie against income of 1996/97 first. If Yaz's income was sufficiently high in that tax year, this could result in an income tax refund of £(9,800 × 40%) = £3,920.

S 381: 1 mark
Refund: 1 mark

In addition, no payment on account will be needed for 2000/01, since the tax in 1999/00 will be covered by the PAYE deducted, and, indeed, there will be a refund position. No income tax will be due until 31 January 2002. Therefore there is a cashflow advantage, although this will be offset by a higher liability in 2000/01 if the profit forecast is correct.

P on A: 1 mark
Conclusion: 1 mark

(b) (i) As Yaz exceeded the VAT registration limit in May 2000, he should have applied to be registered by 30 June 2000 and then would have been registered from 1 July 2000. In this case, as his sales to the general public would have been at the same selling price, output tax would have been additional income. The input tax on the stock purchased in December 1999 (to the extent retained at 1 July 2000) the printing equipment; and the standard rated expenses incurred in the six months before registration, can be recovered. However, the input tax on the advertising campaign could not be recovered as it was incurred more than six months before registration.

Additional income: 1 mark

Mock exam: answers

The additional profit is therefore:

	£	£	Notes
Output VAT			Output VAT: 1 mark
q/e 31.3.00 £19,400 × 17.5%		3,395	
q/e 30.6.00 £28,600 × 17.5%		5,005	
		8,400	
Less: (1) input tax on goods sold			Input VAT: 2 marks
q/e 31.3.00 £(14,900 + 3,600 − 3,800) = £14,700 × 17.5%	2,573		
q/e 31.6.00 £(16,700 + 3,800 − 4,400) = £16,100 × 17.5%	2,817		Advertising/ Pretrading: 2 marks
(2) input tax on advertising not recoverable £1,400 × 17.5%	245	(5,635)	
Increased profit		2,765	

(ii) **A default arises whenever a trader submits his VAT return late, even if a VAT repayment is due.** As Yaz's VAT return to 31.3.00 was late HM Customs & Excise would have served a surcharge liability notice on him. **This notice would specify a surcharge period running from the date of the notice until the anniversary of the end of the period for which he was in default** (ie until 31 March 2001).

If a further default occurs during the specified surcharge period, the original period will be extended to the anniversary of the end of period in which the new default occurs.

Extend period: 1 mark

In addition, if there is a late payment of VAT (as opposed to simply a late return), a default surcharge will be incurred as follows:

Surcharge: 1 mark

Default in period	*Surcharge as % of VAT outstanding at due date*
1st	2%
2nd	5%
3rd	10%
4th and over	15%

(iii) Under the annual accounting scheme, a trader only has to submit a VAT return once a year. However, throughout the year, the trader makes payments on account of the ultimate liability under direct debit. If the annual turnover is £100,000 or more, the trader must pay 90% of the previous year's net VAT liability in nine monthly payments starting in the fourth month of the year. At the end of the year, the trader completes an annual return and submits it within two months of the end of the year, together with any balancing payment.

Return: 1 mark

Payments: 1 mark

Late payments of instalments are not a default for the purposes of the defaults surcharge, although the trader may be expelled from the scheme.

From an administration point of view, the annual accounting scheme is beneficial and should ensure default surcharges are avoided. However, **Yaz must be registered for at least 12 months before he can apply to join. He must be up-to-date with his returns at that date. His expected taxable turnover for the next twelve months should not be in excess of £300,000.**

Advantages: 1 mark

Joining: 1 mark

(c) *Employed/self employed*

There is no single test as to whether a person is employed rather than self-employed. The following tests have, however, been used as a guideline:

(i) control – if Yaz can tell Albert how to do his work, this is likely to indicate Albert is employed.

Notes **Mock exam: answers**

(ii) integration – if Albert's work is integral to Yaz's business, Albert may be an employee.

Tests:
1 mark each

(iii) mutuality of obligations – does Yaz have to offer Albert work and does Albert have to accept work offered? If so, Albert may be an employee. Such mutuality may be built up over a period of time.

(iv) separate business – is Albert in business 'on his own account'? If so, he is more likely to be an independent contractor. Factors here would include taking financial risks; profiting from good management; having his own premises and equipment.

Consequences:
1 mark

If Yaz incorrectly treats Albert as not employed when he is in fact an employee, Yaz will be liable for loss of tax due to his failure to operate PAYE and Class 1 NIC.

Marking guide

				Marks	
(a)		Schedule E		1	
		Schedule D Case I adjustment		2	
		1999/00 assessment		1	
		PA/Tax liability		1	
		Collected under PAYE		1	
		Final payment/payment on account		1	
		Trading loss		1	
		S 381 ICTA 1988 claim		1	
		Income tax refund		1	
		Tax liability/payment on a/c		1	
		Conclusion		1	
			Available	12	
			Maximum		10
(b)	(i)	*Additional profit*			
		Income		2	
		Input VAT on goods sold		2	
		Pre-trading expenditure		2	
			Available	6	
			Maximum		5
	(ii)	Extend default surcharge period		1	
		Default surcharge level		1	
			Available/maximum		2
	(iii)	VAT return annually		1	
		Payments on account		1	
		Advantages		1	
		Joining scheme		1	
			Available	4	
			Maximum		3
(c)		Control test		1	
		Integration test		1	
		Mutuality of obligations test		1	
		Separate business test		1	
		Incorrect treatment		1	
			Available/maximum		5
			Maximum		25

Tutor's hint. For individuals indexation is only available until April 1998.

Examiner's comment. The question covered several recent changes and there is little excuse for candidates who did not read the relevant articles covering those changes.

(a) **Agnes' CGT liability**

Agnes is entitled to retirement relief because:

(i) she is at least 50 years old;
(ii) she is a full time working director of ABC Ltd;
(iii) she owns at least 5% of the ordinary share capital;
(iv) ABC Ltd in a trading company.

Conditions: 1 mark

The relief will be restricted as follows.

CBA/CA: 1 mark

(i) The gain eligible for relief is restricted by the ratio of the market value of ABC Ltd's chargeable business assets to its chargeable assets;

$$\frac{500,000 + 1,050,000 + 400,000}{500,000 + 1,050,000 + 400,000 + 700,000} = \frac{1,950,000}{2,650,000}$$

(ii) The limits for retirement relief are restricted by $6\frac{1}{2}/10$ since Agnes has only been both a shareholder and full time working director for five years and six months.

Limits: 1 mark

As the freehold office building is sold at the same time as her shareholding and it has been let rent free to ABC Ltd it is treated as an associated disposal. Retirement relief is therefore available on the disposal, the qualifying period being also six years and six months.

Associated disposal: 2 marks

Capital gains tax liability

	£	£	£
Capital gain on shares in ABC Ltd (W1)			576,571
Gain eligible for relief			
$£576,571 \times \frac{£1,950,000}{£2,650,000} = £424,269$			
Retirement relief			
$£200,000 \times 6\frac{1}{2}/10$		130,000	
50% (£424,269 – £130,000)		147,135	
			(277,135)
			299,436
Capital gain on freehold office building (W2)		110,066	
Retirement relief			
$800,000 \times 6\frac{1}{2}/10$	520,000		
Less: used	(424,269)		
	95,731	(47,866)	
			62,200
			361,636

Eligible gain: 1 mark

Relief: 1 mark

Relief: 1 mark

The assets disposed of are business assets that have been owned for two years.

Gain remaining after taper relief:

Gain/tax: 1 mark

	£
(£361,636 × 85%)	307,391
Less annual exemption	(7,100)
	300,291
Capital gains tax at 40%	£120,116

Mock exam: answers

Workings

1 Shareholding in ABC Ltd

	£
Deemed proceeds (£20,000 × £30)	600,000
(MV as Agnes, Betty and Chloe are connected persons)	
less: cost	(20,000)
	580,000
Indexation allowance to April 1998 £20,000 × $\dfrac{162.6-138.8}{138.8}$	(3,429)
Gain	576,571

Gain: 1 mark

2 Freehold office building

	£
Sale proceeds	200,000
Less: cost	(78,000)
	122,000
Indexation allowance £78,000 × $\dfrac{162.6-141.0}{141.0}$ (0.153)	(11,934)
Gain	110,066

Gain: 1 mark

(b) IHT Liabilities

31.12.99 PET

	£
Value transferred (£600,000 − £400,000)	200,000
BPR £200,000 × 100% × $\dfrac{(3,500,000-700,000)}{3,500,000}$	(160,000)
	40,000
Annual exemption 1999/00	(3,000)
1998/99	(3,000)
Value of PET	34,000
Chargeable transfers in previous 7 years	Nil
Nil band remaining	231,000
IHT liability £34,000 × Nil%	Nil

Value: 1 mark
BPR: 2 marks
A/E: ½ mark
IHT: ½ mark

30 June 2002 Death estate

	£	£
Death estate (prior to transfers)		400,000
Cash proceeds (£400,000 + £200,000)	600,000	
Less CGT liability (see part (a))	(120,116)	
		479,884
Chargeable estate		879,884
Chargeable transfers in previous 7 years		34,000
Nil band remaining (£231,000 − £34,000)		179,000
IHT liability		
£197,000 at Nil%		Nil
£682,884 at 40%		273,154
		273,154

CGT: 1 mark
IHT: 2 marks

(c) Interest free loan of £200,000

As Chloe is a participator the following tax implications apply:

(i) ABC Ltd must pay an amount of tax of £50,000 (£200,000 × 25%).

(ii) This is due on 1 July 2001 (9 months after the end of the accounting period in which the loan is made).

Payment tax: 1 mark

(iii) If part of the loan is repaid before 1.7.01, the tax charge is not due on the part repaid.

(iv) The tax will be refunded when the loan is repaid (repayment is made 9 months after the end of the accounting period in which the loan is repaid).

Refund: 1 mark

(v) There are no tax implications in respect of the above for Chloe unless the loan, or part of it, is written off.

(vi) However, since Chloe is not a director or employee of the company the 'benefit' of an *interest free loan* will not be caught under Schedule E. Thus Chloe will be treated as though she had received a dividend from the company equal to the amount that would have been chargeable under Schedule E had she been an employee.

Chloe's position: 2 marks

(d) **Purchase of shares by ABC Ltd**

(i) Agnes will be taxed on £422,222 (£380,000 × 100/90) in 1999/00

Additional income tax liability

	£
£422,222 × 32.5%	137,222
Less: tax credit (422,222 × 10%)	(42,222)
	95,000

Agnes: 2 marks

(ii) Since ABC Ltd is a close company and the purchase of own shares is an alteration in that company's unquoted share capital (purchased shares are cancelled) there has been a disposition by the participators of the company for IHT purposes. A transfer of value by the close company is apportioned amongst the participators according to their respective interests in the company immediately prior to the transfer (ie a 20% interest for Agnes). Such transfers are not PETs but rather are chargeable lifetime transfers.

CLT: 2 marks

Mock exam: answers

Marking guide		**Marks**
(a) *Retirement relief*		
Qualifying conditions		1
Restriction to 65%		1
Restriction to chargeable business assets		1
Associated disposal		2
Calculation of CGT liability		
Capital gain		1
Proportion relating to chargeable business assets		1
Retirement relief		1
Gain on freehold office building		1
Retirement relief on associated disposal		1
Annual exemption/CGT		1
	Maximum/Available	11
(b) *Potentially exempt transfer*		
Value transferred		1
Business property relief		2
Annual exemptions/IHT liability		1
Estate at death		
Capital gains tax deduction		1
Calculation of IHT liability		2
	Maximum/Available	7
(c) *Payment of tax*		
Repayment of loan		1
Tax position of participator		2
	Maximum/Available	4
(d) Assessment on shareholder		2
IHT		2
	Available	4
	Maximum	3
	Maximum	25

ACCA – *Paper 11 Tax planning (Finance Act 1999) (1/00)*

REVIEW FORM & FREE PRIZE DRAW

All original review forms from the entire BPP range, completed with genuine comments, will be entered into a draw on 31 July 2000 and 31 January 2001. The names on the first four forms picked out will be sent a cheque for £50.

Name: _____ Address: _____

How have you used this Kit?
(Tick one box only)
☐ Home study (book only)
☐ On a course: college _____
☐ With 'correspondence' package
☐ Other _____

Why did you decide to purchase this Kit?
(Tick one box only)
☐ Have used complementary Study Text
☐ Have used BPP Kits in the past
☐ Recommendation by friend/colleague
☐ Recommendation by a lecturer at college
☐ Saw advertising
☐ Other _____

During the past six months do you recall seeing/receiving any of the following?
(Tick as many boxes as are relevant)
☐ Our advertisement in *ACCA Students' Newsletter*
☐ Our advertisement in *Pass*
☐ Our brochure with a letter through the post

Which (if any) aspects of our advertising do you find useful?
(Tick as many boxes as are relevant)
☐ Prices and publication dates of new editions
☐ Information on Kit content
☐ Facility to order books off-the-page
☐ None of the above

Have you used the companion Study Text for this subject?   ☐ Yes   ☐ No

Your ratings, comments and suggestions would be appreciated on the following areas

	Very useful	Useful	Not useful
Introductory section (Advice on revision and practice, Question and Answer checklist, etc)	☐	☐	☐
Interactive checklists	☐	☐	☐
Tutor's hints	☐	☐	☐
Examination-standard questions	☐	☐	☐
Content of answers	☐	☐	☐
Marking schemes	☐	☐	☐
Mock exam	☐	☐	☐
Structure and presentation	☐	☐	☐
Icons	☐	☐	☐

	Excellent	Good	Adequate	Poor
Overall opinion of this Kit	☐	☐	☐	☐

Do you intend to continue using BPP Study Texts/Kits?   ☐ Yes   ☐ No

Please note any further comments and suggestions/errors on the reverse of this page.

Please return to: Katy Hibbert, BPP Publishing Ltd, FREEPOST, London, W12 8BR

ACCA – Paper 11 Tax planning (Finance Act 1999) (1/00)

REVIEW FORM & FREE PRIZE DRAW (continued)

Please note any further comments and suggestions/errors below

FREE PRIZE DRAW RULES

1   Closing date for. 31 July 2000 draw is 30 June 2000. Closing date for 31 January 2001 draw is 31 December 2000.

1   Closing date for 31 July 2000 draw is 30 June 2000. Closing date for 31 January 2001 draw is 31 December 2000.

3   No purchase necessary. Entry forms are available upon request from BPP Publishing. No more than one entry per title, per person. Draw restricted to persons aged 16 and over.

4   Winners will be notified by post and receive their cheques not later than 6 weeks after the draw date. Lists of winners will be published in BPP's *focus* newsletter following the draw.

5   The decision of the promoter in all matters is final and binding. No correspondence will be entered into.

See overleaf for information on other
BPP products and how to order

ACCA Order

To BPP Publishing Ltd, Aldine Place, London W12 8AA
Tel: 020 8740 2211. Fax: 020 8740 1184

Mr/Mrs/Ms (Full name) _____
Daytime delivery address _____
_____ Postcode _____
Daytime Tel _____ Date of exam (month/year) _____

POSTAGE & PACKING

Study Texts
	First	Each extra
UK	£3.00	£2.00
Europe*	£5.00	£4.00
Rest of world	£20.00	£10.00

Kits/Passcards/Success Tapes
	First	Each extra
UK	£2.00	£1.00
Europe*	£2.50	£1.00
Rest of world	£15.00	£8.00

Master CDs/Breakthrough Videos
	First	Each extra
UK	£2.00	£2.00
Europe*	£2.00	£2.00
Rest of world	£20.00	£10.00

Grand Total (Cheques to *BPP Publishing*) I enclose a cheque for (incl. Postage) £ _____
Or charge to Access/Visa/Switch
Card Number _____
Expiry date _____ Start Date _____
Issue Number (Switch Only) _____

		6/99 Texts	1/00 Kits	1/00 Psscrds	2/00 Tapes	2/00 Videos	Master-CDs
FOUNDATION							
1	The Accounting Framework	£18.95 ☐	£9.95 ☐	£5.95 ☐	£12.95 ☐	£25.00 ☐	£34.95 ☐
2	The Legal Framework	£18.95 ☐	£9.95 ☐	£5.95 ☐	£12.95 ☐	£25.00 ☐	£34.95 ☐
3	Management Information	£18.95 ☐	£9.95 ☐	£5.95 ☐	£12.95 ☐	£25.00 ☐	£34.95 ☐
4	The Organisational Framework	£18.95 ☐	£9.95 ☐	£5.95 ☐	£12.95 ☐	£25.00 ☐	
CERTIFICATE							
5	Information Analysis	£18.95 ☐	£10.95 ☐	£5.95 ☐	£12.95 ☐	£25.00 ☐	
6	The Audit Framework	£18.95 ☐	£10.95 ☐	£5.95 ☐	£12.95 ☐	£25.00 ☐	
7	The Tax Framework (Finance Act 99) (8/99 Text, 1/00 P/C, 1/00 Kit)	£18.95 ☐	£10.95 ☐	£5.95 ☐	£12.95 ☐	£25.00 ☐	
8	Managerial Finance	£18.95 ☐	£10.95 ☐	£5.95 ☐	£12.95 ☐	£25.00 ☐	£39.95 ☐ (1/00)
PROFESSIONAL							
9	Information for Control and Decision Making	£19.95 ☐	£10.95 ☐	£5.95 ☐	£12.95 ☐	£25.00 ☐	
10	Accounting and Audit Practice (Accounting)	£15.95 ☐	£10.95 ☐	£5.95 ☐	£12.95 ☐	£25.00 ☐	£39.95 ☐ (1/00)
10	Accounting and Audit Practice (Auditing)	£13.95 ☐	£10.95 ☐				
11	Tax Planning (Finance Act 99) (8/99 Text, 1/00 P/C, 1/00 Kit)	£19.95 ☐	£10.95 ☐	£5.95 ☐	£12.95 ☐	£25.00 ☐	£39.95 ☐ (1/00)
12	Management and Strategy	£19.95 ☐	£10.95 ☐	£5.95 ☐	£12.95 ☐	£25.00 ☐	
13	Financial Reporting Environment	£19.95 ☐	£10.95 ☐	£5.95 ☐	£12.95 ☐	£25.00 ☐	
14	Financial Strategy	£19.95 ☐	£10.95 ☐	£5.95 ☐	£12.95 ☐	£25.00 ☐	
INTERNATIONAL STREAM							
1	The Accounting Framework	£18.95 ☐	£9.95 ☐				
6	The Audit Framework	£18.95 ☐	£9.95 ☐				
10	Accounting and Audit Practice (Accounting)	£15.95 ☐	£10.95 ☐				
10	Accounting and Audit Practice (Audit)	£13.95 ☐					
13	Financial Reporting Environment	£19.95 ☐	£10.95 ☐ (9/99)				

SUBTOTAL £ _____

We aim to deliver to all UK addresses inside 5 working days. Orders to all EU addresses should be delivered within 6 working days. All other orders to overseas addresses should be delivered within 8 working days.
* Europe includes the Republic of Ireland and the Channel Islands.